Teaching History
in an Uncivilized World

by

Philip Bigler

1998 National Teacher of the Year

AppleRidge
PUBLISHERS

The opinions expressed in this manuscript are solely the opinions of the author and do not represent the opinions or thoughts of the publisher. The author has represented and warranted full ownership and/or legal right to publish all the materials in this book.

Teaching History in an Uncivilized World
All Rights Reserved.
Copyright © 2012 Philip Bigler
V2.0

This book may not be reproduced, transmitted, or stored in whole or in part by any means, including graphic, electronic, or mechanical without the express written consent of the publisher except in the case of brief quotations embodied in critical articles and reviews.

Apple Ridge Publishers

ISBN: 978-0-578-11329-6

Library of Congress Control Number: 2012918740

PRINTED IN THE UNITED STATES OF AMERICA

Dedicated with thanks to all of my many students at Oakton, W.T. Woodson, Bethesda-Chevy Chase, McLean, Thomas Jefferson High School for Science and Technology High Schools, & at James Madison University

Also By Philip Bigler

LIBERTY & LEARNING: The Essential James Madison. with Annie Lorsbach

BE A TEACHER: You Can Make a Difference. with Stephanie Bishop

HOSTILE FIRE: The Life and Death of Lt. Sharon A. Lane

FAILING GRADES: A Teachers Report Card on Education in America. with Karen Lockard

WASHINGTON IN FOCUS: A Photographic History of the Nation's Capital

IN HONORED GLORY: Arlington National Cemetery, the Final Post

For additional information please see

www.appleridgepublishers.com

Cover Art: Thomas Cole's painting "Destruction" (4th in series) from the Course of Empire Series (1836). Oil on Canvas, 39 ¼ X 63 ½ inches, negative #6048c. Used with permission from the New York Historical Society.

Table of Contents

FOREWORD
Frank Charles Winstead

Georgia's Outstanding Young Educator, STAR Teacher,
& Outstanding Principal

Philip Bigler, the 1998 National Teacher of the Year, is uniquely qualified to write a book that breaks new ground in the teaching of a discipline that is often dreaded by students, frequently assigned to the least capable teachers ("Anyone can teach social studies"), and minimized by the general public. *Teaching History in an Uncivilized World* is a vital book for all who care about the difficult and complex task of making history relevant, exciting, and yes, fun, in the classroom and beyond the walls of the schoolhouse.

Phil Bigler is a master teacher who represents all that is noble and uplifting about the teaching profession. He is blessed with the Four Characteristics of a Great Teacher as described by Francis Smith in the PBS program, *To Light a Fire: Great Teachers in America.* Smith said, "The great teacher loves his subject. The great knows his subject. The great teacher loves and honors his students, and the great teacher has humility." By this or any measure of excellence, Phil Bigler is a great teacher.

In large measure because of dismal teaching, we have had two generations of students pass through our schools who are profoundly lacking in knowledge of the history of this great country. Here is the big and troubling question: "Can this nation survive long-term with a population that is almost completely ignorant of the people, documents, and events that shaped the great country in the history of the world?" While I fear for the future, Phil Bigler offers a ray of hope.

For educators who want to dramatically improve the teaching of history by bringing relevance and instructional excitement to the classroom, Phil provides a blueprint. His methods take the reader light years beyond the traditional instructional approach that too often has consisted of this deadly pronouncement—"Read the chapter and answer the odd numbered questions."

David McCullough, the recipient of two Pulitzer Prizes, two National Book Awards, and the Presidential Medal of Freedom has stated, "Teachers are the most important people in our society." From observing my colleagues in teaching for some 48 years, I have learned that the really good teachers are driven to become better because they are passionate about what they do. They recognize that the late Mary Bicouvaris, the 1989 National Teacher of the Year, was correct when she stated, "Teaching is the most important job in the world."

Enjoy and learn as Philip Bigler helps teachers, principals and central office administrators understand how to teach history with joy, passion, excitement, and high expectations to their students as they try to navigate their way in an often uncivilized world.

Magnolia, Texas

Immortal Rome was at first but an insignificant village, inhabited only by a few ruffians, but by degrees it rose to a stupendus height, and excelled in arts and arms all the nations that preceded it...[but eventually it sank] into debauchery, and made it at length an easy prey to barbarians.

John Adams

TEACHING HISTORY
IN AN UNCIVILIZED WORLD

CHAPTER I

Civilization Begins Anew
With Each Child

*If the children . . . are untaught, their ignorance and vices will in
future life cost us much dearer in their consequences, than it would
have done, in their correction, by a good education.*

Thomas Jefferson 1818

On August 3rd, 2008 Aleksandr Isayevich Solzhenitsyn
died in Moscow at the advanced age of 89. He had lived
an exemplary, noble life as a novelist, civil rights advocate and political dissident. Imprisoned in 1945 during World War
II for criticizing Stalin, he spent the next eight years of his life in
the dictator's gulags (*Glavnoe Upravlenie Lagerei*—Main Administration of the Camps) with another three years in "permanent"
internal exile. Solzhenitsyn was liberated only after Stalin's death
as the new Premier, Nikita Khrushchev, began to implement his
de-Stalinization policies. For a time, Solzhenitsyn taught school
while he struggled to publish his many writings in a society where
free speech and unorthodox thinking were outlawed. Eventually, though, he published and received international acclaim in the
west where he was awarded in absentia the Nobel Prize for litera-

ture in 1970. A few years later, the *Gulag Archipelago*, was printed in Paris. This incredible indictment of the totalitarian communist state under Stalin had been covertly smuggled out of Russia and caused an immediate sensation. It was promptly denounced by Soviet authorities and Solzhenitsyn was arrested for treason, stripped of his citizenship and expelled from the U.S.S.R. for his anti-Soviet behavior. He would ultimately receive political asylum in the United States where he resided for the next 18 years in a self-imposed seclusion at his home in the tranquil mountains of Vermont.[1]

Solzhenitsyn continued to write and was incredibly prolific. His life's work include such classics as *One Day in the Life of Ivan Denisovich*, *In the First Circle*, *August 1914*, *Cancer Ward* and, of course, the *Gulag Archipelago*. Collectively, these books exposed the communist state for all of its hypocrisy, brutality and immorality and through the power and truth of his writings, Solzhenitsyn has been rightfully credited with helping destroy the very foundations of the corrupt Soviet system. Truly, he remains one of the seminal figures of the 20th century, ranking in historical significance with such western notables as Winston Churchill, Franklin Roosevelt, and Pope John Paul II.

In the fall of 2008, I casually mentioned to my Education 360 students at James Madison University that Solzhenitsyn had died over the summer. I was stunned by the blank looks on their faces, for not one of these aspiring teachers had ever heard of Alexandr Solzhenitsyn. These were good, smart young people, ranking among the so-called intellectual elite of the United States. All had successfully graduated from high school, passed their many state competency exams, done well on their SAT tests, and had been admitted to college, yet throughout their entire academic careers, no history teacher or college professor had ever mentioned the existence of a man named Aleksandr Solzhenitsyn or of the brutal Soviet Gulag system. This was truly astonishing and bordered on educational malpractice since, as author Deborah Kaple accurately notes:

> The Soviet Gulag surely ranks as one of the most evil political creations of the twentieth century, along with Hitler's Holocaust in Europe, Pol Pot's slaughter of millions in Cambodia, and Mao Zedong's serial campaigns that killed millions of Chinese citizens. The Gulag stands alone as the longest-running program of state-sponsored killing in that very bloody century.[2]

But it would be unfair to solely blame the students for their ignorance. Indeed, they are enrolled in our schools and universities to learn important, meaningful things and it is the sacred obligation and responsibility of their teachers and professors to provide them with a quality, substantive education. Unfortunately, many of our schools, colleges and universities have discarded academic rigor and nowhere is this perilous decline in standards more evident than in the lack of basic historical literacy.

There are many culprits in the decay of our nation's culture and civilization but the American news media remains one of the worst offenders. Aleksandr Solzhenitsyn's death was barely mentioned on the regular evening and cable news broadcasts, yet these same networks chose to interrupt their regular programming for live coverage of the motorcade taking socialite Paris Hilton (feel free to substitute Lindsay Lohan, Snooki, the Kardashians, Charlie Sheen, Britney Spears, O.J. Simpson or any recent celebrity narcissist) to a Los Angeles jail. No wonder that our contemporary students are completely lost when asked to sort out the trivial from the important. Journalistic standards have plunged to an all-time low while substance has been abandoned in a never-ending quest for the sensational and the lewd.

This glorification of ignorance was made even more apparent when a famous American athlete visited Greece to play a series of exhibition basketball games in 1994. This much revered sports star was earning a multi-million dollar salary that translated roughly into $2,500 per minute of playing time. At a press conference in Athens, one reporter asked him if he had visited the Parthenon while in the city. The Parthenon is, of course, the ancient temple to the goddess, Athena, who is the city's patron. It has become universally recognized as the symbol of classical democracy. Perched high upon the Acropolis, the Parthenon dominates the city's skyline and can be seen from virtually anywhere. Yet amazingly, this sports celebrity response to the question was, "I can't really remember the names of all the clubs we went to."[3] Although it certainly does concern me that this individual had never heard of the Parthenon, what is truly inexcusable is that fact that he had absolutely no intellectual curiosity. It is a disturbing sign of the times.

Our current generation of American students, the so called "millennials," is far different from previous ones. They are the first to have grown up wholly in the computer age. They are used to sophisticated technology, rapid communication, and instant access to information, all of which have led to shortened attention spans and little desire for hard work or deferred gains. Increasingly, they have become wholly dependent upon online sources for their knowledge and this leaves little time for books, serious literature, rational judgment or thoughtful study. Nicholas Carr in his book, the *Shallows*, effectively chronicles the evolution of the contemporary distracted mind. It requires constant stimulation but people are losing the ability to focus and concentrate. Solitude and thoughtful reflection are no longer possible with the need to be constantly online, coupled with the ubiquitous use of the cell phone.

Today's students are exposed to voluminous amounts of digital material but are oblivious to its quality, none of which has been screened for perspective or accuracy. Historical relevance is determined by the number of "hits" generated by enigmatic search engines. A quick Google search for Aleksandr Solzhenitsyn, for instance, revealed just 64,300 hits compared to a staggering 9.6 million for Miss Hilton. With such lopsided statistics, it is easy to understand the muddled thinking of many of our students. As teachers, we must motivate our students and help them convert mounds of facts and data into meaningful knowledge. This task, though, has been made increasingly difficult by the fact that virtually all of our school libraries have been converted into modern media centers. Book collections have dwindled and have been replaced by computer terminals and ephemeral digital resources. Books are viewed with contempt by many students as anachronistic relics of an earlier era. Nicholas Carr quotes a Florida State University graduate and Rhodes Scholar who unabashedly states, "I don't read books. I go to Google, and I can absorb relevant information quickly. Sitting down and going through a book from cover to cover doesn't make sense. It's not a good use of my time, as I can get all the information I need faster through the Web."[4] Likewise, another high school student in the PBS documentary, "Growing Up Online," boasts about reading Shakespeare's *Romeo and Juliet* in just five minutes using the resources of Sparknotes, a website that boasts without embarrassment that it has "translated" the bard into "the kind of English people actually speak today."[5] At risk are our nation's basic historical memory, common culture and literary traditions.

Obviously, these are challenging times for today's classroom teachers. I have the utmost respect for public school educators, most of whom are hardworking, honest, and dedicated professionals but this does not excuse the educational establishment for the abysmal state of history education in the United States. Far too much time in our schools is wasted on nonsense and it is our students who truly suffer. Indeed, it is astonishing how little academically is really expected of American students despite the proliferation of A's and B's on report cards. They have been pampered and spoiled, told they were exceptional, deified to the point that they revel in their own personal self-esteem while their international counterparts and global competitors routinely surpass them in math and science scores. Far too many of our students will graduate from high school without ever having read a serious book or attempting a source-based research paper.

In 2007, venture capitalist Robert Compton produced an extraordinary documentary entitled *Two Million Minutes*. The title is derived from the cumulative amount of time students have during their four years of high school. The film compares the lives of typical American teenagers to their counterparts in India and China. The contrast is striking—the foreign students are all highly motivated and disciplined; they take their studies seriously and have a strong desire to achieve academically. To them, a quality education is absolutely essential since it is their way to escape poverty and is their sole opportunity to achieve economic success. By contrast, in the United States, there is little economic pressure for students to succeed nor are there serious consequences for failure. The typical high school student enjoys an active social life filled with sports, video games, social networking, texting, television, dating and a myriad of other activities. Students are not bothered by any real educational challenges and their teachers seem to exert little influence over their lives. This stark assessment is confirmed in the documentary film about high school, *American Teen*, which shows school more as a place to socialize with friends than to actually study.[6]

There have been numerous educational studies which have generated countless statistics that document this abysmal view of American education. According to the *Two Million Minutes* website: "Less than 40 percent of U.S. students take a science course more rigorous than general biology, and a mere 18 percent take advanced classes in physics, chemistry or biology. Only 45 percent of U.S. students take math coursework beyond two years of algebra and one year of geometry. And 50 percent of all college freshmen require remedial coursework."[7] The same dire state exists for history and social studies education. Professor E.D. Hirsh has extensively documented the general ignorance of students about history. In his book, *The Making of Americans*, he states:

> A lack of knowledge, both civic and general, is the most significant deficit in most American students' education. For the most part, these students are bright, idealistic, well meaning, and good natured...Yet most of them lack basic information that high school and college teachers once took for granted.[8]

This lack of historical knowledge is especially perilous for the American republic since the quality of our nation's representative government fundamentally depends upon an informed, enlightened and virtuous citizenry. Indeed, the Founding Fathers were universal in their belief that an educated populace provided the best bastion of defense against political tyranny. James Madison, the Father of the Constitution and the nation's fourth president, wrote that our schools "ought to be favorite objects with every free people. They throw that light over the public mind which is the best security against crafty and dangerous encroachments on the public liberty."[9]

I began my teaching career in 1975 and have been actively involved in education for well over 35 years now. I have always believed teaching is a noble, serious profession. Indeed, a quality teacher is the single most important factor in a child's education and it is our obligation to motivate and inspire our students to learn. We are, literally, on the front lines in an ongoing war against ignorance. For the most part, I have waged my own fight against stupidity within the confines of my classroom, but on April 24, 1998, I was recognized for my many years of work as a high school history teacher when I was named the National Teacher of the Year during a Rose Garden ceremony at the White House by then president, Bill Clinton. It was an incredible honor. On that special day, the President remarked:

> For more than 20 years, his students haven't just studied history, they have lived it. He's transformed his classroom into a virtual time machine, challenging students to debate each other as members of rival ancient Greek city states; as lawyers before the Supreme Court; as presidential candidates named Thomas Jefferson and John Adams.
>
> Through these historic simulations, his students have learned lessons about democracy and the meaning of citizenship, lessons that will last a lifetime -- lessons we want

every American to know...We need more teachers like Philip Bigler and all our other honorees in every classroom in America today. For it is they who can make our schools the best in the world. It is they who can guarantee that America will have another American Century in the 21st century. (President Bill Clinton, April 24, 1998)

The President's vision for another "American Century" is certainly an admirable and worthy goal, but as those of us who have studied history know well, human progress is neither inevitable nor preordained. A nation's culture and its fundamental principles are fragile things which must be nurtured and preserved. In my personal

President Bill Clinton, Secretary of Education Richard Riley, Senator Charles Robb and me at the White House Rose Garden Ceremony for the 1998 National Teacher of the Year. I had been teaching history and humanities in the Fairfax and Montgomery County public schools for 23 years at the time of my recognition. (White House photo)

philosophy of education, I once wrote that: "An old proverb asserts that 'Civilization begins anew with each child.' As an educator, I have found this statement to be both a vision of optimism as well as a dire warning. On one hand, our students are the intellectual heirs to Plato, Aristotle, Augustine, and Newton; the inheritors of a rich legacy of human progress traversing three millennia. Conversely, if we fail to successfully teach and educate our young people we are just one generation removed from barbarism." (See Appendix C) These are the high stakes that we face today in our nation's public schools and we are living in perilous times.

When Aleksandr Solzhenitsyn was living in internal exile in Kok-Terek, Kazakhstan—sick, unpublished, a criminal of the state—he secretly buried his numerous writings and manuscripts in hopes that

The funeral of Aleksandr Isayevich Solzhenitsyn (1918-2008). Solzhenitsyn was one of the seminal figures of the 20th century. Despite his historical significance, many contemporary students have never heard of the great writer and political dissident. (Getty Images)

they would someday be discovered and read by some future generation. Yet even with the awesome power of the Soviet Union mobilized against him, the state was unable to silence Solzhenitsyn, and all of his books and writings were eventually published. He would later write, "No one can bar the road to truth, and to advance its cause I am prepared to accept even death."[10] It is thus ironic that in the United States today we have accomplished what the Soviet Union failed to do by raising an entire generation of students where Aleksandr Solzhenitsyn's name is unknown and his works are unread. There is no more important or critical job in America today than teaching history, for we are engaged in a daily struggle against the barbaric forces of ignorance and a fight for the preservation of human civilization.

Endnotes

1 Joseph Pearce (2001), *Solzhenitsyn: A Soul in Exile*. Grand Rapids: Baker Books, pp. 214-215.

2 Deborah Kaple, Ed. (2011), *Gulag Boss: A Soviet Memoir*. New York: Oxford University Press, p. xviii.

3 "Between Me and You: Quotes of the Year" (1995), *Time Annual 1994: The Year in Review*. New York: Time, Inc., p. 20.

4 Joe O'Shea quoted in Nicholas Carr (2010), *The Shallows: What the Internet is Doing to Our Brains*. New York: W.W. Norton & Company, pp. 8-9.

5 Sparknotes, http://nfs.sparknotes.com (accessed July 1, 2011).

6 *American Teen*, http://www.americanteenthemovie.com (accessed July 12, 2010).

7 *Two Million Minutes*, http://www.2mminutes.com (accessed July 6, 2010).

8 E.D. Hirsch (2009), *The Making of Americans: Democracy and Our Schools*. New Haven: Yale University Press, p. 11.

9 James Madison quoted in Jack Rakove, Ed. (1999), *Madison: Writings*. New York: Library of America, p. 791.

10 "Aleksandr Solzhenitsyn quotes," Thinkexist.com, http://thinkexist.com/quotes/alexander_solzhenitsyn/3.html (accessed July 31, 2010).

CHAPTER II

Be A Teacher

Sir Thomas More: Why not be a teacher? You'd be a fine teacher. Perhaps even a great one.

Richard Rich: And if I was, who would know it?

Sir Thomas More: You, your pupils, your friends, God. Not a bad public that...be a teacher.

Robert Bolt from the play: *A Man for All Seasons*

O n December 7, 1941, the Japanese launched a devastating surprise attack against American military forces stationed in Pearl Harbor, Hawaii. The USS *Arizona* was sunk along with three other battleships but the American carrier fleet was fortuitously at sea and spared destruction. Still, it was a severe blow and over 2,400 servicemen were killed. The following day, President Franklin Roosevelt asked Congress to avenge "the unprovoked and dastardly attack" with a declaration of war. The resolution quickly passed unanimously in the Senate and was approved in the House as well, but with one lone dissenting vote, that of Montana Congresswoman, Jeannette Rankin. A

The USS Shaw *exploding after being struck by two Japanese bombs at Pearl Harbor, Hawaii. Over 2,400 American soldiers and sailors were killed in the attack which led to a declaration of war by the United States.*
(National Archives)

committed pacifist, Rankin had voted against a similar resolution proposed by Woodrow Wilson in 1917 and she justified her principled opposition by claiming that: "As a woman, I can't go to war and I refuse to send anyone else. It is not necessary. I vote no."

The United States immediately began the process of mobilizing its enormous economic resources for the war and millions of young men patriotically volunteered to serve in the United States military. My father, Charles E. Bigler, was only 17 years old and was still a senior at Palm Beach High School in Florida. His mother insisted that he graduate before enlisting so it was not until sev-

Ensign Charles E. Bigler (second row, second from the left) poses with his fellow pilots and crew members. The Grumman TBM Avenger *was a carrier-based torpedo bomber with a crew of three.* (Philip Bigler)

Ensign Charles E. Bigler in the cockpit of his plane. Bigler was stationed at Grosse Isle, Michigan in 1945 while awaiting deployment to the Pacific theater. (Philip Bigler)

eral months later, on October 19, 1942, that he was finally able to join the United States Navy. Still just 18 years old, he was initially sent to the University of South Carolina for pre-flight instruction. He would spend the next two years of his life at various training facilities throughout the south learning to fly the Grumman TBM *Avenger*, the same type of carrier-based torpedo bomber that was then being piloted in the Pacific by Lt. George H.W. Bush.

My dad was commissioned as an ensign on September 2, 1944 and he proudly received his aviator wings. He was then stationed at Grosse Isle, Michigan where he and his fellow fliers were to await deployment to the Pacific theater to participate in the much anticipated invasion of Japanese homeland.

Like all Americans, he carefully watched the military progress in the war. The news from the European front was far more encouraging than that from the Pacific where the allied forces were struggling through the horrific battles of Iwo Jima and Okinawa. On April 30, 1945, Adolph Hitler and his mistress, Eva Braun, committed suicide in the Füherbunker during the Russian siege of Berlin. The Italian dictator, Benito Mussolini, had been captured by Italian partisans and unceremoniously executed just two days earlier. With the Nazi and Fascist leadership either dead or in hiding, the German army unconditionally surrendered to allied forces on May 8, 1945. Throughout the United States, there were spontaneous and enthused VE (Victory in Europe) Day celebrations and on that joyous day in Detroit, Michigan, Ensign Bigler met and fell in love with a young, beautiful waitress from Iowa, Bernice Ola Rains. As with many wartime relationships, their courtship was brief and the two were married shortly after the atomic bombings of Hiroshima and Nagasaki abruptly ended the fighting in World War II. Mercifully my father and countless other sailors, Marines and GI's would be spared the dreadful prospect of assaulting the Japanese home islands.

With the return to peace, the nation quickly demobilized its massive military forces. After four years of sacrifice and privation, the American people yearned for a return to normality. My father left active duty and moved to southern Florida with his new bride, where he hoped to avail himself of the generous educational opportunities offered World War II veterans under the newly passed GI Bill. He enrolled at the University of Miami in Coral Gables and finished his bachelor's degree in Business Administration in just two years. In 1948, he entered law school and supplemented his meager income by towing advertising banners over the crowded Miami beaches with a bi-plane he jointly owned with a couple of his buddies who were also former Navy pilots. Their ambitious and profitable enterprise ended abruptly when a fierce hurricane struck the east Florida coast and destroyed their uninsured airplane while grounded on the airport's tarmac.

Life was difficult for my parents during their early years of marriage. My mom and dad lived quite modestly since there was little money or time for luxuries or other frivolities. Compounding their problems was the fact that the post-war international situation was rapidly deteriorating. Political tensions between the United States and the Soviet Union intensified as Josef Stalin attempted to exert his influence over Eastern Europe and Asia. In June, 1950, the world was stunned when communist North Korea launched a full scale invasion of South Korea. President Harry Truman responded by ordering United States military forces under the command of General Douglas MacArthur into action, and soon American soldiers were engaged in a major land war in Asia, albeit under the auspices of the newly formed United Nations. My father, who was still in the naval reserves, was ordered to return to active duty in February, 1951, forever ending his hopes of becoming a lawyer. He would instead make the United States Navy his career for the next twenty years and he did so without either complaint or regret.

My brother, Bob, had been born the previous September and I was born two years later, in 1952. The two of us were part of the huge post World War II baby boom generation and our parents wanted to spare us the difficulties they had experienced in their youth during the great depression and World War II. We grew up in an era of backyard bomb shelters and the daily threat of nuclear annihilation, but as children we were shielded from the stark realities of global geopolitics. For us, the Eisenhower years were a time of innocence when our family watched the "Mickey Mouse Club," "Leave It to Beaver," "Ozzie and Harriett," and "Roy Rogers" on our new black and white television set. On weekends, we played pickup baseball and went to see the Saturday double-feature without fear or the need for parental supervision.

My father, like most military officers, was assigned a new duty station by the Navy every couple of years and he would be deployed for a time overseas as part of the Taiwan Patrol Force. Life for American military families has always been difficult and challenging. It is necessarily punctuated by regular disruptions and forced separations but like other military dependents, Bob and I were expected to be resilient and uncomplaining. Our mother, of course, bore the brunt of these adversities but she stoically maintained family discipline and order. She made sure that her two boys were raised devout Roman Catholics and we both served as altar boys having carefully memorized the responses for Tridentine Latin Mass by the age of eight (*Ad Deum qui lætificat juventútem meam*). In this pre-Vatican II world, the Catholic Church was a mystical sanctuary which provided all of us with a sense of permanence and immutability. There was little moral ambiguity—we didn't eat meat on Fridays, went to Mass on Sundays and on holy days of obligation, and were held to a higher standard than our protestant peers. Our religious faith provided Bob and me with a strong ethical anchor as well as a strict sense of right and wrong. We had a clear awareness of good and maintained our vigilance against perceived evil. It was, in many ways, a wholesome age when the local parish priest could actually be the real life incarnation of the mythical Father O'Malley so memorably portrayed by Bing Crosby in *Going My Way* and *The Bells of Saint Mary's*.

Still, our transient existence meant that Bob and I never developed any real long term, childhood friends or relationships. We were constantly moving and being forced to adapt to new surroundings, new schools, and new teachers. As Pat Conroy so eloquently describes in his book, *My Reading Life*:

> I think being a military brat is one of the strangest and most interesting ways to spend an American childhood.
> The military brats of America are an invisible, unorganized federation of brothers and sisters bound by common experience, by our uniformed fathers, by the movement of families being rotated through the American mainland and to military posts in foreign lands…We grew up strangers to ourselves. We passed through our military childhoods unremembered. We were transients, billboards to be changed, body temperatures occupying school desks for a short time. We came and went like rented furniture, serviceable when you needed it, but unremarked upon after it was gone.[11]

Our parents, though, always instilled in us the importance of a good education and my mother, in particular, oversaw our learning, enrolling us in quality schools, daily checking our homework, and she demanded that we show proper respect and reverence for our teachers. Education was undoubtedly the number one priority in the Bigler household.

In truth, I did not see any of this as a particular hardship at the time and I enjoyed the adventure of living in different parts of the country. But by the time I graduated from high school, I had attended nine different schools in four states. This could have been a prescription for academic disaster, but during those years I was

My mother, Bernice Bigler, reading to Bob and me at our home in Springfield, Virginia circa 1957. Education was always a priority in the Bigler household despite regular moves. I attended nine schools before graduating from high school.
(Philip Bigler)

fortunate to have had many dedicated teachers. There were two in particular, though, that would have a profound influence on my life.

In 1965, we moved from Westminster, California to Jacksonville, Florida where my father was assigned as a computer system analyst to the Fleet Intelligence Center for Europe (FICEUR). It was a top secret position and his office building on post was perpetually guarded by the Shore Patrol; its windows were sealed shut and covered by steel metal plates.

I was 13 years old and about to enter the eighth grade. This is an especially critical stage for adolescent boys since it is in middle school when far too many young men give in to the temptations of peer pressure, teenage angst and youthful insecurities.

The public schools in Jacksonville were still in a state of turmoil due to court-ordered desegregation, and many remained unaccredited. Despite considerable financial hardship, my parents decided to enroll Bob and me in the local parochial schools which had maintained their reputation for academic excellence through these turbulent years. Bob was sent to Bishop Kenny High School while I attended Sacred Heart School (SHS). It was located on Blanding Boulevard only a few miles from the naval airbase. Sacred Heart was a relatively new school. It had been established in 1960 by a group of four devout Sisters of Mercy. They had come from Clonakilty, Ireland on a mission to establish a school which would "view each student as a unique child of God" and "provide a safe, nurturing, and supportive learning environment where students can achieve their full potential and individuality."

Most of the buildings at Sacred Heart were still modest, temporary structures and the school's water supply came from wells which were tainted with sulfur. Although it was harmless to drink, the water gave off a horrible stench that smelled like rotten eggs and permeated the campus. The classes were routinely overcrowded but this did nothing to diminish the high academic and moral expectations of the sisters, priests and parents. The boys, of course, were expected to wear neatly pressed white shirts, black slacks and red, logo emblazoned SHS clip-on ties, while the girls' uniforms consisted of the characteristic Catholic plaid skirt, white blouse, bobby socks and saddle shoes.

I was fortunate that year to have as my eighth grade teacher one of the school's founders, Sister Mary Josephine O'Leary, RSM. She was a remarkable, sincere woman who took an active interest in the educational and spiritual well-being of all of her students. She had an incredible gift for making each one of us feel special and loved. I desperately wanted to please her so I worked hard and diligently in all of my subjects, earning A's and B's in everything except spelling. Nothing, it seemed, could inspire or motivate me to memorize the endless lists of vocabulary words. Sister Jo forgave me for this minor transgression and she continued to nurture my educational development. Like all great teachers, she was a wonderful role model who cared first and foremost about the well-being of her students. As one of her former pupils recently posted on Facebook, "I thought she had to be a saint when I was younger. I never met anyone like her before or since. Also, it was amazing how she knew everyone's names." Sister Josephine devoted almost 50 years of her life to teaching before finally retiring and her legacy continues through the lives of the countless students she inspired to become better human beings.

Three years later in 1968, I had another exceptional teacher who would make a profound difference in my life. By now, I was a junior in high school and once again the new kid in class since my father had retired from the Navy and we had relocated in 1968 for the last time as a family. Dad had begun a second career working with computers at IBM in downtown Washington, DC. That year, I had Colonel Ralph Sullivan as my US/Virginia history teacher at Oakton High School. He was a gruff, no-nonsense Marine who had just returned from two combat tours as a helicopter pilot in Vietnam. Col. Sullivan was not a particularly innovative or charismatic teacher. He spent most classes lecturing from his podium in the front of classroom. The only technology he used was an overhead from which he projected his handwritten transparencies onto a screen. Still, he had an incredible knowledge of history and his lectures were not mere renditions of dates and facts but rather were complex interpretations of the people, stories and events that made history exciting. In the spring, he took the class on a memorable field trip to the Gettysburg battlefield in Pennsylvania. I will never forget the excitement of that day walking through the sacred fields where thousands of soldiers had gallantly fought and died and where ultimately the union was preserved. The Civil War was no longer a mythical event confined to the pages of a stale textbook but was rather a seminal moment in our nation's history whose outcome had been shaped by the real life decisions of politicians, soldiers, patriots, and yes, even rogues and villains.

I learned a lot of history that year from Col. Sullivan but I also gained the critical understanding that in my life, there will always be more to learn and new books to read. I also discovered that to be an effective teacher, you have to be a perpetual student and live a life of the mind. These prospects intrigued and inspired me to pursue a career in education.

While it is obvious what an impact a great teacher can have upon his students, I also learned the harm that can be done by a single ineffective instructor. In 10th grade, I had a geometry teacher who had earned some minor notoriety at Bishop Kenny High School as the father of a famous rock star. The priests and nuns found this to be a mildly interesting novelty but they were completely oblivious to his son's avant-garde reputation and notorious antics, including posing for a well-known poster sitting on a toilet. This fascinating artifact, of course, was covertly smuggled into the school and caused quite a sensation for its scandalous content.

As amazing as it sounds by today's standards, we had 40 boys in our math class. The girls, of course, attended school across the street in a strictly enforced segregation that was designed to limit adolescent temptations. Despite our large classes and the high testosterone levels, there was a strict discipline and order imposed by the school and the rules were enforced punitively with paddles and after school detentions. In our geometry class, though, chaos reigned. Every day, several of the boys conspired to ask intentionally bizarre questions that were designed solely to get the teacher off topic. He readily complied and spent the day pontificating about nonsense while the rest of us were more than content to sit idly by, bored and ignorant, with our geometry books unopened and unused. We were all equally complicit in this ongoing plot since none of us had any desire to study or work hard. We never took any tests nor did we do any homework. Since the teacher never bothered to learn our names, for "assessment" at the end of each grading period, he would eventually call the roll to identify who we were and then generously hand out B's to mollify us so that we wouldn't complain to our parents or to the administration.

After 30 weeks of doing virtually nothing, rumors about what was truly going on in our class were running rampant. One afternoon, the principal suddenly appeared unannounced in the back of the room to observe a lesson. It was immediately obvious to her that we hadn't learned anything during the entire school year and the very next day, we had a brand new, novice teacher from Jacksonville University as our replacement instructor. He tried his best to teach us a year's worth of geometry in the final few weeks of class but it was a hopeless task. I had always been very good at math and I enjoyed the subject, but because of this one course, I never mastered Euclidian geometry and it would plague me for the rest of my academic career as I struggled through trigonometry and elementary calculus. It proved the axiom that one bad teacher can cripple a child for life.

I graduated from Oakton High School in June, 1970. Our ceremony was held on the school's football field and was memorable only for the plague of cicadas which had emerged from their 17-year hibernation to ruthlessly attack the graduates in their caps and gowns while we waited to receive our Fairfax County diplomas. The following month, on the occasion of my 18th birthday, I made the obligatory visit to the local selective service board to register for the draft. The Vietnam War was still raging and political discontent had escalated dramatically after four students were killed by National Guard troops at Kent State University earlier that May. In truth, I was not philosophically opposed to the war but I was looking forward to going to college and continuing my education. It was perhaps selfish on my part but the selective service system had instituted a system which classified all male college students as 2-S or temporarily deferred from military service. For all practical purposes, this meant that you would not be drafted as long as you remained in school and in good academic standing. It was a controversial law and many have justifiably claimed that it was unfair and even discriminatory. It proved beneficial for me, though, since the next year when a draft lottery was introduced, my "random sequence number" was 88, meaning a relatively high risk of being conscripted had it not been for my 2-S status.

I had applied to several Virginia colleges and was accepted at most of them. Unlike today's contemporary students, I didn't agonize over my choice of colleges. I eventually decided to attend Madison College solely because that was where my girlfriend wanted to go. It was not my most intelligent decision but it proved to be an ideal school for me. At that time, Madison was a small, liberal arts school nestled in the beautiful Shenandoah Valley just two hours away from my home in Fairfax. It had a stellar reputation for producing high quality teachers. Founded in 1908 as a normal school for women during the early national efforts to improve and professionalize the teaching profession, it had grown steadily since its founding and had expanded its curricular offerings. The college had only recently admitted men as full-time, boarding students but despite its growth and development, Madison had successfully preserved its intimate campus atmosphere. The college's administration continued to place a high premium on quality undergraduate instruction and these years were, in many ways, the golden days of the university—an idyllic time when classes were small, the professors were committed, and the acquisition of knowledge was cherished.

The history department was located, appropriately, in one of the oldest buildings on campus, Jackson Hall. Under the leadership of its chairman, Dr. Raymond Dingledine, the department had an outstanding reputation for excellence and I reveled in the challenging, thought-provoking courses and seminars. Our history professors expected us to read voraciously and I spent many agreeable hours studying in the campus library or reading quality books in my dorm room. As history majors, we were expected to write well-researched, source-based papers in every class to develop our skills as future historians. In Dr. Lee Congdon's modern European history class, I spent an entire semester researching the evolution of Nazi nihilist propaganda during the Third Reich. I became so interested and engrossed in the topic, that I made special arrangements with the National Archives in Washington to watch an original 35mm print of Leni Riefenstahl's "documentary" of the 1934 Nuremberg

Party Congress, *Triumph of the Will.* It was the first time that I came to fully appreciate the axiom that "one cannot deal with pure evil, with the naked, full-conscious evil that neither has nor seeks justification."[12] Through this and other challenging assignments, I discovered the joy of academic research and was able to improve my writing skills. I was determined to make history my life's work and hoped to inspire students to pursue this incredible course of study.

I graduated on schedule from Madison in May, 1974, receiving both my Bachelor's degree in history and a teaching license from the

Bernice Bigler (mother), Philip Bigler, Charles Bigler (father), and Ora Lee Schwarz (grandmother) at Madison College, May, 1974. I graduated with a Bachelor's degree and a teaching license but was unable to find employment in the schools for over a year. (Philip Bigler)

Commonwealth of Virginia. I felt well-prepared to accept the challenges of teaching in a public school classroom, but as the Nixon administration was drawing to a tragic and unexpected end due to the Watergate scandal, the American economy simultaneously faltered. There were virtually no openings in the schools for social studies teachers. Despite having meticulously typed dozens of letters to various school systems and having mailed out countless numbers of resumes, I never secured a single job interview that year. With my immediate teaching prospects so dismal, I decided to accept a graduate assistantship with the history department at Madison for the following academic year. It was a viable alternative to the stark realities of unemployment and would, at least, give me a temporary reprieve. I would also be able to use my time productively by improving my core content knowledge while refining my teaching philosophy and pedagogy.

Over the next year while still in graduate school, I continued to apply for teaching positions but nothing substantive ever transpired. It seemed that every day, the mailman delivered another standardized rejection letter, all of which further contributed to deflating my already fragile ego. For some masochistic reason, I started to decorate my office wall with these pitiful letters. By the end of the spring semester, in a true testament in futility, I had wallpapered the entire office and I had no job prospects whatsoever.

I had finished most of my course work by the summer of 1975, so I returned home to Fairfax. I was a 23-year old college graduate, living at home with my parents. Although it did nothing to advance my career goals, I had a job working 40 hours a week as an over-educated cook at the Hot Shoppes cafeteria at Tyson's Corner shopping center for a little over the minimum wage. In my spare time, I decided to expand my job quest to include all of the local private and parochial schools in the DC metropolitan area. My persistence finally paid off when, in late July, I was invited to interview for a history opening at a prestigious private academy located in the northern Virginia suburbs.

I was thrilled to have finally an opportunity to present myself personally for a teaching position, so I spent hours prepping for my scheduled interview with the school's headmaster. I even researched the school's history and familiarized myself with its curricula. I was well aware of the importance of first impressions, so in order to present a professional, dignified appearance, I purchased an expensive, three-piece suit. I knew, of course, that there were several other applicants competing for this same job but I was confident that no one would be able to match my enthusiasm for teaching.

On the appointed day, I arrived early so that I would have time to covertly tour the school grounds. I was impressed by the school's well-manicured fields, orderly classrooms and immaculate hallways. It was obvious that this was a place of privilege, wealth, and pedigree. At the assigned time, I met the headmaster who greeted me politely and then escorted me into the inner sanctum of his office. After a few minutes of casual conversation, he began to interrogate me about more substantive topics including my teaching philosophy and ideology. I answered most of the questions without too much difficulty and it seemed that the interview was progressing nicely. My confidence was soaring until the headmaster began to explain the essentials of the position and its many responsibilities. Although the school had all grades from kindergarten through 12th, he explained, I would be expected to teach only the upper level middle and high school students. If hired, I would be assigned five separate and distinct social studies classes, each consisting of a different curriculum requiring its own specific preparation. The salary was a paltry $6,500 per year and there were no health or retirement benefits included. Along with my individual teaching responsibilities, I would also be expected to coach the school's football team and, incredibly, to drive a small school bus every morning. I was shocked—I sat there for a moment in stunned silence trying to regain my composure and to digest all that I had just heard. But regardless of how ridiculous the class schedule and expectations were, I still felt that this was my one opportunity to start my teaching career so I assured the headmaster that everything was acceptable and that I would be honored to come to work at the school.

I left the interview a bit anxious but confident that I had made a good impression. I had done everything I could possibly do to secure the job so there was nothing else for me to do but to await a final decision. The next few days were, of course, pure agony. Each time the telephone rang, I was convinced that it was the principal calling to offer me the position. The school was in no hurry to fill its vacancy and it took several days before the anticipated phone call finally came. Instead of the headmaster, though, it was the school's secretary who had the lamentable task of informing me that they had selected another candidate for the position. She courteously wished me well on my continuing search for another teaching position but I was totally dejected.

It was now early August and the new school year was scheduled to begin in just a few weeks. I had exhausted all of my options and so, in utter frustration, I drove down to the local Air Force recruiting station in Falls Church to enlist in the military. To my chagrin, a sergeant informed me that all of the armed services were downsizing with the end of American participation in the Vietnam War and that there were no openings for someone with my educational background and experience. I had been rejected yet again.

Miraculously, a few days later I received an unexpected call from the assistant principal of my alma mater, Oakton High School. It seemed that one of their history teachers had suffered a heart attack over the summer and was still recuperating on short-term disability. The school desperately needed someone to cover his classes for the first grading period while he was home regaining his health. The AP wondered if I would be interested in a long-term substitute position at the school. It was made perfectly clear to me that this would be a short term, proposition—the job would end in early November and I would then have to leave.

I didn't hesitate for a second and gladly accepted the offer. This was finally my opportunity to be a teacher and to have my own classroom and my own students. Even if it would be just for a short time, I would at least be able to fulfill my dreams.

Endnotes

11 Pat Conroy (2010), *My Reading Life*. New York: Nan A. Talese/Doubleday, p.186.

12 Ayn Rand (1999), *Atlas Shrugged*. New York: Plume Publishing, p. 303.

CHAPTER III

Cause, Effect, & Consequences

Youth is the best season wherein to acquire knowledge, tis a season when we are freest from care, the mind is then unencumbered and more capable of receiving impressions than in an advanced age.

Abigail Adams

I officially began my teaching career at precisely 8:00 AM, September 2, 1975. I had spent most of the previous week attending the vast array of required faculty and departmental meetings that are, for some reason, deemed necessary to begin every new school year. In between these tedious and routine meetings, I somehow managed to decorate my new classroom by hanging historic flags from the ceiling and covering the bare walls with colorful posters and motivational sayings. The room was transformed from a drab, sterile place into an inviting, vibrant learning environment. I also spent many long hours carefully preparing my first week of lesson plans, most of which were focused upon the early English explorers and the establishment of the Jamestown colony in 1607.

Even though I was a brand new teacher, I was not assigned a mentor to assist me during these critical first days of teaching. In truth, no one really offered me much in the way of advice or encouragement nor did they share with me any innovative ideas or lesson plans. I was left pretty much on my own but I was keenly aware that my professional responsibilities as a novice teacher were essentially the same as those of the more experienced, veteran educators who had been in the classroom for decades. I was humbled by this realization and was keenly aware that I had much to learn. It was certainly going to be an interesting and challenging semester.

Over the Labor Day weekend, I carefully and neatly inscribed the names of my assigned students into my new gradebook. I was well aware of the fact that the vast majority of these students would enter my class with no prior interest in American history. Many would be openly skeptical about the course's relevancy to their contemporary existence but it would be my job to inspire them and to capture their imaginations. My ultimate goal was to teach them to love history as much as I did. In order to do this, though, I knew I would have to provide them with a credible, coherent rationale for why studying the past was important.

Tony Hendra, the English writer and satirist, offered an exceptionally eloquent justification for history in his book, *Father Joe*. He explained, "...history [is] not simply a catalog of the dead and buried and benighted, but rather a vast new world to be pioneered; that if you approached the past generously, so to speak—its people as humans, not facts, as modern in their time as we were in ours, who thought and felt as we do, the dead would live again, our equals, not our old-fashioned, hopelessly unenlightened, and backward inferiors."[13] The past must be treated with respect and with honesty by teachers. We need to avoid the easy temptation of vilifying our ancestors for their past mistakes while pretending to be their moral superiors. Our students have to be trained to learn to look at historical events within the context of the period, free to make their own judgments while learning to think independently and critically. My fondest hope was that my classroom would be an academic sanctuary where, as Thomas Jefferson's stated, it would: "… be based on the illimitable freedom of the human mind. For here we are not afraid to follow truth wherever it may lead, nor to tolerate any error so long as reason is left free to combat it."

Through my own personal study of history, I had rejected the popular premise that you can somehow predict future events by studying the past. Indeed, no contemporary political or societal circumstances are ever identical so thus no outcomes can ever be the same. Moreover, I also shunned the concepts of economic and political determinism which portrayed people as hapless victims of history. No, throughout time the ultimate fate and destiny of nations has been determined by the decisions and choices made by individuals. The resulting consequences have been determined by their actions (or in some cases, inaction) which have ultimately decided the course of human destiny. As such, our very concept of civilization has proven to be extremely fragile.

The American Founding Fathers were acutely aware of these realities and they fully comprehended the pivotal role that they were playing in shaping history. As Thomas Paine so astutely observed in his revolutionary treatise, *Common Sense*, "We have it in our power to begin the world over again." The Founders' remarkable efforts to formulate a constitutional government with proscribed, limited powers—one that would likewise maximize human freedom and liberty—were predicated upon a careful and scholarly study of the past. In 1776, coincidentally the same year that Thomas Jefferson penned the Declaration of Independence, the British historian, Edward Gibbon, published the first volume of his epic work, *The Decline and Fall of the Roman Empire*. The book caused an immediate sensation throughout the British Empire since it seemed to constitute an overt and prophetic warning both to the British Parliament and King George III. Gibbon argued persuasively that the gradual loss of civic virtue among the Roman citizenry coupled with the consistent failure of the nation's political leadership to address serious problems caused the world's greatest empire to dissolve into venality. A slow and systematic decay and degeneration of Roman society resulted, so that by the fifth century, barbarian hordes (Visigoths and Vandals) from the north were able to successfully invade and sack the empire's once proud capital. The great Christian theologian, St. Augustine, attempted to explain the triumph of the pagan hordes in his epic book, *The City of God*, but their victory was total and complete, ending with the abdication of the last Roman emperor, Romulus Augustus, in 476 AD. Europe now descended into what would later become known as the Dark Ages, a stagnant period which would last almost a millennium. "Immortal Rome," the American patriot John Adams lamented, "was at first but an insignificant village… but by degrees rose to a stupendous height, and excelled in arts and arms all the nations that preceded it…[but ultimately] it [sank] into debauchery, and made it at length an easy prey to Barbarians."[14]

Gibbon's landmark work was far more than a mere rendition of dates and facts. *The Decline and Fall of the Roman Empire* was a brilliantly written and compelling narrative illuminated its readers with its clear and vivid explanation of history. Gibbon argued conclusively that even the greatest and most powerful nations could collapse if their leaders and citizenry failed to respond effectively to social challenges and political crises. It was a classic example of what I liked to refer to as historical cause, effect, and consequences. Interestingly, Aleksandr Solzhenitsyn would express these same sentiments two centuries later in his prophetic warnings to western democracies about the dangers of tyrannies during the 20th century.

John Adams believed that the study of history provided a "solid instruction" for young people and he urged his son, John Quincy, to read it extensively. The former president realized how dangerous ignorance of the past was to a free, republican society. In his retirement years, Adams was increasingly alarmed by the fact that the post-Revolutionary generation was becoming complacent and took for granted the rights and liberties that had been so painfully won during America's struggle for independence. These younger Americans were guilty of the common mistake of assuming that what had occurred in the past had been inevitable, that there could have been no alternative outcome. What they failed to appreciate, however, was the actual chaos of the times; abject and total failure had been a very real possibility and there had been immense peril in the Founders' decisions and actions. It was not mere hyperbole when they solemnly pledged in the Declaration of Independence, "our Lives, our Fortunes and our sacred Honor." If the American Revolution had been unsuccessful, history would have dismissed these men as traitors rather than patriots.

My overall philosophy of history was still evolving but I knew from the start that I was doing important work. I was on the front lines in the ongoing battle against ignorance and the stakes for our state and nation were enormous. What I would teach my students in class would hopefully help them prepare for life and translate into becoming productive citizens who would live meaningful lives.

The start of each school year is always an exciting time. There are very few professions that allow people to start over; but for teachers, every September is essentially a new beginning. What happened the previous school year, either good or bad, no longer really matters. Instead, teachers have the unique opportunity to re-create themselves and to re-establish their reputation with their current students.

I was excited about the prospect of beginning the new school year but I was a bit apprehensive as well. I hoped and prayed that all of my preparation would be adequate and that my new students would accept me despite my inexperience. My teaching schedule consisted of five sections of eleventh grade United States/Virginia History.

High school juniors are, in many ways, an ideal age group to teach. The students are generally more mature and they see this year of high school as the one that matters the most. Indeed, colleges and universities tend to look more closely at these grades as evidence of academic promise and ability. For most students, they will also take the SAT's for the first time, so there is a clear message that academics do matter, at least if they have any hopes of attending a decent college. Likewise, it is the students' eleventh grade teachers who write most of their college recommendations, so the students tend to be better behaved.

Despite all of my college and academic preparation, I still had an enormous amount to learn about how to be an effective teacher. It would take a few years before I was completely comfortable with the curriculum and would be able to adjust to the incredible work load. I discovered that it takes an enormous amount of talent and skill to inspire and motivate students on a daily basis and those truly great teachers who can do this routinely should be cherished and revered.

I desperately wanted to be a good teacher during that first year but I was forced to settle for being a diligent and sincere one. I have since forgiven myself for all of the mistakes that I made during these early days of my teaching career, and I now realize that a more realistic goal for me would have been to strive to have simply more good days than bad.

Before our academic classes could actually begin, all of the teachers first had to meet with their assigned administrative homerooms. Nothing has ever been concocted by the educational establishment that more effectively drains the enthusiasm of students and teachers than these marathon, two hour bureaucratic sessions.

My own homeroom consisted of 30 students who were grouped alphabetically by grade level for the convenience of the guidance department. Although we would be required to meet with them on a monthly basis for various clerical reasons, it was hard to form any lasting bond with these students or even to establish any real rapport.

The entire homeroom period was devoid of any substantive instruction. It consisted wholly of completing various administrative tasks. I took attendance, passed out student schedules, assigned lockers, reviewed bus schedules, distributed federal survey forms, went over student rights and responsibilities, collected past due fees and fines, read announcements, and alphabetized forms. It was incredibly boring and tedious work and despite the advent of modern technology, these routine chores continue to multiply, to the dismay of educators.

Finally, the principal made an announcement over the school's PA system releasing us from this purgatory and the real school year could actually begin, albeit now with seriously abbreviated academic periods. When I met my students for the first time, they seemed to like the prospect of having a young, idealistic teacher as their instructor. I was relieved that none of them were yet aware of my second class status as a long term substitute.

I was obsessed with preparation and I spent hours of meticulous planning to ensure that I had everything ready for my first day. Over the long Labor Day weekend, I wrote my course syllabus which carefully explained the course requirements and class expectations, and then typed it onto stencils. I arrived early Tuesday morning to run off the needed 150 copies on the history department's antiquated ditto machine. All of the students loved to receive the freshly printed handouts so they could inhale the fragrant fumes of the ditto fluid which permeated the paper. It certainly called into serious question the effectiveness of our school's anti-drug policies. Unfortunately, the quality of the ditto stencils deteriorated with each copy so that the characteristic royal blue ink slowly faded into illegibility. I would always have to read the syllabus out loud to the afternoon classes so that they didn't miss anything important.

I felt pretty comfortable with the content of the American history curriculum. Since the course was supposed to be arranged chronologically, I started predictably with the colonial period. It is an era especially important to Virginians since the first English settlement was established in Jamestown. I had taken all of the classes in colonial history that had been offered by Professor Clive Hallman while in college and this even included an amazing three week seminar which featured a week of intensive study at Colonial Williamsburg.

Content knowledge is a vital component to effective teaching, but to effectively motivate students to learn, it takes far more. I made a lot of neophyte mistakes during these early days of my teaching career as I struggled to develop my own classroom identity and personal teaching style. I initially tried to model myself after my own high school teachers, which meant that I tended to lecture a little too much, relied too heavily on the textbook, and gave too many multiple choice tests. It was competent but uninspired teaching, but I still tried to make my classes interesting and fun. I liked to take the students to the school library to conduct historical research and I assigned several projects including having them publish their own patriotic Stamp Act newspaper in protest of British taxation policies. For review, we often played a rousing and fierce game of classroom Jeopardy. Through all of this, the students were patient and understanding and we began to develop a positive connection based upon mutual respect.

I never worked so hard in my life. I spent every waking hour reading, studying and preparing lesson plans. In this pre-digital world, I had few resources to guide me so I had to rely upon my own creativity and innovation. Every class proved to be a unique challenge and I tried to learn from my mistakes and was constantly seeking ways to improve my instruction. I knew that to make history relevant and interesting for teenagers, it was important that I not only be able to relate the facts of a period, I had to be able to assess the content for its historical significance. I quickly discovered that the better prepared I was, the more comfortable I felt in the classroom, but this also meant that I had little social life—I was totally devoted to school.

By late September, I was beginning to become reasonably comfortable with my role as a high school history teacher. I was unaware that Fairfax County had failed to adequately staff several of their schools over the summer, including Oakton. Our school's World History classes were impacted the most by this staffing issue and were seriously overcrowded. Indeed, several of the teachers were complaining loudly and frequently to the administration about what they rightfully saw to be an intolerable situation. Many had classes with over 35 students and there were not enough desks. Some students were forced to sit on the floor during class while others chose to perch themselves on the classroom's radiator. Regardless, it was not conducive to a quality learning environment and it was obvious that something had to be done soon. After weeks of lobbying, the principal finally received authorization from the county's centralized personnel office to hire an additional social studies teacher in an effort to reduce class size. Although I was unaware of it at the time, for once my luck was beginning to improve. Since I was already working at the school, I would be the logical choice for the new job.

One afternoon, I was summoned over the school's PA system

to the main office. I was terrified and convinced that I must have done something dreadfully wrong when I heard that the assistant principal to want to meet with me. The AP was a nice guy and he kindly reassured me that the purpose for this unexpected meeting was benign. Indeed, he wanted to offer me a contract for full-time employment as a social studies teacher. It seemed that my perseverance had finally paid off.

The assistant principal then went on to explain that the teacher I was replacing would be returning in just a few weeks. And despite having been in the classroom for over 30 years, he had never taught any subject but American history. It would be easier for the school just to hire another long term substitute to take over my current schedule rather than risk alienating this teacher. Thus, I was informed that I would be reassigned to teach five newly created sections of 9th grade World History. These classes would be formed by involuntarily transferring several students from their existing classes into my newly created ones. What made matters worse was that the students would be selected wholly at the discretion of their current history teachers. The practical consequence of this inane policy was that it provided the World History teachers with an extraordinary opportunity to reduce their overall class load by purging their class rolls of their least motivated and most disgruntled students.

The new schedules were delivered by the guidance department to the unsuspecting students late Friday afternoon in a clever effort to lessen the overall impact. I left school that day knowing that most of my "new" students would be extremely unhappy about having their lives disrupted this late into the grading period. I spent a restless and agonizing weekend trying to think of ways to appease the students' hurt feelings and help them cope with this change in a positive and mature manner.

I had additional concerns as well about the World History curriculum. I wasn't nearly as comfortable with the course content and I was intimidated by what seemed to be an impossible amount of material to cover satisfactorily. How can a teacher possibly condense 1,100 years of Roman history into a short three week unit? How was I going to get the students excited about the technological accomplishments of the ancient Chinese empire? Why would the Stoic philosophy of Epictetus be relevant to a contemporary teenager? How could students fathom the horrors of the French Revolution and the resulting Reign of Terror when Hollywood movies and the national television news daily glorified such slaughter? These were fundamental, serious questions and I would be destined to spend the entire year grappling with them.

On Monday morning when my new classes convened, my worst fears were realized. All of the students were in foul, sullen moods. When I tried to engage them in conversation, they were unresponsive while a few—admittedly a small but significant few—were openly hostile. I quickly surmised that the course content was going to be initially secondary to the necessity of gaining control of these disgruntled classes. Yet I never had any real, substantive training in college about how to effectively manage a dysfunctional classroom or how to impose effective discipline or how to deal with indifferent students.

Most of my discipline problems involved relatively minor infractions of school rules such as refusing to do class work or just sleeping in class, but there certainly is nothing more obnoxious in our world than a bored teenager. Others, though, were more serious and bordered upon open insubordination. I soon discovered that the threat of bad grades or of parent conferences did little to deter this unacceptable behavior or to improve the situation. For weeks I struggled to get the students interested in World History and to learn to behave civilly. I tried everything I could think of including showing 16 mm films, providing detailed study guides, creating worksheets, assigning class projects, and attempting class discussions. I did make some inroads with those students who were willing at least to try but there were still far too many students who refused to engage. My classes were rapidly becoming an embarrassment and an educational disaster.

The prospect of failure proved to be a great motivator and I was willing to experiment and to try anything to improve my instruction. One day in late autumn after yet another miserable class, I went down to the social studies work room and spent a few hours scouring through a stack of educational catalogs in an effort to discover some new ideas or inspired lesson plans. I happened upon an advertisement for a historical simulation game entitled *Grand Illusion*. It purported to provide a series of highly motivational lesson plans that would effective dramatize the climatic events surrounding the outbreak of World War I. It came with a wide range of teaching materials including a set of primary source documents, a vinyl LP record, a laminated map of Europe in 1914, and an extensive teaching manual. Although the simulation cost a staggering $50, I was so desperate that I immediately went home and wrote a check to the company despite my pauper's income of just $9,500 annually.

When the long anticipated simulation finally arrived a few weeks later, I spent several hours carefully reading over the teacher's guide. This was something truly revolutionary—a unit that would be entirely student-center and whose ultimate outcome would be decided by the decisions of the students. They would be facing the same difficult

Amy Campbell presides over a 1914 peace conference during a "Grand Illusion" simulation at Oakton High School circa 1978. Historical simulation games help make history come alive for the students and they became active, enthusiastic participants in their own learning. (Philip Bigler)

challenges that faced their historic counterparts in Austria-Hungary, Germany, France, Italy, Great Britain, the Ottoman Empire, Russia, and the United States. The ultimate fate of the Balkans as well as the territorial aspirations of their respective countries would lie in the hands of a group of contemporary high school students in Room 142 at Oakton High School. The prospect was exhilarating and I had an important epiphany—my role as a high school history teacher was not just to impart knowledge but also to facilitate authentic learning.

When the students reported to class the next day, they were shocked to see that our classroom had been transformed into a site for an international peace conference. Each team had been assigned a separate space which was indicated by their country's flag. There they discovered a packet of top secret material that listed their goals and national aspirations, while detailing their objectives for success in the simulation. Many of these objectives, though, proved to be in direct conflict with those of other nations, so to achieve victory would require cunning, diplomacy, and ingenuity.

Something quite magical happened in my classes over that week. The students actually became active participants in their own education. They began to discuss among themselves how they hoped to "win" the game and began making covert alliances with some of the other groups. The students carefully studied the territorial map of Europe that was prominently posted in the front of the room, and attempted to initiate negotiations with friendly, allied nations. The more powerful, militaristic countries postured and threatened, while the poor, hapless Serb contingent helplessly appealed to Russia, their Slavic kin, for help against the growing threat of an Austrian-Hungarian invasion. It was fun. It was also authentic, content-based learning.

The power of this type of lesson became even more apparent to me some 25 years later when I went to a local trophy store to purchase some awards for a few of my students. The store clerk was a gentleman in his early 40's and turned out to have been one of my students from that first year at Oakton High School. Although he had never gone on to college or pursued his education much beyond high school, the first thing he said to me was: "I was Bosnia-Herzegovina when we played *Grand Illusion* in class my freshman year. What's going on in the Balkans today sure looks a lot like 1914." I was impressed; he was aware and informed about current events based upon what we had learned in class years prior. It was one of the most gratifying moments of my entire teaching career.

From this point on in my career, using historical simulations in my classes became an key part of my teaching pedagogy. It was gratifying to see my classes finally evolving into a place where serious, substantive learning took place. I loved seeing the students master new material while acquiring vital content knowledge. Moreover, they were gaining an important sense of historical perspective. It seemed that I had truly found my life's calling.

Things were going well until that spring. The local newspapers were reporting on an ominous political situation that was developing between the Fairfax County School Board and Board of Supervisors. The two were engaged in a nasty fight over the next year's fiscal budget and neither side was willing to compromise. Matters were only made worse when one of the supervisors was widely quoted as saying that teachers were the highest paid *part-time* employees in the state. The contentious negotiations made the disputes we had dramatized earlier that year in class between Russia and Germany in 1914 seem mild by comparison.

By mid-April, there was a stalemate with no solution in sight. Without a guarantee of adequate funding, the school board issued over 900 teacher "pink slips," euphemistically referred to as RIF (reduction in force) notices. Under the precept of "last hired, first fired," I, along with all of my fellow first year teachers, were formally advised at the end of the third grading period that our teaching contracts would not be renewed for the following year. It was devastating and discouraging. I personally felt that this callous action on the part of our school board was arbitrary and malicious since these politically motivated dismissals were not in any way performance-based. The immediate consequence for me was that it ruined my naïve sense of idealism. I finally began to understand the harsh reality that in American public schools, many decisions are not made in the best interest of the students.

My ultimate fate had not been resolved by the time school adjourned in mid-June for summer vacation. The assistant principal, however, met with me before I left and was kind and reassuring; he firmly believed that the ongoing political feud would ultimately be resolved and that I would be rehired. Fortunately, I had already planned for a busy summer so there was little time to dwell upon my precarious employment situation.

I was enrolled in two challenging graduate-level summer classes at George Mason University—"The History of the Cold War" and "Educational Research Methods and Statistics." I was also scheduled to take my final comprehensive oral exams for my Master's degree, so I had to spend a good deal of time studying and preparing. It also proved to be an interesting summer from the historical perspective since the United States celebrated the bicentennial of the American Revolution on July 4, 1976. The gala was a welcomed distraction for the nation after the painful collapse of South Vietnam the previous year and from the aftermath of the Watergate scandal. In mid-July, the Democrats chose to nominate a virtually unknown governor and peanut farmer from Georgia named Jimmy Carter for president, while the Republicans reluctantly settled upon Gerald Ford as their candidate in Kansas City. Although Ford was technically the incumbent, he had assumed office by virtue of the XXV Amendment and had never been elected on a national ticket. Many of the Republican Party faithful were unenthusiastic, preferring the former governor of California, Ronald Reagan, to the current president.

As the summer progressed, just as my principal had prophesized, a settlement was finally reached in the budget impasse and the school board offered me a new teaching contract. It was a relief and I was eager to put all of the residual bitterness behind me and to begin a brand new school year. The guidance department sent me my teaching schedule in early August and it was perfect. I would be teaching three sections of freshmen World History and two classes of 11th grade American history. Because of space limitations, though, I was assigned to a vacant Home Economics classroom. It was located adjacent to the high school cafeteria and meant that I would be isolated from my peers in the Social Studies department, who were all teaching on the opposite side of the school. Although the room was spacious, it was hardly an ideal environment for teaching history. My students' desks were surrounded by several unused sewing machines, ironing boards, and other household implements. My first priority was to strategically place flags and posters around the classroom to camouflage these domestic implements so that my room would be a suitable place for studying the historical past.

At a student pep rally during my early years at Oakton High School. I was RIF'ed due to budget issues during my first two years as a classroom teacher.
(Philip Bigler)

My previous year's worth of experience had greatly improved my overall confidence and teaching skills. I still didn't consider myself to be a "great" teacher but I was certainly competent and was pleased that my instruction was continuing to improve. I was also popular with the students and was actively involved in a wide variety of extracurricular school activities. I attended most of our "Cougar" football games and volunteered to sponsor Oakton's new ice skating club. Likewise, I was regularly enlisted to chaperone student sock-hops, and that fall my students even convinced me to participate in a "donkey basketball" game.

This annual spectacle was extremely popular with the students and always proved to be a lucrative fund raiser. The game pitted a team of faculty members against several well-liked seniors. The premise was that each participant, protected from potential injury and hazard by only a standard-issue football helmet, would be assigned a donkey and they would then ride around the basketball court in an attempt to score a goal. The animals were equipped with special, customized rubber horseshoes to ensure that their hooves did not damage the court's highly polished hardwood floors. The donkeys, of course, were not house-broken and that aspect particularly appealed to the juvenile humor of the student body.

It seemed to me to be a harmless if somewhat sophomoric activity so I agreed to participate. At the pre-game meeting, the owner of the donkeys went over the sparse rules of the game and then casually inquired about who was the youngest member of our faculty team. Although in retrospect this should have made me suspicious, I innocently identified myself and was then assigned to an innocuous looking grey-and-white donkey affectionately known as "Honey Pot."

A referee signaled for the game to begin and everyone successfully climbed onto the backs of their donkeys to commence play. When I attempted to do the same, though, Honey Pot immediately became agitated and began to buck and kick. He threw me onto the hardwood floor and the crowd erupted into laughter. I tried to recover my composure but it proved futile since unbeknownst to me, Honey Pot held the distinction of being the only donkey in the game that had never been successfully ridden (a distinction he still has as far as I know). So I spent the remainder of the evening frustrated, being repeatedly thrown to the ground by the triumphant Honey Pot. For me, the whole thing soon ceased to be funny and became a painful embarrassment. I didn't like being laughed at and decided then and there that I would never again allow myself to be put into a situation that would demean or humiliate me before my students. It became an essential tenet of my teaching philosophy—a teacher must always maintain his dignity and remain a positive role model for his students.

At least all of my classes were going well. I particularly enjoyed planning lessons and trying new activities that would get the students enthused about learning history. The kids were willing learners and the months flew by as I was hitting my stride as a teacher. The nation's economy, though, remained stubbornly sluggish, mired by high unemployment, ongoing stagflation and high energy costs. Once again, the school board was locked in a predictable feud with the Fairfax County Board of Supervisors over adequate school funding. It was all becoming pretty tiresome and I, like most of my colleagues, felt that we were helpless political pawns in the annual budget chess game. I tried to ignore the partisan politics and concentrate on my students and my lessons. I was, thus, completely unaware of the fact that during a late night session of the school board, a decision had once again been reached to RIF dozens of teachers. In accordance with the terms of the negotiated teacher contracts, layoff notices would have to be delivered immediately in order to meet a mid-April deadline.

I was teaching my third period World History class when I was interrupted in mid-sentence by a surprise knock upon the door. Such disturbances are routine in high school and usually entail something minor, such as a note from the guidance department requesting to see an individual student, or a message from the office informing a student that their parents had delivered their missing lunch. I was therefore surprised to see the assistant principal standing next to a somber looking gentleman. It was immediately obvious that both were uncomfortable and the stranger identified himself as one of the county's human resource officers. He quickly handed me a piece of paper and directed me to sign the document indicating that I had been officially informed that due to the actions by the school board, my teaching contract would not be renewed for the 1977-78 school year.

I was taken totally by surprise and hastily scribbled my signature across the bottom of the paper without comment. I silently asked myself, "What kind of profession does this to people? What did I do to deserve to be treated in such a callous manner?" Dejected, I returned to my desk and told my students that they could use the remainder of the class period to finish their homework assignment. I tried to avoid eye contact and pretended to focus on a stack of student papers in front of me. The students were eerily quiet, an amazing thing in itself for 14-year olds; no one spoke and they all recognized that something terrible had just happened. After a few painful minutes, one brave little girl quietly asked, "Mr. Bigler, did something just happen?" I tried to regain my composure and told the class that I had just received a layoff notice which meant that I wouldn't be returning to Oakton the following year.

Endnotes

13 Tony Hendra (2004), *Father Joe: The Man Who Saved My Soul.* New York: Random House, p. 238.

14 John Adams quoted in David McCullough (2001). *John Adams.* New York: Simon & Schuster, p. 39.

CHAPTER IV

Reading, Romanovs
& Professionalism

*Parents or professors who do not encourage their young to tackle
big jobs commit a moral crime against those young people. For we
know that when the young are properly challenged, they will rise to
the occasion and they will prepare themselves for the great work that
remains to be done.*

James Michener

It was another long and excruciating summer. By early August, I
still didn't know if the county's budget impasse would ever be
resolved and I had not been recalled nor had I heard anything
from the school. I finally swallowed what was left of my pride and
went into Oakton to see if I could find out any current news. I was
politely informed that staffing for the fall was still uncertain and
that I should continue to "have patience" but this ongoing ambiguity
was aggravating and only added to my growing sense of frustration
and disillusionment. I was now facing the very real prospect of being unemployed and I had several financial obligations and com-
mitments including an apartment lease and a regular car payment.
My parents, as usual, were totally supportive and they reassured

me that they would be there to help me out financially if needed, but I found it appalling that a 25-year old college graduate would still be dependent upon the generosity of his parents. What troubled me most, though, was the lack of respect that I was beginning to feel as a classroom teacher. It seemed that to the politicians, accountants and bureaucrats that ran and directed the school system, teachers were just another fiscal commodity to be manipulated in a vast, impersonal educational apparatus where the bottom line of a ledger sheet dictated policy. In such a callous and arbitrary system, the overall quality of education suffered and an individual teacher's dedication, skill and commitment meant little. In the span of just two years, my naïve sense of idealism had been severely tarnished and it was being replaced by a growing sense of mistrust.

Miraculously, just a few days before teachers were scheduled to report back to school from summer vacation, all of the RIF's were again rescinded and I was rehired. It was an enormous relief, but when I returned to school I discovered that due to overcrowding, I had been exiled to a temporary classroom which was, in fact, a cheap, gutted metal house trailer that had been moved over the summer onto a tennis court. It proved to be a horrible teaching environment. Unlike modern temporaries, this trailer was so narrow that it was like teaching in a hallway since the student desks could only be arranged one way—three across and ten deep. To make matters even worse, the "classroom" was located a good distance away from the main building and across a faculty parking lot. The isolated location prevented it from being wired to the school's public address system and it was impossible to hear bells or fire alarms due to the persistent loud noise generated by the unit's window air condition-

American history students with me at Oakton High School. My temporary class-room was an old, gutted house trailer that was located on an unused tennis court. It proved to be an awful teaching environment where the students were forced to sit in cramped quarters. (Philip Bigler)

ers. Likewise, whenever it rained, the noise generated by the water striking the metal was deafening and the students would arrive at the door soaked to the skin and miserable after having made a mad dash from the main building across the parking lot littered with pools and puddles. Yet regardless of these hardships, I was determined to make the 1977-1978 a successful academic year. I had, in fact, finally accumulated enough seniority within the school system that I would not get laid off for the first time in my career.

The seventies were, in general, a difficult era to begin a teaching career since the American public schools were undergoing a radical transformation. Due to the incredible societal upheavals of the previous decade, the schools, like much of society, had lost their traditional sense of mission and focus; there was a widespread cynicism prevalent among the education elite. Disillusioned by the Vietnam War, Watergate, political assassination and scandal, the schools attempted to reinvent themselves by becoming "relevant" and they did this by abandoning the so-called authoritarian rules and regulations of the past. As educator Diane Ravitch accurately notes:

> [Many school reforms] were intended to liberate students from burdensome requirements. Still others proceeded in the spirit of A. Neill's Summerhill, where any sort of adult authority was strictly forbidden. Tear down the walls between the classrooms, said some reformers. Free the children, free the schools, abolish all rules and requirements. Let the English teacher teach math, and the math teacher teach English. Let students design their own courses and learn whatever (or if ever) they feel like learning whenever (or if ever) they feel like learning. Get rid of graduation requirements, college entrance requirements, grades, tests, and textbooks. Down with the canon. On it went, with reformers, radicals, and revolutionaries competing to outdo one another.[15]

It was, in truth, absolute insanity. Throughout the country, billions of taxpayer dollars were being frivolously wasted in the construction of new, holistic schools that were built without walls or well-defined classrooms. There was also a movement towards "values education," where students were assigned absurd scenarios and then asked to speculate about the value of life or some other moral conundrum. At Oakton, we avoided the worst excesses of the decade but we did have a specially designated smoking court which allowed students to enjoy a cigarette or two between classes, during break and at lunch time. This area quickly became a student sanctuary and swiftly degenerated into an adult-free, no-man's land where drugs were readily available. It was common for the smell of marijuana to permeate the air and we frequently had to have a "stoned" student removed from class. Likewise, we abandoned the repressive dress codes of the past and this allowed the students to proclaim their freedom by wearing their colorful polyester bell-bottoms, "hot pants," mood rings, and Earth Shoes to school. The hallways seemed to be populated by the cast of *Hair*.

The public schools were seen as ideal laboratories for human experimentation by liberal university professors. Fueled by lavish federal grants, they used the nation's classrooms to test their esoteric theories and hypotheses without any fear of accountability or the resulting consequences. Each year, teachers were mandated to implement some new initiative, the latest educational fad, which was purported to be the revolutionary answer to all of the problems faced by American public education. In history, for instance, we were mandated to devote a significant amount of instructional time each week to a discussion of current events. The students, of course, had little historical background or academic substance by which to form rational arguments or opinions, so these classes became little more than an exercise in futility. Another year, several teachers decided to abandon the traditional (and proven) chronological approach to history in order to experiment with a thematic method which emphasized general trends such as war and peace, immigration, reform movements, and political unrest. The end result was that most students had no concept of cause and effect or any linear sense of time. They left their history classes even more befuddled and confused.

Yet probably the most egregious sin of the period was the imposition of a rigid tracking system which removed struggling students from their mainstream classes and assigned them to special sections. Although like most educational "reforms," this was well-intentioned and intended to help these challenged students, but academic tracking actually served to isolate and further alienate them. Most of these students suffered from severe learning disabilities and what they needed was not academic exile but intensive help, inspired instruction, and positive intervention. To aggravate matters, someone got the bright idea to brand these special classes with a cruel acronym, "AUS," which stood for "Academically Unsuccessful Students." No wonder that school was a daily humiliation for these children and their own personal purgatory.

Reading remains the single most fundamental skill needed for academic success. I always encouraged my students to read great books related to history.
(www.comstock.com)

While teaching one of the special sections of AUS World History, I quickly became aware that virtually all of my students suffered from severe, fundamental reading problems. It was their basic lack of literacy that was preventing them from achieving any real success in school. Indeed, reading impacts every aspect of a child's educational development including vocabulary acquisition, writing proficiency, and content knowledge. As one of my wise colleagues observed, the first three grades of elementary school should be primarily devoted to teaching students how to read; after that, we expect that students will be able to read to learn.

Yet reading skills continue to decline in our public schools. In 2011, the *Washington Post* reported alarmingly that "SAT reading scores for graduating high school seniors this year reached the lowest point in nearly four decades."[16] The fact that we continue to fail to educate a literate generation amounts to little more than educational malpractice since reading proficiency is, undoubtedly, the single most important skill that a child must acquire during his educational development. Throughout my entire teaching career, I have found nothing—no computer program, no film, no class project—that can adequately replace the learning experience of reading a quality book. Indeed, as author Pat Conroy so eloquently writes, books remain a civilization's gateway to the past and hold the keys to our imagination:

> Books permitted me to embark on dangerous voyages to a world of painted faces of mandrills and leopards scanning the veldt from the high branches of a baobab tree. There was nothing my mother could not bring me from a library…If I close my eyes I can conjure up a whole country of the dead who will live for all time because writers turned them into living flesh and blood. There is Jay Gatsby

floating face downward in his swimming pool or Tom Robinson's bullet-riddled body cut down in his Alabama prison yard in *To Kill a Mockingbird*.[17]

The multi-talented comedian/song-writer and original host of the "Tonight Show," Steve Allen, created a wonderful television program entitled "Meeting of Minds" which aired on PBS from 1977-1981. The series earned critical acclaim and won several awards for its creativity, excellence and quality. The premise of each episode was to bring four diverse and significant historical figures together, freed from the limitations of time, to discuss, argue and defend their philosophies, ideals, and attitudes. In such a mythical setting, it was thus possible to have an energetic discussion conducted between Theodore Roosevelt, Cleopatra, Thomas Aquinas and Thomas Paine or to host a hypothetical meeting between Sir Francis Bacon, Socrates, Emiliano Zapata, and Susan B. Anthony. It was a scintillating idea and one that I adapted for use with my own classes by having the students create and present their own unique scenarios and scripts.

Allen, himself, was a voracious reader and he explained the importance of reading to human civilization and to historical memory:

> I perceive the magic, wondrous power of reading, and it disturbs me that many others do not share this insight. The great majority on our plant, which not very long ago we imagined was generally civilized, is still illiterate...Of course we are all relatively illiterate in the sense that though there are hundreds of languages in the world, even many educated people can read only one and perhaps an additional one or two stumbling. But hundreds of millions, even in the twentieth century, can read nothing at all. This means that much of the best of human achievement, from all cultures, down through the long march of history, is largely closed to them. If they

happen to live within walking distance of an ancient temple, a great cathedral, a sculpture by Michelangelo, a painting by da Vinci, if they are able to hear a performance of a symphony by Brahms or Beethoven, they are fortunate indeed, but few illiterates are so situated. And the degrading, dehumanizing social circumstances which may have contributed to their illiteracy make it extremely unlikely that they will avail themselves of even such opportunities as might present themselves. For the man who cannot read, Dostoevski and Bacon might as well have lived on another planet, Aristotle and Aquinas might as well have never been born.[18]

I have been personally fortunate that books have always been an important part of my life, thanks to my parents and my teachers. Books gave me an incredible gift—a gateway into the historical past or, as Tony Hendra observes in his book, *Father Joe*, "...a way to live extra lives, to cheat the limits of flesh and blood, to roll the rock back from the tomb and free the resurrected dead."[19]

When I was in college, Dr. Raymond Dingledine, the Chairman of the History Department, once told me that books were to the historian what test tubes are to the scientist. I never forgot these words of wisdom, and I spent countless hours in our university's library which became a sacred sanctuary for me where I could concentrate on learning and exploring the collective wisdom of human civilization. When I finally became a teacher, I was determined to make reading the cornerstone of my curriculum. I used every opportunity to discuss important books with my students and I encouraged them to read outside of the classroom by offering special incentives such as extra-credit for additional book reports. In class, I tried to assign highly motivational reading materials to my classes and every year, I designated a special corner of my classroom totally devoted to reading. The area was filled with dozens of my own personal paperback books which were available for the students to peruse or check out and there were also ample supplies of *National Geographic* and *American Heritage* magazines as well as piles of current newspapers, journals and news magazines.

For my students with learning disabilities, it was particularly important to make reading accessible, since most books were intimidating to them. But just like any acquired skill, reading requires discipline and hard work. It takes time, effort and practice, but the more you read, the more you will ultimately comprehend and learn.[20] It was my passion to help my students gain an appreciation for the beauty of the written word and to discover the quiet dignity in reading a book. Sadly, our World History textbook conspired against these goals. Its encyclopedic approach to history coupled with its incredibly poor prose carefully camouflaged with colorful pictures, graphics, and charts destroyed any magic that the subject might have held for students. Truly, no sane person would ever venture to read a high school textbook for pleasure. But despite their recognized mediocrity, our nation's school systems persist in spending billions of taxpayer dollars on these poor, rudimentary texts which are routinely stuffed into a student's locker where they rot unopened and unread. Our students would be far better served if the money was spent on high quality books and highly motivational learning resources.

The AUS class was a huge challenge for me but these students, like everyone else, deserved a quality education. I realized that to be a truly good educator, it is important that you learn how to effectively adapt your teaching techniques, methods and instruction to accommodate a wide variety of student abilities and learning styles. For these understandably frustrated students, I tried to do this by providing them with individualized instruction, hands-on activities, project-based learning, group activities, and a wide variety of audio-visual resources. It was incredibly difficult to be creative and inspiring each and every day but teaching is a demanding profession; it requires an enormous amount of skill and talent to motivate teenagers.

I also knew that it was imperative for me to overcome my students' pre-existing mistrust of school as well as their suspicion of teachers. I needed first to build trust with them and then work to establish a positive rapport and connection with my class as a whole. To do this, I relied upon the advice that was once given to me by a good friend and colleague, Frank Winstead. Frank is an advocate of what is referred to as "Wayside Teaching." As first explained by Professor John Loundsbury, wayside teaching is the opportunity that all teachers have for positive interactions with their students outside of the traditional classroom setting, those chance meetings that occur "between classes, when walking in the halls, after school, and in dozens and dozens of one-on-one encounters, however brief."[21] Each day, I tried to have at least one positive, personal connection with all of my students. This may have been little more than engaging them in a casual conversation about an interest or hobby or it could have been simply taking the opportunity to greet and acknowledge them by their given name as they entered my classroom. It required just a little bit of effort but it was vitally important since it showed the students that at least one teacher cared about them as human beings and it had an incredibly positive effect on their attitude towards my class.

I was pleased was the overall progress I was making with my students, but one boy, Robert, remained a persistent and frustrating problem.[22] He was completely unmotivated and totally disengaged. No matter what lesson or engaging activity I prepared, he would spend virtually the entire class period gazing out the window, obviously wishing that he could be anywhere but in my classroom.

Robert was a tall, handsome young man who possessed a gifted jump shot along with delusional dreams of starring in the NBA. He needed to pass my required course in order to remain academically eligible to play on the school's basketball team. But to do that, I insisted that he put forth a modicum of effort as well as learn the fundamentals of the curriculum. To the everlasting credit of the Oakton High School athletic department, the coaches were fully supportive of my efforts in the classroom, and they tried to dissuade Robert about any fantasies he may have had about his basketball prowess. Like me, they urged him to concentrate on his studies; it was in school where his ultimate future would be determined.

Every day before class, I would encounter Robert in the hallway locked in an amorous embrace with his girlfriend. These overt and totally inappropriate public displays of affection are discouraged in high school but they seemed to be inevitable when dealing with passionate, hormonal teenagers. Using my best "wayside teaching" techniques, I would interrupt Robert and his girlfriend by engaging them in conversation. They both were always polite and respectful but I still was perplexed about how I would get Robert interested in my World History class.

The county's curriculum required that we teach the students

about the historical influence and impact of the world's great religions. We were expected to include units on Judaism, Christianity, Islam, Buddhism, Hinduism, and Taoism. I knew, though, that when dealing with the delicate subject of religion, it is vitally important that teachers be informed about the content and sensitive to a student's beliefs. No public school teacher has the right to challenge a child's religious beliefs, nor is it acceptable for educators to proselytize or impose their own personal opinions upon their students.

Over the previous summer, Pope Paul VI had died after a long 15-year reign. His immediate successor, John Paul I, lived only 33 days and died in late September. It was one of the shortest papacies in history and necessitated yet another conclave in Rome.[23] I read in the newspaper that the ceremonies were to be broadcast live by each of the three major television networks and, in an era without videotape or digital resources, it would provide me a unique opportunity to help engage my students. By showing a portion of the news coverage, I hoped that it would ultimately make my unit on the Middle Ages more interesting and relevant. It would certainly help establish a historical link to the past and bridge the gap between an era of fiefs, kings, castles, knights, damsels, chivalry, crusades, monks and monasteries to the present time of 1970's disco music, boom boxes, and platform shoes.

As I rolled the massive television cart I checked out from the library into the classroom, I noticed that Robert was strategically seated in his usual desk in the very back of the classroom. I switched on the news coverage and intentionally turned down the volume so I could personally narrate the events that were occurring in Rome at that very moment. I began my instruction by explaining the importance of the church to Medieval Europe after the collapse of the Roman Empire in 476 AD. I then directed the students to pay close attention to the procession of the cardinals at St. Peter's basilica. These so-called "princes of the church" were resplendent in their bright red robes and had gathered from around the world in the Vatican to select one of their number as the new pontiff. The selection would be made by secret ballot behind the locked doors of the Sistine Chapel surrounded by Michelangelo's incredible frescoes.

Robert seemed to be actually paying attention to what I was saying and it was gratifying that I had finally found something that had piqued his latent interest. For the first time that semester, he actually raised his hand to ask a question: "Are the cardinals powerful?" I wasn't completely sure what he meant by this but since it appeared to be a major breakthrough, I carefully explained that the cardinals were, indeed, very important and significant religious leaders within the hierarchy of the Catholic Church, hence they were "powerful" and influential.

Robert then questioned: "Can they fly anywhere they want?"

I was puzzled by this seemingly bizarre diversion and answered tersely: "Yes, of course, if they are on official duties, they can pretty much fly to wherever they need to go."

Robert then loudly proclaimed to the entire class: "I want to be a cardinal."

By now, it was increasingly obvious that this was going nowhere so I told Robert that it would be impossible for him to be a cardinal since each member of the clergy had all taken a solemn vow of celibacy and thus couldn't be married nor could they have girlfriends.

A momentary look of puzzlement came over Robert's face as he tried to digest this startling revelation and then he suddenly blurted out: "You mean all of those old men are virgins?" The entire class erupted into laughter. It should have been one of those so-called teachable moments but I was so startled and embarrassed that I didn't have any response. The entire episode proved to be a metaphor for my year with Robert. Although we had good rapport, I never did truly reach him and he did only the minimal amount of work to justify my passing him. History, though, would forever be a mystery to Robert while he remained enamored with sports.

Robert would eventually play, with a good deal of success, small-time college basketball, but once he used up his eligibility, there would be no degree, no NBA contract, and no future. Like so many of our struggling high school students today, he had been blindly seduced by the impossible dream of professional sports and was lured to destruction, just like the ancient mariners of Greek mythology who were seduced by the intoxicating song of the sirens and foolishly crashed their ships onto treacherous shoals.

A few years later, I read in the newspaper that Robert had been murdered in Washington, DC in a drug-related drive-by shooting. It was such a tragic and useless waste of a human life, and I have always wished that somehow Robert could have discovered the simple joy of being a student and the privilege of having the unencumbered opportunity to learn. It would have provided meaning and direction in his life. As Ellen Wayles Randolph Coolidge, Thomas Jefferson's granddaughter, once so beautifully wrote: "I have often thought that the life of a student must be the most innocent and happy in the world...the pursuit of knowledge unlike other pursuits is subject to no disappointments."[24]

A couple of years later, we were informed that Oakton would be assigned a new principal. There was a palpable sense of apprehension throughout the school since the principal is the single most important factor in shaping the overall school environment. At minimum, they are expected to be academic leaders, skilled managers, and good communicators while those who are truly outstanding can transform schools and inspire academic learning by fostering a climate of mutual respect and seriousness of purpose. They also value, appreciate and empower their teachers and staff.

Fortunately, the school was in excellent shape with a quality, dedicated and hardworking faculty. We were blessed with students who were, for the most part, well-behaved, motivated and high achieving. None of this seemed to matter to the new principal who we met for the first time at the August opening faculty meeting. He was arrogant and confrontational, and proceeded to alienate the entire faculty with his condescending and authoritarian attitude. It was all unnecessary and foolish and within days, the staff's morale plummeted under the new oppressive and despotic regime. I was personally insulted and disillusioned. I had never accepted the teacher lounge premise that administrators and teachers were adversaries. Indeed, I believed that a child's education is the product of the work of many dedicated and committed individuals. This includes not only the classroom teachers but the custodians, cafeteria workers, bus drivers, administrators, parents, and guidance counselors.

Each individual has their own unique role to play and if our schools are going to truly be successful, it is essential that we work together.

Given the increasingly tense political situation at Oakton, I was determined to spend the year avoiding any unnecessary confrontation or conflict with the new regime. For the first time, I became essentially a foxhole teacher—I came to school, closed my classroom door, taught my students, and tried to stay off the principal's radar. The sole positive thing was that my teaching schedule was ideal. I had my usual allotment of American history classes along with two elective classes in Russian history. In those days, the public schools were still encouraging elective courses and I had a full complement of 32 students in each of my two sections.

Russian history held a particular relevance for students during the waning months of the Carter administration. The brief era of détente that had existed between the United States and the USSR ended abruptly on December 27, 1979 when the Soviet Union invaded neighboring Afghanistan, providing a vivid and tangible expression of what was known as the Brezhnev Doctrine. The Soviet premier asserted that all socialist revolutions were permanent and irreversible; he would enforce this belief brutally and without compromise, first against Czechoslovakia in 1968 and now against Afghanistan. With Soviet tanks once again on the move, the truth of Aleksandr Solzhenitsyn's warnings to the West about Communist motives became even more apparent.

All of my students were eager learners and they wanted to understand Soviet intentions within the context of Russia's long and rich history. We began the course by looking at the physical and demographic geography of the modern USSR and then proceeded to study the nation's history chronologically, beginning with its humble, tribal origins in Kiev and the eventual establishment of the Rurikid dynasty. We also discussed the historical, artistic, and spiritual significance for Russia of its adoption of Orthodoxy after the conversion of Saint Vladimir in 987 AD. During the ensuing weeks, we studied the expansion of the country, the rise of Moscow, and the curious circumstances that led to the establishment of the Romanov dynasty.

Tsar Nicholas II, the last of the Romanovs. The students watched the epic film, Nicholas & Alexandra, *in my elective Russian history class at Oakton High School. It dramatically personalized the story of the royal family as they struggled to cope with the realities of the 20th Century.* (Library of Congress)

For over 300 years, these monarchs, from Michael through Nicholas II, would rule Russia "by the grace of God," and would reign with absolute power as the "Emperor and Autocrat of all the Russias."[25]

The first quarter ended with the students listening to the delightful and humorous song, "Rasputin," by the German disco group, Boney-M. We all laughed at the humorous and historically inaccurate refrain, "Ra, Ra, Rasputin, Lover of the Russian queen, there was a cat that really was gone."[26] I then showed the students a rented 16-mm copy of the epic film, *Nicholas and Alexandra*. Based upon Robert Massie's best-selling book, the film begins with the birth of Alexi, the Tsar's hemophilic son and sole heir to the throne. It then skillfully dramatizes and personalizes the struggles and flaws of the royal family as this ancient autocracy tried to cope with the stark realities of the 20th Century. In 1914, Nicholas faces the gruesome prospect of going to war with Germany after the assassination of the Archduke, Franz Ferdinand. The Tsar's most trusted advisor, Count Sergei Witte (portrayed brilliantly in the film by Lawrence Olivier), urges Nicholas not to mobilize his military forces and prophetically warns of the consequences of modern warfare:

> None of you will be here when this war ends. Everything we fought for will be lost, everything we've loved will be broken. The victors will be as cursed as the defeated. The world will grow old, and men will wander about, lost in the ruins, and go mad. Tradition, restraint, virtue, they all go. I'm not mourning for myself, but for the people who will come after me, they will live without hope. And all they will have will be guilt, revenge, and terror. And the world will be full of fanatics and trivial fools.[27]

The Tsar foolishly ignores Witte's advice and shortly afterwards, Russia enters World War I. Within weeks, the nation experiences a series of demoralizing military defeats. Millions of Russians die on the battlefield and the war leads to mass starvation, political turmoil, and ultimately the Tsar's ultimate abdication and arrest.

The climax of the film occurs when Nicholas II, his wife Alexandra, and his children—Tatiana, Olga, Marie, Anastasia, and Alexi, are slaughtered by the Bolsheviks while imprisoned at the Ipatiev House in Yekaterinburg.[28] It is a powerful, poignant scene and I watched as the students sat in stunned silence while many of them were trying to suppress their tears. It showed the power of history to impact the students emotionally as well as intellectually.

During the second quarter, we took an in-depth look into the causes and consequences of the two revolutions of 1917. When Lenin seized control of the government on October 25th (Julian calendar), the communism era began and the Union of Soviet Socialist Republics (USSR) was proclaimed in 1922. Unilateral peace with Germany and a brutal civil war followed as Lenin ruthlessly consolidated his power. Lenin died on January 21, 1924 and after a brief power struggle with Leon Trotsky, Josef Stalin emerged victorious. For the next three decades, Stalin's cold-blooded, barbaric regime led to a general purge of Soviet society and resulted in the deaths of millions of innocent people. It also led to the arrest and imprisonment of a young Army artillery officer, Aleksandr Solzhenitsyn, under provisions of Article 58 of the Soviet criminal code for "anti-Soviet propaganda."[29] The students were learning the truth about the abuses of absolute power and the inherent dangers in a totalitarian state. Russian-American novelist, Ayn Rand, having fortuitously fled the Soviet Union in 1925, aptly explained that in Stalin's Russia, life for prisoners in the gulags differed from that of ordinary citizens only in the matter of degree—both were essentially slaves to the all-knowing, all-powerful state.

Although I had taken a good deal of Russian history while an undergraduate in college, I knew that to effectively teach my students, I still needed to learn more. I had reached an epiphany early in my teaching career that to be a good teacher you had to be continually learning, reading, and studying. So I enrolled in some night classes that were being offered in Northern Virginia through the University of Virginia, including one entitled, "The History of Stalin." Likewise, despite my notoriously poor linguistic abilities, I even took a semester in Russian language. Although I never came close to learning the language let alone achieving fluency, I at least mastered the Cyrillic alphabet and was then able to assist my students in learning and writing their Russian patronymics. To them that year, I was officially known as Tsar Fillip Karlovich and they proclaimed themselves to be my loyal and devoted *mozhik* (peasants). We chose as our class motto: "Tradition, Honor, Tsar," and we emblazoned it throughout the classroom. Each day learning became great fun and not only did we study the history of Russia, we also read excerpts from the classics of Russian literature including the works of Pushkin, Gogol, Tolstoy, Turgenev, Bulgakov, and Pasternak. Everyone was assigned to read Aleksandr Solzhenitsyn's *One Day in the Life of Ivan Denisovich* and I supplemented this assignment by playing passages from the text on a record player. I gave the students the option and opportunity to read Arthur Koestler's classic, *Darkness at Noon.*

We also listened to a good deal of Russian music and for the first time, the students gained an appreciation of such composers as Borodin, Rimsky-Korsakov, and Mussorgsky. They also finally understood that Tchaikovsky's famed *1812 Overture* was, in fact, about Russia's triumph over Napoleon during the battle of Borodino rather than about America's second war of independence against Great Britain.[30]

What I was most proud of, though, was that I earned the respect of my students without sacrificing my standards or expectations on the seductive altar of popularity. This was not some nonsense elective focusing on life-skills or enhancing self-esteem, but rather a substantive, intellectually challenging, content rich course. It proved conclusively that high school students can and will do advanced work if it is meaningful and properly presented. At the end of the year, one young lady wrote to me: "I have learned so much from you. You are an exciting, dedicated teacher who has gained the love and respect of his students." Other students gave me notes saying: "In all the classes I've had I learned the facts but never the reasons of past events. In your class I have learned things that are unforgettable," and "I believe I have learned more from your teaching than in the past 4 years combined—and had more fun." These letters became personal treasures to me since too often we don't know the impact that we have on students since, as the proverb says: "Teachers sow seeds of harvest unseen."

To make the class even more pertinent, I made arrangements with a student travel company to take several of my most interested students to the Soviet Union over our spring break. Eventually, about 25 students signed up for this promising adventure, but throughout the year, the international political situation continued to rapidly deteriorate. President Jimmy Carter feebly protested the Soviet's invasion of Afghanistan by cancelling the United States' participation in the scheduled 1980 Moscow Summer Olympics and he then imposed a series of punitive restrictions on American citizens travelling to Russia. Just three weeks before our scheduled departure, our travel company felt justifiably compelled to cancel our trip, which left me with the painful task of breaking the news to my students. They were disappointed and heartbroken over this lost opportunity. Since most were graduating seniors, they were convinced that they would never be able to visit Russia. I promised them that even though most of them would be in college, I would try and reschedule the trip for a future date.

The next fall, the travel ban on trips to the Soviet Union was finally lifted, so I negotiated a contract with a local, independent private agency to make arrangements for my former students to go to the USSR that December. In those days, American travel agencies served as mere intermediaries since all travel by westerners was carefully controlled and manipulated by the Soviet state agency, Intourist.

The day after Christmas, 1980, our reconstituted group left Washington-Dulles Airport on what would prove to be one of the most enlightening learning experiences of our lives. We initially flew to New York's JFK airport where we transferred to a regularly scheduled Finnair flight to Helsinki. The following morning we were scheduled to connect to another Finnair flight to Moscow.

It was particularly exciting and appropriate to be travelling to the

USSR during mid-winter. The cold and snow had always played a major role throughout Russian history and was credited with helping destroy various invading armies including those of both Napoleon and Hitler. So it seemed fitting that when we finally landed in Finland, it was snowing heavily. As we waited for our next flight in the terminal, we were informed that due to the inclement weather, our departure to Moscow would be delayed. Over the next several hours, the delay would be extended time and again as we tried to pass time playing Uno and other card games. Finally, after ten hours of waiting, we were allowed to board our connecting Finnair flight, but a few minutes later, the pilot informed us that the Soviet air traffic controllers had ordered a ground hold. So we anxiously waited on the tarmac for yet another two hours before we were finally permitted to take off.

The flight between Helsinki and Moscow was relatively short but the pilot had to follow a very strict and narrow flight pattern since any slight divergence was seen as a provocative violation of Soviet border security.[17] Finally, the pilot announced over the intercom that if we looked out our windows, we would be able to see the shimmering lights of Moscow below the clouds, but because we had been unexpectedly denied landing rights by the Soviets and we were being forced to return to Finland.

It was all incredibly disappointing and petty but soon after we returned to Helsinki, Finnish airline officials graciously made arrangements for us to spend the night in a local hotel. We were able to get just a few hours of sleep before we returned to the airport to try again. This time our flight to Moscow proved uneventful, but after the plane taxied to the arrival gate, it was immediately surrounded by Russian military troops. It was a surprising and intimidating welcome to Brezhnev's USSR.

I had given strict instructions to all of the students about the rigid customs procedures for entering the USSR. They were not to bring any western magazines or reading materials (including Bibles) that could be considered provocative, lascivious, or subversive. At best, any such materials would be confiscated by the border agents but mere possession of these contraband items could also lead to detainment and an uncomfortable interrogation. This was not a game and fortunately the students took my warnings seriously. Still, that did not alleviate our horrendous experience with Soviet customs. Our American passports were carefully scrutinized and our visas were examined for a prolonged period of time. Once we cleared this obstacle, we had to face the incredibly long luggage inspection lines. After over two hours, our group was finally approaching an agent when suddenly a Soviet official appeared and declared that our line was now closed and we had to start the entire process over. It was stupid and infuriating but we had no option except to comply. As soon as we had vacated our places in the original line, it was suddenly reopened to accommodate a group of Eastern Europeans in an apparent show of communist solidarity. We were obviously being singled out for punishment for American foreign policy decisions.

We didn't escape from the customs area until after three o'clock in the afternoon. Because of Moscow's far northern latitude, it was already dark. We had effectively lost an entire day of our trip and when we were met by our ever-cheerful Intourist guide, she promptly informed us that since we were late, she had cancelled our tour of the Kremlin and had instead substituted a visit to the Exhibition of Economic Achievement which featured such scintillating exhibits as: "The Worker and the Collective Farmeress (sic)." After a lot of arguing, I finally convinced her that my history students would benefit far more from a visit to the Kremlin than to some propaganda monument to the anemic Soviet economy.

When we boarded the Intourist bus, I discovered that our group had been randomly joined by several other Americans who were visiting the Soviet Union. It proved to be an eclectic assembly of characters, to say the least. One man was a conniving restaurant owner from New Jersey who was in Russia secretly working as a black marketeer. He was there with the intention to smuggle out icons, historical artifacts, and other valuable items whose export was strictly forbidden by Soviet law. There were also several devout Jewish girls who wanted to secretly help Russian *refuseniks* escape religious persecution and emigrate to Israel. There was even an Orthodox priest and his son who were there to visit Russian churches in order to gain a better sense of the status of the church in this officially atheistic country.

During the bleak and grey winter months, Moscow was a city devoid of color. The only exception was the omnipresent red and yellow propaganda banners that bore pictures of Lenin or Marx and featured various slogans celebrating the "all-caring, all-knowing," Soviet state. It was as if we had been somehow transported directly into a scene from George Orwell's *1984*.[32]

Over the next nine days, we learned the true value of human freedom and gained a renewed respect for the privileges we enjoyed

One of the omnipresent propaganda signs located throughout Moscow. It reads, "The Work of Lenin Lives and Triumphs." (Philip Bigler)

The Cruiser Aurora *docked in the ice-laden Neva River. This was the view from my hotel room in Leningrad during our student trip to the USSR.* (Philip Bigler)

(and too often took for granted) as American citizens. We witnessed long lines of Soviet citizens standing patiently in queue for simple subsistence goods; we visited Orthodox cathedrals which had been desecrated by the state and converted into museums of atheism; we saw the war monuments and cemeteries that reminded us of the incredible losses Russia experienced during World War II; and we observed the gargantuan Stalinist-gothic architecture that dominated the Moscow skyline. In Leningrad, my hotel room had an incredible view of the cruiser, *Aurora*, which was credited with firing the first shot of the Bolshevik revolution in October 1917. While in the city, our group also toured the magnificent art collections at the Hermitage museum (formally the tsar's Winter Palace) and was able to personally see the famed jeweled imperial Easter eggs crafted by Fabergé. We were also given the opportunity to visit the Fortress of Peter and Paul, where we were able to actually see the graves of all of the tsars, but we took special note of the fact that the remains of Nicholas II and his family were still missing. On New Year's Eve, we all joined hundreds of other foreign tourists in celebrating the beginning of 1981, confined together in a huge ballroom at the hotel. It was a life-changing trip for all of us and it certainly confirmed my belief that travel can be a powerful learning experience.

After we returned to the United States, though, I found that little had changed with my teaching situation. It now seemed even more untenable for me to continue to work under the totalitarian conditions imposed by an inflexible, dictatorial regime. For the first time, I seriously began to question my choice in a vocation. I certainly did not feel that I was being treated as a professional nor was I being accorded much respect. I was now approaching my 30th birthday and felt that this was the time to for me to make a fundamental change in my life. So after the conclusion of the 1982 school year, I submitted my formal resignation to Fairfax County. It proved to be the best decision of my life.

Endnotes

15 Diane Ravitch, (2010) *The Death and Life of the Great American School System: How Testing and Choice are Undermining Education*. New York: Perseus Books Group, p. 23.

16 Michael Chandler, "SAT Reading Scores Hit Lowest Point in Decades," The *Washington Post*. September 14, 2011, p. A-1.

17 Conroy, pp. 4, 11.

18 Steve Allen, (1978) *Meeting of Minds*. Los Angeles: Hubris Press, pp. 1-2.

19 Hendra, p. 77.

20 When I was growing up, I used to spend hours reading Hardy Boy's mysteries. As a young man, I also enjoyed the John Jakes' series, *The Kent Family Chronicles*. Although these books were not great literature, reading them helped me learn the discipline necessary to read a book. The Harry Potter phenomenon has done much the same for our current generation of students. It has been amazing to see young people excited about reading and with maturity, hopefully they will transfer this desire to more substantive literature.

21 John Loundsbury quoted in Philip Bigler and Stephanie Bishop, eds., (2007) *Be A Teacher: You Can Make a Difference*. St. Petersburg, Florida: Vandamere Press, p.47.

22 Not his real name.

23 John Paul I was the eleventh shortest papacy in history, lasting only 33 days. In 1590, Pope Urban VII died after being in office for just 12 days.

24 Ellen Wayles Randolph Coolidge quoted in Virginia Scharff, (2010) *The Women Jefferson Loved*. New York: HarperCollins Publishers, p. 339.

25 Tsar Nicholas' full title read: "We, Nicholas II, by the grace of God, Emperor and Autocrat of all the Russias, of Moscow, Kiev, Vladimir, Novgorod, Tsar of Kazan, Tsar of Astrakhan, Tsar of Poland, Tsar of Siberia, Tsar of Tauric Chersonesos, Tsar of Georgia, Lord of Pskov, and Grand Duke of Smolensk, Lithuania, Volhynia, Podolia, and Finland, Prince of Estonia, Livonia, Courland and Semigalia, Samogitia, Belostok, Karelia, Tver, Yugra, Perm, Vyatka, Bulgaria and other territories; Lord and Grand Duke of Nizhni Novgorod, Sovereign of Chernigov, Ryazan, Polotsk, Rostov, Yaroslavl, Beloozero, Udoria, Obdoria, Kondia, Vitebsk, Mstislavl, and all northern territories; Sovereign of Iveria, Kartalinia, and the Kabardinian lands and Armenian territories - hereditary Lord and Ruler of the Circassians and Mountain Princes and others; Lord of Turkestan, Heir of Norway, Duke of Schleswig-Holstein, Stormarn, Dithmarschen, Oldenburg, and so forth, and so forth, and so forth."

26 Available at the Lyrics Depot at: http://www.lyricsdepot.com/boney-m/rasputin.html.

27 See the Internet Movie Data Base for quotes from the film at http://www.imdb.com/title/tt0067483/quotes.

28 There is an excellent website on the Ipatiev House and the execution of the Romanov's at: http://www.romanov-memorial.com/. For years, there were rumors that Anastasia had survived the executions. This has been conclusively proven to be untrue, but the students loved to speculate about its possibility, especially when Walt Disney makes a cartoon feature popularizing the myth.

29 Solzhenitsyn writes extensively about this in his book, *The Gulag Archipelago*.

30 This myth is perpetuated by the fact that the 1812 Overture is a featured piece on the 4th of July.

31 Author Alexander Dallin writes, "Borders are seen as the battle lines between civilizations—as surrogate front lines." The stark reality of this attitude led to the Soviet shoot down of flight KAL 007 in September 1983. The regularly scheduled Korean Boeing 747 inadvertently strayed over Soviet airspace while en route to Seoul. Soviet military jets shot down the plane, killing all 269 passengers and crew. See Alexander Dillion's excellent book on this incident, *Black Box: KAL 007 and the Superpowers*.

32 In Moscow, we stayed at the Cosmos Hotel, which had been specially built for the 1980 Moscow Olympic Games. It was located on *Prospect Mira* (Peace Avenue) near the gargantuan Ostankimo TV tower and across the street from the Monument to Explorers of Outer Space. In Leningrad, we stayed at the Hotel Leningrad, which was located on the banks of the Neva River, in close proximity to the Finland railway station where Lenin famously returned from exile in 1917.

CHAPTER V

Hallowed Ground

Historians ought to be precise, faithful, and unprejudiced; and neither interest nor fear, hatred nor affection, should make them swerve from the way of truth, whose mother is history, the rival of time, the depository of great actions, witness of the past, example to the present, and monitor of the future.

Cervantes

I t was the job that I had always dreamed of—or at least that was what I thought at the time. On October 19, 1983, I was hired as a civilian historian for the United States Army and was assigned to Arlington National Cemetery. I had been technically unemployed for the previous 16 months after having quit my teaching job but although I wasn't actually working, I was hardly idle. I enrolled in graduate school at the College of William and Mary in Williamsburg after being offered a full scholarship to study at the university's newly constituted American Studies department.

It was an intellectually-rich time for me since I had grown and matured as a student and was liberated from all of the social temptations of college. I was totally engrossed in my studies, which focused primarily on early American history and literature. I was living in Williamsburg, Virginia in a boarding house located just off of Capitol Landing Road and immediately adjacent to the restored colonial capital and within close proximity of both the Jamestown and Yorktown historic sites. Most of my time outside of the classroom was devoted to reading and to writing my thesis which was entitled, "John Leacock's 'The Fall of British Tyranny' in the Whig Propaganda Offensive: The Personalization of the Revolution." As with most such academic exercises, it was an esoteric topic, but my goal was to show that literature could be used as an effective weapon for transforming the American Revolution "from a war on constitutional issues to a struggle against evil personalities."[33] Despite all of my hard work and effort, I am virtually certain that this tome has never been checked out of the Swem Library by a student or has ever been read since its completion. Still, the academic process, which was, at times, tedious and frustrating, taught me discipline and perseverance. It also allowed me to reassess my goals and life-priorities during my daily contemplative ten-mile runs along the Colonial Parkway.

I also got married that year while in graduate school. My wife, Linda, was a Spanish teacher who I met while we were both teaching at Oakton High School. We were married on October 16, 1982, in a civil ceremony which was performed on the portico of the Arlington House Mansion. It had once been the pre-Civil War home of Robert E. Lee and featured a beautiful panoramic view of the nation's capital. Its strategic location and commanding position along the west bank of the Potomac River led federal forces to seize the property at the onset of the war, and in 1864, the grounds were converted into a cemetery to bury the nation's war dead. A good friend, Phil Walsh, had once served as a Park Ranger at Arlington House and he helped make the arrangements for our wedding. It would later seem to be particularly fortuitous since I was destined to go to work at Arlington Cemetery just one year later.

I was working with another historian, Tom Sherlock. Tom had been at Arlington since graduating from the University of Maryland and we soon became good friends and colleagues. He taught me an enormous amount about the history of the cemetery and we both enjoyed working together.[34] Our office was actually located in the basement area of the Memorial Amphitheater and was linked by a tunnel to the Tomb Quarters where the Tomb Guard resided while on duty. We were responsible for compiling and maintaining the cemetery's history and for the preservation of its historical records, including the original burial ledgers which dated from May, 1864. Often, we were asked to provide VIP tours for visiting dignitaries at the behest of various government agencies, including Congress, the Department of Defense, and the White House. I personally conducted tours for Ron Ziegler, President Nixon's press secretary, and for Larry Linville, who played Major Frank Burns in the television series M*A*S*H. Our office also supported the military with major ceremonies conducted at the Tomb of the Unknown Soldier. This required us to work closely with State Department Security and the United States Secret Service.[35]

My tenure at Arlington happened to coincide with the nation's 40th anniversary commemorations of World War II. It was an appropriate time for the nation to thank the millions of veterans of the "Great Generation" for their service. These men and women selflessly postponed their careers and delayed starting families to engage in a titanic struggle against fascism and tyranny which would ultimately determine the fate of modern civilization. These real-life

"Private Ryan's" regularly made a solemn pilgrimage to Arlington in order to pay honor to their compatriots who had paid the ultimate sacrifice during war. The rows of thousands of white headstones provided a silent testament to the horrific cost of the war as well as to their valor.

Many veteran organizations visited the Tomb of the Unknown Soldier to place a wreath, complete with military ceremonies. During this time, I had the privilege of meeting personally hundreds of authentic American heroes. I met soldiers who fought during the Battle of the Bulge; Navy sailors who survived the surprise Japanese attack on Pearl Harbor; Native-Americans veterans who operated as military "code talkers;" and countless of other brave and valiant men.

One of my most memorable days at Arlington occurred in January, 1985. It was an atypically cold winter in Washington and the unusually frigid, arctic temperatures had necessitated the cancelling of many of the planned inaugural festivities for President Ronald Reagan's second term. Even the customary outdoor swearing in ceremony at the U.S. Capitol had to be moved indoors to the Rotunda and, of course, the inaugural parade down Pennsylvania Avenue had to be cancelled. Yet despite the adverse weather conditions, the many visitors to our nation's capital were determined to visit Arlington to watch the hourly changing of the guard ceremony. Indeed, the sentinels continued to maintain their stoic, uninterrupted 24-hour, 365 day vigil at the Tomb.

One late afternoon, I went upstairs from my office to check on things in the Amphitheater's trophy room. There was a small crowd gathered inside the building for warmth and all of them were watching the sentinel on duty as he regularly took his 21 measured steps across the mat while guarding the Tomb. I quickly spotted among the crowd two very distinguished-looking gentlemen; both were wearing a Medal of Honor (MOH).

The Medal of Honor is the nation's highest and most prestigious decoration for valor.[36] Created during the Civil War, it is rarely awarded and then only for "…conspicuous gallantry and intrepidity at the risk of his or her life *above and beyond the call of duty* while engaged in an action against an enemy of the United States."[37] Those individuals who receive the medal have all performed heroically on the battlefield and their actions truly defy the imagination. The criterion for the MOH requires that the deed:

> …must be proved by incontestable evidence of at least two eyewitnesses; it must be so outstanding that it clearly distinguishes his gallantry beyond the call of duty from lesser forms of bravery; it must involve the risk of his life; and it must be the type of deed which, if he had not done it, would not subject him to any justified criticism.[38]

With such stringent standards, it is not surprising that most of the modern day recipients of the MOH have received their decoration posthumously.

I introduced myself to the two men and then escorted them downstairs to the Tomb Guard quarters so that they could meet the sentinels as well as autograph our Medal of Honor reference book. I noted that one of the veterans had obviously suffered some very serious burns.

All MOH citations are carefully documented, recorded, and

compiled by the military. As the two men toured the guard quarters, I took the opportunity to look up and read about the men's awards in a volume of citations that we kept in the historian's office. One of our special visitors was Desmond Doss. He was originally from Lynchburg, Virginia and was a devout and practicing Seventh-day Adventist. As a religious conscientious objector during World War II, he refused to carry a weapon into battle but still joined the Army as a private and served as a medic with the 77th Infantry Division. He earned his Medal of Honor for his heroic actions during the climatic and bloody battle of Okinawa in 1945. Without personal regard for his own life, Doss rescued several wounded American soldiers while under heavy enemy fire. He was wounded three times but continued to minister to the injured and dying. In the words of his MOH citation, "Through his outstanding bravery and unflinching determination in the face of desperately dangerous conditions Pfc. Doss saved the lives of many soldiers. His name became a symbol throughout the 77th Infantry Division for outstanding gallantry far above and beyond the call of duty."[39]

Accompanying Doss that day to Arlington was his friend, Staff Sergeant Henry "Red" Erwin, U.S. Army Air Corps. During the Second World War, Erwin served with the 29th Bombardment Group. He was part of a B-29 crew assigned to the *City of Los Angeles* and in April, 1945, they were assigned a combat mission which called for their plane to drop a series of phosphorous bombs off the coast of Japan to mark a pathway for a squadron of trailing planes. During their bomb run, one of the phosphorous bombs misfired and kicked back into the fuselage of the plane. The errant bomb struck Sgt. Erwin in the face and caused severe burns which "obliterated his nose and completely blinded him."[40] The resulting smoke from the accident quickly filled the interior of the plane and obscured the pilot's vision, causing the plane to descend in a potentially deadly dive. Yet despite his incredibly painful wounds, Erwin somehow managed to grab the still smoldering incendiary bomb and clutched it under his arm. He carried it the entire length of the aircraft and was finally able to dispose of it through an open window. The pilot was then able to regain control of the plane and saved it from certain destruction. Erwin collapsed in agony and was, according to one account, "burned beyond recognition and charred over the upper half of his body." Still, he remained con-

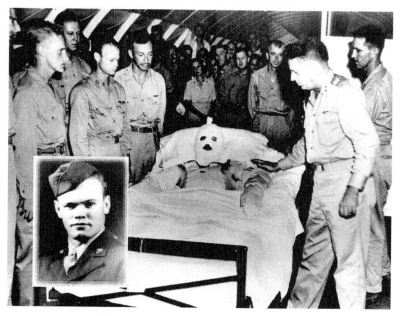

Staff Sergeant Henry Erwin after being awarded his Medal of Honor for bravery. Erwin served on board the B29 bomber, City of Los Angeles *and was severely burned during a bombing raid off of the coast of Japan in 1945.* (U.S. Army)

scious as the pilot flew back to a recently established American airbase on the captured island of Iwo Jima, some two hours away.

At the hospital, none of the doctors or nurses expected that Erwin would survive his devastating wounds. Advised of Erwin's heroic actions on board the *City of Los Angeles*, General Curtis LeMay quickly awarded him the Medal of Honor during a hastily arranged ceremony conducted at his bedside. Although permanently disfigured, Erwin miraculously recovered from his injuries but only after undergoing 43 operations. Yet here on that cold day in January, 1985, Erwin was proudly wearing his medal. [41] Such were the daily experiences of working at Arlington National Cemetery. It was an incredible privilege to meet authentic American heroes and, for the first time in my life, I was encountering the real-life history that I had previously only read about in books.

In fact, Arlington continues to present a powerful narrative of our nation's entire history. Interred throughout its rolling 624 acres are the dead from all of America's wars, from the American Revolution through our most recent military operations in Iraq and Afghanistan. Among the dead are famous generals, aviation pioneers, Supreme Court justices, politicians, presidents, patriots, and even a villain or two. I always enjoyed the tranquility of Arlington, and frequently would walk through the various sections reading the headstones and inscriptions, discovering new facts and information, and learning about the legacy of the thousands of people who were buried at Arlington. When my mother died in February 1989, she, too, was buried at Arlington. Her grave is located in Section 7A, a beautiful area just a short distance below the Tomb

My mother's grave at Arlington National Cemetery. She is buried in Section 7A, near the Tomb of the Unknown Soldier. The inscription reads, "Each Headstone Represents a Story Waiting to be Told, A Past to be Remembered."
(Philip Bigler)

of the Unknown Soldier. Nearby are the graves of such notables as General Jimmy Doolittle, Heavyweight Champion Joe Louis, *Challenger* Pilot Michael Smith, and Hollywood movie actor Lee Marvin.[42] On the back of her black, marble stone, I had engraved the following inscription from my book, *In Honored Glory*: "Each headstone represents a story waiting to be told, a past to be remembered."[43] I hope that these words will forever serve as a silent affirmation of the importance of learning history and our need as a nation to remember the sacrifices of those who came before us.

Certainly the singular most important event that occurred during my two year tenure at Arlington was the burial of the Vietnam Unknown Soldier. The decision to inter a soldier from that conflict was part of a nationwide effort to make amends to the millions of veterans who had served honorably in Vietnam but who were never thanked for their service nor properly welcomed home. The war had been divisive and costly, claiming the lives of 58,212 Americans. All of their names are now forever enshrined on the glistening panels of Maya Lin's Vietnam Memorial in Washington, a powerful chronicle of the human toll of war.

The tradition of selecting and interring an unknown soldier in a place of honor began shortly after the armistice ending hostilities in World War I. The first American unknown was buried in 1921 at Arlington on the plaza of the Memorial Amphitheater in ceremonies that were presided over by President Warren G. Harding. In 1958, the government also buried unknown soldiers from World War II and the Korea Conflict in crypts flanking the main tomb. These graves were marked with flat, white marble stones inscribed with the dates of the two conflicts—1941-1945 for World War II and 1950-1953 for Korea. But once again the Vietnam War proved to be problematic. Although there were over 2,500 Americans still classified as missing in action (MIA), advanced and sophisticated identification techniques which had been perfected by the U.S. Army Central Identification Laboratory in Hawaii had proved so successful that in 1984 there were only four sets of remains that were still classified as unidentified. In order to bury a Vietnam Unknown, it would require a drastic alteration to the traditionally rigorous criteria for such a selection. The decision to proceed with a funeral would not be without considerable controversy. Indeed, Ann Mills Griffiths, the executive director of the National League of Families of American Prisoners and Missing in Southeast Asia, warned, "We are opposed to the interment of any remains now held" and hope that all of the remains could eventually be identified and returned to their individual families.[44]

There was enormous political pressure on the President and Congress to bury an unknown at Arlington. The interment would finally bring some closure to the war and accord to the Vietnam veterans the same respect that had been extended to their compatriots from World War I, World War II, and Korea. As Secretary of the Army, Jack Marsh, recalled, "President Reagan and Caspar Weinberger wanted to go forward with it, as a way to honor those who served and as a way to reach closure on the Vietnam era."[45]

Although Tom and I were not personally privileged to the behind the scenes maneuvering or the ongoing classified discussions, we always assumed that any remains that were under consideration for an unknown had to be those of a military aviator. Only the catastrophic nature of a plane crash could explain the paucity of bones that prevented a positive identification.[46] In early spring, we received word at Arlington that we were to proceed with the planning for a state funeral for a Vietnam Unknown Soldier and that the ceremonies would take place on Memorial Day. President Ronald Reagan would personally preside over the ceremonies.

It was the most important event at Arlington since the burial of President John F. Kennedy some two decades before. Over the Memorial Day weekend, the Unknown was granted the rare privilege of lying-in-state in the Capitol Rotunda. There thousands of Vietnam Veterans and other American citizens slowly passed by his flagged-draped casket during the 24-hour vigil. That Monday, the casket was placed on a horse-drawn caisson for the final journey to Arlington National Cemetery. The long and solemn procession paused briefly near the Vietnam Memorial and there hundreds of Vietnam veterans, many dressed in their military fatigues and proudly wearing their military decorations and unit insignia, spontaneously joined the march across the Memorial Bridge to the Tomb. At the Memorial Amphitheater, President Reagan awarded the Unknown the Medal of Honor and delivered an eloquent eulogy just prior to the actual burial:

> Today we pause to embrace him and all who served us so well in a war whose end offered no parades, no flags, and so little thanks ... A grateful nation opens her heart today in gratitude for their sacrifice, for their courage and their noble service. Let us, if we must, debate the lessons learned at some other time. Today we simply say with pride: Thank you, dear son, and may God cradle you in His loving arms.[47]

The burial of the Vietnam Unknown Soldier at Arlington National Cemetery on Memorial Day, 1984. I had the privilege to work on the ceremonies while serving as one of the historians at Arlington. (Ronald Reagan Library)

Every day that I worked at Arlington was memorable. As an active military cemetery, the cemetery was conducting on average some 20 funerals per day.[48] So death became something very real to me. The vast majority of burials were for retired military servicemen and their spouses. Most of these individuals had lived long and full lives so the final military honors that were rendered at their gravesites were, in many ways, a celebration of their honorable service to our country. But I soon learned that Arlington also dealt regularly with terrible tragedies, disasters, and calamities.

On October 23, 1983, a terrorist successfully evaded base security at the Marine compound located at the Beirut International Airport in Lebanon. He detonated a powerful car bomb which totally destroyed the Marine Barracks, killing 241 American servicemen. The soldiers had been deployed to the region as part of a multinational peacekeeping force and most were still asleep in their bunks with the attack occurred. Over the next two weeks, we dealt with the tangible result of the terrorist attack, burying 21 of the Marines who had perished in the explosion. They were all painfully young and their deaths seemed irrational and pointless. All of the soldiers were interred in adjacent graves in Section 59; each grave was marked with an identical white government headstone which contained the individual's name, rank, date of birth, and the inscription "Killed, Lebanon: October 23, 1983." Several months later, a cedar of Lebanon tree was planted nearby and a plaque was dedicated which reads: "This cedar of Lebanon tree grows in loving memory of the Americans killed in the Beirut terrorist attack and all victims of terrorism throughout the world."[49] It was at Arlington that I finally began to gain a true appreciation for what is important in life. I now

First Lady Nancy Reagan visits wounded soldiers from the Marine Barracks bomb-
ing. The terrorist attack upon the American compound resulted in the deaths of
241 soldiers; 21 of these casualties were buried at Arlington National Cemetery.
(Ronald Reagan Library)

understand that we could never truly know what the future holds for us, so it is important to live life fully and with meaning. As the great psychologist and holocaust survivor, Viktor Frankl, once wrote, "Man must decide for better or worse what will be the monument to his existence."[50]

As much as I enjoyed working at Arlington, I began to reassess my ultimate life goals and this meant that I first had to seriously examine the real reasons why I had left teaching. I knew that I had been frustrated by the impersonal bureaucracy, hurt by my two layoffs, and discouraged by the poor pay, but none of these external factors actually had anything to do with teaching kids. Indeed, I missed sharing my enthusiasm for history with my students and the sense of satisfaction I received from seeing them learn material for the first time.

I finally appreciated the powerful impact that good teachers have on their students and realized that being a teacher was, in fact, an important and significant job. I decided that I would return to the classroom at the first opportunity, and this time, I would ignore the little frustrations and petty problems and focus on making a difference.

Memorial Day at Arlington National Cemetery. (National Archives)

Endnotes

33 Philip Bigler. (1984) "John Leacock's 'The Fall of British Tyranny' in the Whig Propaganda Offensive: The Personalization of the Revolution." Master's Thesis, The College of William and Mary, p. v.

34 I worked with Tom Sherlock, who was the other historian at Arlington. Tom continues to work at the cemetery and has had a distinguished career with the federal government.

35 I was fortunate to work on two visits by President Ronald Reagan. The last year I was at Arlington, our office handled the cemetery's preparations for 11 heads of state, including visits by Francois Mitterrand of France and Prime Minister Yitzhak Shamir of Israel.

36 For more information on the Medal of Honor, see http://www.cmohs.org/.

37 *Ibid.*

38 *The Congressional Medal of Honor: The Names, The Deeds.* (1984) Forest Ranch, California: Sharp & Dunnigan Publications, p.1.

39 The citation for Desmond Doss reads as follows: "He was a company aid man when the 1st Battalion assaulted a jagged escarpment 400 feet high As our troops gained the summit, a heavy concentration of artillery, mortar and machine gun fire crashed into them, inflicting approximately 75 casualties and driving the others back. Pfc. Doss refused to seek cover and remained in the fire-swept area with the many stricken, carrying them 1 by 1 to the edge of the escarpment and there lowering them on a rope-supported litter down the face of a cliff to friendly hands. On 2 May, he exposed himself to heavy rifle and mortar fire in rescuing a wounded man 200 yards forward of the lines on the same escarpment; and 2 days later he treated 4 men who had been cut down while assaulting a strongly defended cave, advancing through a shower of grenades to within 8 yards of enemy forces in a cave's mouth, where he dressed his comrades' wounds before making 4 separate trips under fire to evacuate them to safety. On 5 May, he unhesitatingly braved enemy shelling and small arms fire to assist an artillery officer. He applied bandages, moved his patient to a spot that offered protection from small arms fire and, while artillery and mortar shells fell close by, painstakingly administered plasma. Later that day, when an American was severely wounded by fire from a cave, Pfc. Doss crawled to him where he had fallen 25 feet from the enemy position, rendered aid, and carried him 100 yards to safety while continually exposed to enemy fire. On 21 May, in a night attack on high ground near Shuri, he remained in exposed territory while the rest of his company took cover, fearlessly risking the chance that he

would be mistaken for an infiltrating Japanese and giving aid to the injured until he was himself seriously wounded in the legs by the explosion of a grenade. Rather than call another aid man from cover, he cared for his own injuries and waited 5 hours before litter bearers reached him and started carrying him to cover. The trio was caught in an enemy tank attack and Pfc. Doss, seeing a more critically wounded man nearby, crawled off the litter; and directed the bearers to give their first attention to the other man. Awaiting the litter bearers' return, he was again struck, this time suffering a compound fracture of 1 arm. With magnificent fortitude he bound a rifle stock to his shattered arm as a splint and then crawled 300 yards over rough terrain to the aid station. Through his outstanding bravery and unflinching determination in the face of desperately dangerous conditions Pfc. Doss saved the lives of many soldiers. His name became a symbol throughout the 77th Infantry Division for outstanding gallantry far above and beyond the call of duty."

40 Red Erwin's MOH citation reads, "He was the radio operator of a B-29 airplane leading a group formation to attack Koriyama, Japan. He was charged with the additional duty of dropping phosphoresce smoke bombs to aid in assembling the group when the launching point was reached. Upon entering the assembly area, aircraft fire and enemy fighter opposition was encountered. Among the phosphoresce bombs launched by S/Sgt. Erwin, 1 proved faulty, exploding in the launching chute, and shot back into the interior of the aircraft, striking him in the face. The burning phosphoresce obliterated his nose and completely blinded him. Smoke filled the plane, obscuring the vision of the pilot. S/Sgt. Erwin realized that the aircraft and crew would be lost if the burning bomb remained in the plane. Without regard for his own safety, he picked it up and feeling his way, instinctively, crawled around the gun turret and headed for the copilot's window. He found the navigator's table obstructing his passage. Grasping the burning bomb between his forearm and body, he unleashed the spring lock and raised the table. Struggling through the narrow passage he stumbled forward into the smoke-filled pilot's compartment. Groping with his burning hands, he located the window and threw the bomb out. Completely aflame, he fell back upon the floor. The smoke cleared, the pilot, at 300 feet, pulled the plane out of its dive. S/Sgt. Erwin's gallantry and heroism above and beyond the call of duty saved the lives of his comrades."

41 Desmond Doss died on March 23, 2006; Henry Erwin died in January 2002 and is buried in Alabama.

42 Joe Louis served as a Technical Sergeant in World War II and was given a presidential exception for in ground burial at Arlington; Lee Marvin was eligible for burial as a recipient of the Purple Heart for wounds he sustained during the battle for Saipan in the Pacific.

43 The passage comes from a book I wrote about the cemetery entitled, *In Honored Glory: Arlington National Cemetery, the Final Post*. See page 3.

44 Ann Mills Griffiths quoted in Robert M. Poole (2009). *On Hallowed Ground: The Story of Arlington National Cemetery*. New York: Walker Publishing Company, p. 240.

45 Jack Marsh quoted in Poole, p. 240.

46 This proved to be true. In fact, there had been considerable circumstantial evidnce about the identity of the unknown's remains. When this became public in 1998, many M.I.A. families demanded that the Vietnam Unknown be disinterred and the bones subjected to DNA testing. The military agreed and the Vietnam Unknown was formally identified as being Captain Michael Blassie, an Air Force pilot who was shot down on a mission over An Loc on May 11, 1972. His remains were returned to his family for private burial and the now empty crypt at Arlington now reads, "Honoring and Keeping Faith with American's Missing Servicemen, 1958-1975."

47 Ronald Reagan quoted in Philip Bigler (2005). *In Honored Glory: Arlington National Cemetery: The Final Post*. St. Petersburg, Florida: Vandamere Press, p. 60.

48 Arlington's burial rate has increased dramatically after the attacks of 9-11 and with American military operations in both Iraq and Afghanistan. The active duty deaths coupled with the aging World War II population pushed interments to over 30 per day. It also extended the wait time between a death and a funeral to over two months for a full-honors ceremony. My father died on Christmas Day, 2003 and his funeral did not take place until February 18, 2004.

49 *Ibid.*, p. 103.

50 Viktor E. Frankl (1992). *Man's Search for Meaning*. Boston: Beacon Press, p. 124.

CHAPTER VI

Students First and Foremost

And if all others accepted the lie which the Party imposed-if all records told the same tale-then the lie passed into history and became truth. 'Who controls the past' ran the Party slogan, 'controls the future: who controls the present controls the past.'

George Orwell *1984*

I gladly returned to the classroom in September 1985 after having received a contract to teach history at Bethesda-Chevy Chase High School (B-CC) in suburban Montgomery County, Maryland. My three-year hiatus from teaching had proved to be a rejuvenating experience and had given me a much better perspective on both my life and career. After having worked at Arlington National Cemetery, I now fully understood that our allotted time on this earth is finite and short. Moreover, it is wholly within our own power to formulate our own individual success and happiness. We are the ones who control our own destinies, and for me, that meant that I needed to re-focus my efforts as a teacher by concentrating more fully on my students' academic and intellectual well-being. The myriad of other things that I had found so trivial and frustrating about American public education—the massive bureaucracy, the school politics, the inflated egos—were actually irrelevant. What mattered most were my students and, in reality, I actually had an enormous amount of autonomy within the confines of my own classroom. It was here where I could truly make a difference and it was my professional obligation to by ensure that each one of my students had the opportunity for a high quality, substantive history education.

The only negative thing about my new teaching position at B-CC was geography. The school was located some 20 miles away from my home in Fairfax. My commute required me to navigate Washington's notorious beltway traffic as well as to cross twice daily the infamous Cabin John Bridge. The bridge marked the physical, political, and spiritual border between Virginia and Maryland, and was a common scene of accidents and long traffic delays. Even on relatively good days, the bridge was nearly impassable, clogged with hundreds of cars and trucks. There were no reasonable detours available but I quickly discovered that as long as I left my house in Fairfax by 6:15 AM, I could be reasonably certain that I would be at school by seven o'clock, well in time for the start of my first period class, which was scheduled to start precisely 30 minutes later. A delay of just five minutes or even stopping for a quick cup of coffee and a breakfast donut could prove disastrous, though, since the metro area's rush hour traffic patterns were incredibly fluid and the time needed to traverse Washington's highways would change dramatically. I was proud of the fact that during my entire six year tenure at B-CC, I was only late to school twice, both times due to pre-dawn accidents on that damnable Cabin John Bridge.

B-CC was a wonderful school and had a long and distinguished tradition. It had first opened its doors to students in 1925, when Calvin Coolidge was president and in the same year that F. Scott Fitzgerald published his classic novel, *The Great Gatsby*. In Tennessee, a young biology teacher named John Scopes was on trial for teaching evolution. The resulting courtroom drama was a clash between two American titans, Clarence Darrow versus William Jennings Bryan, and would be later immortalized in the classic film, *Inherit the Wind.*

Over the ensuing decades, through depression and world war, B-CC grew and evolved, as did its reputation for academic excellence which garnished national acclaim. In 1960, the school was recognized as the "best high school" in America by *Time* magazine and both First Lady Eleanor Roosevelt and Senator John F. Kennedy would serve as commencement speakers during senior graduation ceremonies conducted at the school.

By the time I arrived at B-CC in the fall of 1985, the school's once pastoral surroundings had long since disappeared. The proximity of the Bethesda Naval Hospital and the medical facilities of the National Institutes of Health had served as a major catalyst for Montgomery County's rapid growth, urbanization, and economic development. Likewise, the opening of a Bethesda metro subway station the previous year made access to the nation's capital quick and painless. Soon massive apartment complexes, high rise office buildings, and gourmet restaurants were constructed and these corporate enterprises completely surrounded the school's grounds.

The baby-boom era (1945-1964) had led to an influx of students at B-CC and the school responded by continually building new classroom space. This was accomplished by constructing several new wings and adding other physical enhancements but the frequent and somewhat haphazard expansion ultimately created a confusing labyrinth of hallways and passages that would confound teachers, staff, and students for years.[51]

All high school students in Montgomery County were required to take three semesters of American history as part of their graduation requirements. One of the courses was entitled "Contemporary Issues" and its focus was primarily on the political, sociological, and diplomatic development of post-World War II America. It was, in fact, a much needed supplement to the traditional social studies curriculum since it provided educators with the time and opportunity to delve into such critical topics as the Cold War, the Civil Rights movement, the 60's, Vietnam, and Watergate.

I was determined to utilize innovative, highly motivational activities with my classes. To get the students more involved and personally vested in my classes, I incorporated several new historical simulations into my instruction. One of the most intense class activities was a dramatic recreation of the court-martial trial of Lt. William Calley for alleged war crimes committed by American troops at My Lai in March, 1968.[52] This activity served as the climax of my extensive and thorough Vietnam unit.

I devoted four full weeks of instruction to the war and I found that the students were very interested and highly motivated to learn more about this relatively recent period of American history. Although U.S. involvement in the conflict had ended just ten years earlier, the students had no direct personal memories of the era, so it was essentially ancient history to them. By now, though, enough

Returning to the classroom after a three year hiatus. I was determined to make my classes more student-centered by using historical simulations and other innovative classroom activities. (Philip Bigler)

time had elapsed so that it was possible to assess the Vietnam War as a historical event and to discuss it reasonably free from the intense passions and political divisions that had so characterized the period.

Before conducting the trial, it was important to establish a proper context, so we spent a good deal of time reading, studying, and learning about the major political, social, and military aspects of the war. Such important topics as the assassination of President Ngo Dinh Diem, the passage of the Gulf of Tonkin Resolution, the consequences of the Tet Offensive, the global turmoil of 1968, and the impact of the anti-war movement were all carefully analyzed and discussed.

The actual court-martial trial of Lt. William Calley took place over several months during the winter of 1970-1971. In many ways, the trial provided the perfect metaphor for U.S. involvement in Southeast Asia, since it was extremely controversial. Many Americans openly questioned its legitimacy and the wisdom of prosecuting a relatively low ranking army lieutenant for the actions of his troops in a combat zone.

The contentious proceedings had been initiated as a result of a letter written and distributed to several members of Congress by a former soldier, Ron Ridenhour. He alleged that American troops had murdered over 500 women and children during military operations conducted in Quang Ngai province in 1968. These startling accusations gained increased credibility when *Life* magazine published a series of gruesome photographs of the My Lai incident in December, 1969.

For the classroom trial, I was careful to assign the challeng-

Serving as a judge in the war crimes trial of Lt. William Calley. The trial was the culmination of my extensive four week unit on the Vietnam War. (Philip Bigler)

ing roles of prosecuting and defense attorneys to my most accomplished and motivated students. Several other students were asked to volunteer to portray important witnesses who would be subpoenaed by the student lawyers to testify before the classroom's military tribunal. The remaining students would serve essentially as jurors in the trial, while I acted as the presiding judge in order to ensure an orderly and steady progress to the classroom proceedings. In this role, I also ruled on critical legal matters including the admissibility of evidence and the validity of courtroom objections.

The attorneys were the key component to the success of this particular simulation. They had to become experts on the My Lai massacre and were required to collect depositions and gather evidence as well as to develop and present their case in a logical, coherent fashion. It was extremely hard and detailed work, but it is amazing to see what high school students can actually achieve when properly academically challenged. Indeed, one of my most resolute and determined students even went every day after school down to the National Archives to conduct her own research. There she spent hours reviewing volumes of files and records from the actual case. She returned to our class armed with reams of primary source documents.

All of my students, regardless of their individual roles, were expected to conduct background research and to investigate relevant historical precedents. This meant, at a minimum, that they had to familiarize themselves with the ostensible "rules of war" that had been established by the Geneva Convention; the precedents established by the Nuremberg trials of Nazi war criminals; and the historical significance of the Supreme Court ruling in the case of Japanese General Tomoyuki Yamashita.[53] They were also expected to evaluate the legitimacy of American military tactics including the rules of engagement which governed combat operations. This included assessing the validity of declaring large geographic areas "free fire zones" where all inhabitants of the region were to be considered to be enemy sympathizers and openly hostile.

The Calley simulation was content-rich and substantive. I was impressed at how vested, engaged, and emotionally committed the students became in our mythical trial's outcome. Each of my classes was free to reach their own independent conclusions and verdicts. The outcomes were solely predicated upon the quality of the case presented, the effectiveness of the attorneys' arguments, the credibility of witnesses, and the veracity of evidence. Indeed, in some of my classes, Calley was convicted of murdering dozens of innocent civilians while other classes absolved him from personal culpability. What was truly important, though, was that the students were learning to develop and exercise their own historical judgment; they were not merely regurgitating random facts nor were they expected to conform to a pre-ordained orthodoxy of thought. This type of classroom activity provided them with the confidence to think for themselves and the freedom to reach their own rational, fact-based conclusions.

One year, as my Vietnam unit continued to evolve and expand, I had the unique opportunity to invite Everett Alvarez to school to speak to my classes.[54] Alvarez was a Vietnam veteran and a former prisoner-of-war who had been a Navy pilot assigned to the USS *Constellation*. On August 5, 1964, his carrier-based squadron was ordered by President Johnson to conduct the first American retaliatory raids against North Vietnam as a direct result of the Gulf of Tonkin incident. During a bombing run over the town of Hon Gai, Alvarez's A-4 *Skyhawk* was hit by enemy fire and he was forced to eject. Immediately captured by the North Vietnamese, he was held as a prisoner-of-war for the next eight years of his life.[55] Everett Alvarez's poignant story was an odyssey of personal degradation, pain, starvation, and torture. Yet despite all of this physical adversity, he remained stoic throughout this ordeal just as Aleksandr Solzhenitsyn had done while enduring similar hardships during his captivity in Stalin's gulags. The brutal captors of both Solzhenitsyn and Alvarez were able to imprison and humiliate these remarkable men but they were never able to conquer their souls or break their spirit. For my students, Alvarez's honest and forthright stories about Vietnam personalized the war in a way no textbook or lecture could.[56]

One of the obvious advantages of teaching in such close proximity to Washington, D.C. was the access I had to noteworthy digni-

Journalist, author, and political commentator, Chris Matthews, with my principal, Elizabeth Lodal, and me at McLean High School. Matthews was one of the many guest speakers who I regularly invited to address my classes about important political and historical events. (Philip Bigler)

taries, politicians, celebrities and other personalities. I felt strongly that such well-known people (many of whom are openly critical of public education) should regularly visit our nation's schools in order to gain a better understanding of what was actually happening in our classrooms. Over the years, I was fortunate to host such prominent figures as Ben Bradlee (the executive editor of the Washington Post during Watergate); Morton Kondracke (journalist and panelist on the McLaughlin Group); Kathy Bushkin (press secretary for the Gary Hart presidential campaign); Marlin Fitzwater (Press Secretary for both Presidents Ronald Reagan and George H.W. Bush); Mark Shields (political pundit and journalist); and Chris Matthews (author, commentator, and journalist). All of these individuals were gracious with their time, but I firmly believe that they also personally benefited from their interaction with my students.

I particularly enjoyed having the students meet and talk with practicing historians. These visiting scholars would discuss their ongoing research as well as the inherent challenges of writing. One year, I assigned my Contemporary Issues classes the book, *May Day: The U-2 Affair*. It had been recently published by an upcoming young historian named Michael Beschloss and was garnishing widespread acclaim and recognition even amongst the popular press.

May Day was exceptionally well-researched and was a riveting historical narrative about the perilous struggles between the United States and the Soviet Union during the dark days of the Cold War. The Eisenhower administration was particularly concerned about Russian's missile development and its advancements in ICBM technology. The President ordered the CIA to begin a top secret aerial surveillance program to determine the scope and intent of the Soviet program. Francis Gary Powers was engaged in this risky high altitude photographic reconnaissance when his U-2 spy plane that was shot down over the USSR in the spring of 1960.

It was a compelling story and a fascinating read. Beschloss employed a clever literary technique which had been perfected by historian Barbara Tuchman, (*The Guns of August, The Proud Tower, The Distant Mirror, et al.*), to engage his readers. An author begins his historical narrative at its most critical or pivotal moment and then retrogresses into the more distant past in order to explain how all of the relevant people, significant events, and other circumstances culminate in the story's dramatic climax.

In the case of *Mayday*, Beschloss began his book on May 1, 1960, describing in detail the preparations that Francis Gary Powers had to make for his U-2 over-flight of the Soviet Union. His assigned mission (in an era before spy satellites) was to photograph strategic Russian military and rocket installations. Taking off from a clandestine American base in Peshawar, Pakistan, Powers skillfully guided his fragile high altitude spy plane across the border of the USSR in a willful violation of Soviet airspace and in direct violation of international law. A few hours later, while flying over the industrial city of Sverdlovsk (formally Yekaterinburg, the site of Tsar Nicholas' execution), Powers' plane was struck by a Russian anti-aircraft missile. Somehow, despite the high altitude, the American pilot managed to eject from his crippled plane and miraculously survived the crash. Powers was immediately captured and imprisoned by the Soviets, and for the next several weeks, the embarrassing incident provided the Soviet Premier, Nikita Khrushchev, ample political propaganda to denounce and humiliate the United States before the entire world community. The ensuing diplomatic disaster resulted in the cancellation of a previously scheduled diplomatic summit meeting between President Eisenhower and Premier Khrushchev.[57] Khrushchev would later boast, with significant merit, that his shrewd manipulation of the embarrassing U-2 affair had been the primary cause for Vice President Richard Nixon's narrow electoral defeat in the 1960 presidential election.

Despite all of its intriguing political and historical consequences, most contemporary Americans were totally ignorant of this important episode of American history. Yet my high school students at B-CC were exceptionally well-informed and knowledgeable because they had read a significant book and had the opportunity to meet its author. They had gained new insight into the dramatic events of the Cold War through content-rich instruction.[58]

The students themselves often became the source for my classroom speakers. One year a student casually inquired if I would be interested in having her neighbor come to class to speak about his experiences as a United States Secret Service agent. It seemed to be a promising opportunity. After further conversation, I discovered that her family friend was, in fact, Win Lawson, the agent in charge of conducting the advance work for John F. Kennedy's ill-fated trip to Dallas in November, 1963. Lawson was an important historical figure who was also an actual eyewitness to the President's assassination. Although it remained an incredibly painful memory for him, he graciously consented to speak with my students about what actually had occurred in Texas on that tragic November 22nd.

Agent Lawson prefaced his remarks by explaining to the students that he felt personally responsible (unjustly) for having failed to prevent the President's assassination. He was perpetually haunted by the fact that he was the only agent in American history to have lost a president while under direct Secret Service protection. Each and every day he was reminded of this fact during his commute to the Secret Service offices in Washington. As he drove across the Memorial Bridge, in the distance he could always see from the span the flickering eternal flame at Arlington National Cemetery which marked the Kennedy memorial grave.[59]

It was important for Win to help set the historical record straight, since there have been few events in American history that have generated more nonsense than the Kennedy assassination. Indeed, over the last several decades, a vast array of conspiracy theorists, lunatics, and charlatans have successfully confused the American public into believing some of the most outrageous claims, innuendos, distortions and outright lies about President Kennedy's assassination. Despite a complete lack of factual evidence to support their scandalous accusations, these individuals continue to publish volumes of "literature" on the subject, most of which is totally devoid of any historical scholarship or academic integrity.[60] Unfortunately, this rubbish is today even more widely disseminated through the Internet and other electronic media resources.

As a teacher, I insist that my students maintain a strong ethical and scholarly standard when assessing any historical event. By contrast, the modern conspiracy theorists are motivated instead by strong ideological agendas and they willingly forsake the truth. In essence, they hold three axioms in common: 1.) the United States government is engaged in an aggressive cover-up of the assassination and is lying to the American people; 2.) all of the evidence which supports a single gunman or which proves Lee Harvey Oswald guilt has been cleverly fabricated; 3.) and the absence of any credible evidence to support their own claims is due to the fact that the conspiracy was successful.

In reality, the conspiracy theorists are intentionally distorting the historical record, with the most egregious offender being Hollywood movie director, Oliver Stone. His 1991 film on the Kennedy assassination, *JFK*, while admittedly well-made and powerful, is a total fabrication and provably false. Yet Stone is undeterred as he intentionally manipulates actual historical film footage of the events in Dallas and splices it into wholly fictitious scenes in order to promote and advance his own preposterous theories on the assassination. In so doing, he effectively dupes his unsuspecting and ill-informed audience into accepting the most outlandish scenarios as historical fact. Joseph Roquemore in his book, *History Goes to the Movies*, accurately observes: "According to *JFK*, [President Lyndon Johnson] and a cast of hundreds killed Kennedy to keep America in Vietnam. Packed with similar harebrained nonsense, Stone... mangles history throughout."[61] Despite this, it is Oliver Stone's celluloid fable that has become the primary source of "knowledge" for many Americans about the Kennedy assassination and it continues to corrupt the minds of countless high school students.[62]

It was completely understandable that my own students' thinking on the Kennedy assassination was muddled and confused. Like most Americans, they desperately hoped that there was some sort of cosmic meaning in the President's tragic and untimely death. They had a difficult time accepting the idea that John Kennedy's murder was little more than a random act committed by an insignificant nobody who had opportunity, will, and a powerful 6.5 mm. Mannlicher-Carcano bolt-action rifle. Although no one will ever know with absolute certainty what actually motivated Lee Harvey Oswald to kill the president on November 22, 1963, the most likely explanation is that he suffered from what has been referred to as the "Herostratus syndrome." This is when "...a killer may hope, by his attack, to absorb the celebrity of his prey."[63] Indeed, it was only through his heinous act that Lee Harvey Oswald was able to achieve his own personal villainous immortality.

Win Lawson's powerful and unadulterated testimony about the Kennedy assassination, though, helped my students to discern the truth about the assassination and dispelled many of their acquired misconceptions. As agent in charge of the Dallas portion of Kennedy's campaign trip to Texas, Lawson vividly recounted how he visited the city for the first time on November 13th to schedule and coordinate the President's motorcade route. This was done in close consultation and cooperation with the White House staff, who insisted upon maximum visibility for the President and the First Lady since the Dallas trip was the kick off for Kennedy's re-election campaign. Kennedy, himself, had earlier ordered his Secret Service detail to maintain a low profile and insisted that they refrain from riding on the back of his limousine since their presence tended to obscure the public's view.[64] Lawson also worked closely with the local Dallas police department in an effort to effectively allocate their resources as well as to address their own specific security concerns.

On the actual day of the presidential visit, Lawson was at Love Field where he met Air Force One. After the President and First Lady's arrival, he then took his position in the lead car of the presidential motorcade in order to guide and navigate the caravan through the sometimes confusing city streets of Dallas en route to the Trade Mart where the President was scheduled to deliver an address to a large audience of political supporters. But just 30 minutes later as the procession slowly passed through Dealey Plaza, Lawson heard three distinct gunshots, all originating from the sixth floor of the Texas School Book Depository. The President was struck twice by the gunfire and was mortally wounded.[65]

My students sat in complete silence, mesmerized by Lawson as he explained how he ordered the motorcade to divert immediately to Parkland Hospital. Despite their speedy arrival at the emergency room, within the hour the President of the United States was officially pronounced dead.

Win and his fellow Secret Service agents were shocked and devastated but they had no time to grieve. The agents hastily arranged transportation of the martyred President's remains back to Love Field and they helped load the deceased President's casket on board of Air Force One for the return trip to Washington, D.C. Later that day, Lawson would assist in the massive police investigation into the shooting and would be personally present at the Dallas Police headquarters when the assassin, Lee Harvey Oswald, was finally arrested and arraigned. There was no doubt as to what had actually transpired that day in Dallas—there was no conspiracy, no mysterious plot—just a loathsome lone gunman who forever changed history.

With the nation's capital in such close proximity to B-CC, coupled with easy access to the Metro subway system, I was determined to escape the limitations and confines of the traditional classroom whenever possible. I wanted my students to experience all of the city's magnificent museums, art galleries, archives, and governmental institutions.

I enlisted the support of B-CC's administration to have my government classes each semester spend two full school days in Washington. This became known as our "capital internship." I insisted that the students dress professionally and reminded them that they were each a personal emissary of our school.

During the field trip, the students visited the Supreme Court, the National Archives, and the United States Capitol. At each site, they were required to complete a variety of tasks and assignments, which included such things as attending a congressional committee hearing, listening to an oral argument at the Supreme Court, observing a general session of the House and Senate, and visiting their Congressional representative's office. At a prearranged time, the students collectively reassembled on the steps of the House of Representatives and met with our district's elective representative. I also arranged for a class photograph to be taken for a souvenir. Afterwards, they were allowed to enjoy a relaxed lunch at Washington's famed Union Station.

During these halcyon days before the 9-11 terrorist attacks, we had unlimited access to the U.S. Capitol building. The students were

Congresswoman Connie Morella of Maryland addresses B-CC students on the steps of the U.S. Capitol. Meeting with our congressional representative was an important part of our two day field trip to Washington. (Philip Bigler)

able to roam and explore freely and to leisurely enjoy its magnificent art and architecture. They were especially delighted to discover the special underground electric subway that linked the House and Senate office buildings with the main Capitol building. They were also fascinated by the special clocks that were prominently located throughout the Hill and which lit up and sounded bells to signal quorum calls and other special legislative procedures.[66]

It was impossible to duplicate the palatable excitement of being on Capitol Hill in a typical classroom. Moreover, it was important for the students to see our nation's representative government in action. They quickly learned that there were profound differences between the cryptic governmental theories contained within the pages of their textbooks and the often messy reality of Washington politics. When the students returned to school, they were always invigorated and would regale their less fortunate classmates with incredible stories about what they had seen and experienced while on our field trip. They always had the opportunity to meet prominent legislators including such notables as Ted Kennedy, Tip O'Neill, Newt Gingrich, Al Gore, and Jessie Helms. Likewise, they frequently encountered other newsworthy dignitaries and lobbyists who were on the Hill to testify before Congress.

The highlight of these semi-annual Washington excursions was always our attendance at a presidential arrival ceremony held on the South Lawn of the White House. These impressive and prestigious ceremonial events were organized to honor a visiting head-of-state. My good friend, Phil Walsh, was then serving as the chief park ranger at President's Park and he was able to make special arrangements to accommodate my high school students. It was electrifying and thrilling to witness firsthand the military pomp and pageantry associated with the office of the chief executive and it was, of course, always a special honor to see the President of the United States in person.

It was only natural that my history classes were envious of my government students. I assured them that I would take them on their own field trip sometime later in the semester. A trip to the Gettysburg National Military Park in southern Pennsylvania fit perfectly into the American history curriculum since we devoted a good deal of class time to studying the causes, effects, and consequences of the American Civil War.

All good field trips must be content-based and provide a unique learning experience, so to prepare, I had the students read Michael Shaara's historical novel, *The Killer Angels*. In the book, Sharra's main protagonist is Lt. Col. Joshua Chamberlain, the Union commander of the 20th Maine regiment. On the second day of the battle, Chamberlain and his troops were deployed along the rocky ridges of Little Round Top anchoring the extreme left flank of the federal lines. On the afternoon of July 2, 1863, the 358 infantry soldiers of the 20th Maine successfully repelled a determined assault by a combined force of Confederate troops from Alabama and Texas.[67] It was an admirable feat but it was important that my students

Lt. Col. Joshua Chamberlain
(Library of Congress)

learn to think seriously as historians. They needed to investigate and decide for themselves whether or not this particular action was, as Shaara had boldly asserted, the most critical factor in the eventual Union victory at Gettysburg. It would be the essential question that would govern our class' entire trip to the Pennsylvania battlefield.

Field trips are a huge responsibility for teachers since taking large numbers of teenagers out-of-school are inevitably occasions ripe for potential disaster and filled with personal liability issues. They are also significant logistical exercises, so it is vital that there is adequate pre-planning as well as appropriate adult supervision. My first bureaucratic task was to secure individually signed parental permission slips for each and every student. This form was as a basic prerequisite for participation, but it also afforded me the opportunity to detail my expectations by requiring them to sign a contract that bound them to abide by all of our school rules governing student behavior. Next, I then had to devote several hours of time pulling every one of my students' emergency care card from files stored in the main office. These county-required documents contained critical contact and medical information that would be necessary in the event of an emergency.

For my Gettysburg trip, I also had to make special arrangements and negotiate an acceptable financial contract with a private charter bus company. It required three large commercial buses to transport all of my students and parent chaperones; so in order to organize them efficiently, I assigned each bus a historically accurate Union corps number and identified it with its distinctive corresponding badge symbol. Thus "Bus #1" became General John Reynolds' I Corps and it was marked by a prominent round circle; "Bus #2" was General

Dan Sickles' III Corps and it had a diamond symbol; finally, "Bus #3" was General George Sykes' V Corps and it was clearly identified by a Maltese cross. Every student was then given a specially prepared pin-back button which had a corresponding corps badge to indicate their bus assignment. They were expected to wear their buttons throughout the trip which helped facilitate the tedious and repeated task of taking roll. The buttons also allowed my parent chaperones to identify and sort the students out quickly. To maximize content instruction, as the students boarded their assigned buses, they were given a detailed handout to read while en route to Gettysburg. This material provided biographical information about their corps commanders and recounted their troops' actions during the actual battle.

Gettysburg is a short 90-minute drive from the Washington, D.C. suburbs. When we arrived at the visitor's center, our group was met by several licensed battlefield guides. These individuals were knowledgeable historians who were contracted to spend the day with us. Initially, they began our tour by pointing out Gettysburg's distinctive and strategic geographical features which dictated the course of the battle. They then escorted our group to various important battlefield sites where they continued to provide expert commentary about the battle while discussing key troop movements by both George Gordon Meade's Army of the Potomac and Robert E. Lee's Army of Northern Virginia. They also helped interpret the symbolism and meaning of the many regimental monuments and memorials that were scattered throughout the battlefield.

Our lead guide was Blake Chambers. I personally liked Blake because of his easy rapport with my students as well as for his keen

Gettysburg battlefield guide, Blake Chambers, teaching students about the perils of charging an artillery position. (Philip Bigler)

Students charging up Little Round Top in an effort to duplicate the Confederate assault on Union forces on July 2, 1863. (Philip Bigler)

wit and detailed knowledge. He made the trip fun and memorable by halting our caravan of buses at regular intervals and ordering the students to disembark. He would form the surprised students into hastily arranged battle lines and drill them on proper battlefield tactics and maneuvers. Blake taught them how to march and maneuver in proper formation and even explained the technical complexities of loading, aiming and firing a Civil War canon. The culmination of our day at Gettysburg came when Blake ordered the students to charge up the slopes of Little Round Top in an effort to duplicate the assault of the 15th Alabama against Chamberlain's defending forces.

By the time we returned to school late that night, the students were exhausted but inspired. They had gained a new respect for the actions of their ancestors a century before and their class trip to Gettysburg would be something that they would remember for the rest of their lives.

I was truly enjoying teaching again and had, for the most part, been able to avoid much of the bureaucratic nonsense that I had found so frustrating earlier in my career. But for some reason, large school systems seem intent upon making broad policy decisions based upon political expediency rather than for sound educational reasons. The further away an administrator, central office employee, or state official is from the classroom, the more unrealistic their pronouncements become. Indeed, many of these routine educational directives serve only to frustrate and hinder good teachers while such generalized mandates do very little to deter less competent educators. They certainly fail to improve the overall quality of instruction.

One year, we were informed that the county had issued an immediate injunction on using any motion picture film that had received an "R" rating by the Motion Picture Association of America (MPAA). The intention of the policy seemed to be perfectly reasonable since it would prevent inept teachers from exposing their students to the customary Hollywood garbage that contained inappropriate sexual content, glorified drug abuse, or promoted gratuitous violence. The practical reality of this blanket prohibition was that the schools had no autonomy nor were teachers given the academic freedom to exert their professional judgment. There was absolutely no distinction made between salacious films and those with significant artistic merit and quality of content. Good teachers don't waste valuable classroom time just showing a movie; they actually use it as an instructional tool. There are, in fact, numerous R-rated films that are age-appropriate for high school students and which can serve as valuable and legitimate resources for teachers; but rather than risk any controversy, it was far safer to just say no.

The 1989 film, *Glory*, stars Denzel Washington, Morgan Freeman, and Matthew Broderick, and is the dramatic portrayal of Colonel Robert Gould Shaw and the 54th Massachusetts during the American Civil War. The 54th was comprised primarily of freed African-Americans and was organized in 1863 during the nadir year when the Army of the Potomac was demoralized by its repeated defeats by General Robert E. Lee and the Army of Northern Virginia.[68] Among the 54th's more notable recruits were two of the sons of the distinguished abolitionist, Frederick Douglass.

The soldiers of the 54th served admirably throughout the war but their gallantry was forever immortalized by the regiment's brave but

The Shaw Memorial in Boston, Massachusetts.
(Library of Congress)

unsuccessful assault against a heavily fortified Confederate position at Fort Wagner in South Carolina. During the battle, Colonel Shaw was killed, and he was interred in a mass grave along with many of his soldiers.[69] After the war, the famed Irish-American sculptor, Augustus Saint-Guadens, memorialized Shaw with a bronze bas-relief monument. It depicted Shaw on horseback gallantly leading his troops into combat. The Shaw Memorial was dedicated in 1897 and today can be seen on the Boston Commons directly across from the Massachusetts State House. Saint-Guadens' original plaster mold casting has also been fully restored and is on permanent display at the National Gallery of Art in Washington, D.C.[70]

Glory is an evocative and emotional film that represents Hollywood film-making at its very best. It is a powerful teaching tool, since the movie personalizes the Civil War and humanizes the conflict. It skillfully chronicles and documents both the bravery and tragedy of the American Civil War, a conflict which in essence destroyed an entire generation of young men.[71] *Glory* was also branded with an "R" rating by the MPAA because of its "violence and mature themes." This rating is, at best, debatable, but regardless, it condemned the film by placing it within the school system's broad classification of banned films and its use was thus prohibited.

I felt strongly that my students should be able to see the film which I intended to show in conjunction with our study of the African-American contributions to the Union cause during the Civil War. To do so, though, would require an exemption from the county's policy. I had to spend several precious hours carefully drafting a formal written justification for using the film with my high school juniors. Eventually, I was granted a conditional waiver, but I had to secure individual parental permission forms from each of my students and provide them the opportunity to opt out of this particular class should they find the content objectionable. The absolute absurdity of this became even more apparent a few years later when our senior class was permitted to show the disgusting and vulgar film, *Austin Powers: The Spy Who Shagged Me*, as a class fund raiser. Apparently, the educational bureaucracy deemed this film permissible under its written policy since the movie had received only a generous PG-13 rating for its "sexual innuendo and crude humor."

Overall, I was happy and content to be teaching at B-CC. Our school's history department was outstanding, staffed by some truly skilled and dedicated educators. The quality of instruction was exceptional, but B-CC was also undergoing some unwelcome demographic changes. The surrounding community's population was rapidly aging and most of the school's neighborhoods were inhabited by middle aged or retired individuals. Their children had long since graduated from school. Likewise, the area's new high rise apartment complexes were mostly inhabited by young professionals who had careers rather than school-aged children. As a result, B-CC's student census continued to decline but the Montgomery County school board was reluctant to alter the neighboring school boundaries to compensate for the population changes. Such decisions are inevitably emotional and ripe with political controversy. As an ever-smaller school, each year B-CC's administration had to adjust by reducing its staffing. For a while, this was achieved through normal attrition; but in April 1991, I received formal notification from our Human Resources office that as the history teacher with the least seniority in the system, I would be "surplused" the following school year. This meant that although I would still retain my job within the system, I was scheduled to be involuntarily transferred to another school.

There were few viable geographic alternatives for me within Montgomery County. My daily commute was already difficult and too long. To drive to most of the other high schools in the county was impractical, so I decided to contact Elizabeth Lodal, the principal of McLean High School in Fairfax County, to see whether she had any job opportunities available. Within a matter of just a few weeks, Elizabeth had miraculously secured an early teaching contract for me. That fall, I would be teaching classes in World Civilizations and American History, as well as serving as the advisor of McLean High School's *Clan* yearbook publication.

Endnotes

51 Two of B-CC's most notable alumni are comedian Tommy Davidson, bestselling author/historian Laura Hillenbrand.

52 *The Trial of Lt. William Calley* is available through Interact at http://www.teachinteract.com. As will all historical simulations, I modified the lesson plans to fit the needs of my own particular classes.

53 Yamashita was convicted for war crimes committed by his troops during the siege of Manila in 1944. His command and control structure was disrupted by the American invasion and his troops committed numerous atrocities. The courts declared that he bore personal responsibility for these actions as their commanding officer. This became known as the *Yamashita Standard*. The Supreme Court (*327 U.S. 1, 27*) upheld Yamashita's conviction in 1946 and the General was executed on February 23, 1946. The relevance to the Calley case is that commanding officers can be held responsible for the actions of their troops.

54 Students are great sources for classroom speakers. In the case of Alvarez case, one of my students (Jennifer Shaheen) attended church with him and offered to serve as an intermediary.

55 Alvarez's story is recounted in the book, *Chained Eagle*. He was the second American to be captured during the Vietnam War. The first was Captain Jim Thompson, a Green Beret, who was captured on March 26, 1964. Unlike Alvarez, Thompson was unable to readjust to American life after the war and he became alcoholic and suicidal. He died in 2002. See Tom Philpott's excellent book, *Glory Denied: The Saga of Jim Thompson, America's Longest-Held Prisoner of War*.

56 James Stockdale was shot down the following year and would be the highest ranking American officer to be held captive by the North Vietnamese. After his release in 1973, he authored several books on his experiences as a P.O.W. I particular like his book entitled *Thoughts of a Philosophical Fighter Pilot*. Stockdale recounts how his study of Stoic philosophy, particularly the works of Epictetus, helped him survive the deprivations and daily humiliations imposed by his captors.

57 Francis Gary Powers was placed on trial in the Soviet Union. He was eventually convicted and sentenced to ten years in prison. In 1962, he was released in exchange for a Soviet spy. He was killed in 1977 when a helicopter he was piloting ran out of gas. He is buried at Arlington National Cemetery.

58 Michael Beschloss has gone on to become one of the leading historians in the nation and is an expert on the American presidency. He has authored several best-selling books and regularly serves as an expert historian for PBS and NBC.

59 Win Lawson and his fellow secret service agents recounted their stories in a recent book entitled *The Kennedy Detail*. It is an essential read for students seeking the truth about the Kennedy assassination. Also recommended are Jim Moore's *Conspiracy of One*; Vincent Bugliosi's *Reclaiming History*; William Manchester's *The Death of a President*; and Gerald Posner's *Case Closed*.

60 Stephen King came to the conclusion that Lee Harvey Oswald acted alone after doing research for his novel, *11/22/63*. According to the *Wall Street Journal* "Mr. King studies various conspiracy theories. He ultimately dismissed them, drawing the unsettling conclusion that a single person with no political power or charisma managed to alter the course of history by himself." See Alexandra Alter "Stephen King's New Monster," *Wall Street Journal*, October 28, 2011, p. D2.

61 Joseph Roquemore. (1999) *History Goes to the Movies: A Viewer's Guide to the Best (And Some of the Worst) Historical Films Ever Made*. New York: Main Street Books, p. 251.

62 I began teaching the Kennedy assassination in 1976. I was able to get an 8mm copy of the Zapruder film from a company in Canada, and the film became the centerpiece of my presentation. At that time, few people had actually seen the film. Over the years, my presentation grew and expanded as I added new materials, photographs, charts and other resources. It was widely anticipated by the students although it became a bit tedious to me. At B-CC, I taught Abraham Zapruder's granddaughter, Alexandra. She had never seen the film until I showed it to her one day. When we visited the National Archives on a field trip, I tried unsuccessfully to have her grandfather's 8mm camera removed from the vaults to be shown to her and her fellow classmates. Alexandra is currently working at the Holocaust Museum in Washington, D.C. and is the author of *Salvaged Pages: Young Writers' Diaries of the Holocaust*.

63 Albert Borowitz. (2005) *Terrorism for Self-Glorification: The Herostratus Syndrome*. Kent, Ohio: Kent State University Press, p. xii. Herostratus was an arsonist who is accused of destroying the Temple of Artemis (one of the seven ancient wonders of the world) in Ephesus, circa 356 B.C. Through this monstrous act, he gained eternal fame and notoriety. The "Hersotratus syndrome" is a psychosis that motivates many insignificant individuals to commit horrible crimes in a lust for undeserved fame. The students involved in the school shootings at Columbine

would be typical since through their act, they received widespread notoriety, including appearing posthumously on the cover of *Time* magazine.

64 According to Secret Service Gerald Blaine in his book, *The Kennedy Detail*, Kennedy told Agent Floyd Boring that he did not want agents positioned on the back of his car: "It's excessive…and it's giving the wrong impression to the people. Tell them to stay on the follow-up car. We've got an election coming up. The whole point is for me to be accessible to the people." See Gerald Blaine. (2010) *The Kennedy Detail: JFK's Secret Service Agents Break Their Silence*. New York: Gallery Books, 2011, p. 148.

65 Win Lawson's lead car is not seen in the Zapruder film. It had just passed through the area when Zapruder began filming the motorcade.

66 A red light on the clock indicates that the House or Senate is in session. The lights and bells on the clock mean the following: One light/ring indicated the calling for the yeas and nays; two lights/rings indicates a quorum call; three lights/rings is a call for the absentees; four lights/rings indicates adjournment or recess; five lights/rings signals that there are 7.5 minutes remaining in a vote; six lights/rings means that the body's business is concluded.

67 The best historical record about the 20th Maine's role in the battle comes from Charles Hamlin's book, *Maine at Gettysburg,* published in 1898. See Charles Hamlin, et al. (1898) *Maine at Gettysburg*. Portland, Maine: The Lakeside Press, pp. 253-255.

68 After the issuing of the Emancipation Proclamation, the Union army began to actively recruit African American troops. By August, 1863, 14 regiments had been formed to augment the federal forces. By the end of the Civil War, over 180,000 blacks had served in the Union army. The troops were designated by the acronym USCT, for United States Colored Troops.

69 Shaw's grave and that of his men was located on the mouth of Charleston harbor. It no longer exists since the land has long since eroded away into the Atlantic Ocean.

70 The National Gallery of Art has a wonderful website devoted to the Shaw Memorial. They also have slides of the memorial and a series of lesson plans available for free loan to teachers. See the National Gallery of Art's website at http://www.nga.gov for additional information.

71 There were no "great" American presidents from 1865 through 1901. I argue that this was because the nation's greatest talent had been killed during the war. At the same time, I explain to the students that every Republican presidential candidate during this period had to have a notable Civil War record to run for office, since the party continued to run so-called "Bloody Shirt" campaigns, reminding voters that "Every Rebel was a Democrat" and that they should "Vote as You Shot."

CHAPTER VII

The "Brave New World" of Technology

We can give students as many computers and cafeterias and curriculum administrators as we want, but none of it will make any difference without the one thing that makes a classroom work—a dedicated and well-trained teacher.

Rod Paige

According to ancient Greek mythology, it was the Titan god Prometheus who one day stole fire from the heavens and gave this coveted knowledge to mortal man. This divine gift forever freed humanity from its perpetual darkness and metaphorically from everlasting ignorance. For his offense, Zeus punished Prometheus by having the god chained to a rock on Mount Caucasus. There, an eagle would torment the disgraced and fallen god by hungrily devouring his liver. As an immortal, though, Prometheus' agony and suffering would be eternal since his liver miraculously regenerated itself each day, allowing the horrific scene to be repeated in perpetuity. In Aeschylus' tragedy, *Prometheus Bound*, the god still boasted:

> Such help I gave, and more
> …who else
> Can claim that he revealed to man but I?
> …Prometheus founded all the arts of man.[72]

Prometheus was considered to be the champion of humanity, the person singularly responsible for providing mankind with the essential knowledge that would be required for the advancement of civilization. It is from this Greek myth that we derive our contemporary concept of "technology."

Over the past three decades, there has been a remarkable technological renaissance that has virtually transformed all aspects of modern life. The corresponding information revolution has been unprecedented in human history. For the first time, the world's vast intellectual resources are readily accessible and physical location is no longer a major obstacle. Distant repositories of learning and the entire new digital universe are readily accessible through the mere click of a computer mouse.

This is undoubtedly the most exciting time to be a teacher, yet it is astonishing how slow our public schools have been to innovate using the latest technological developments. Likewise, many educators continue to resist modifying or adapting their traditional teaching methods and are failing to meet the rapidly changing demands of modern student learners. As a result, our nation's schools are still mired in the past, moribund and obsolete, while our students are failing to meet the complex challenges of the 21st century.

I first became aware of the vast potential of computer technology shortly after my father was transferred to Jacksonville, Florida in 1965. He was assigned to duty with Fleet Intelligence and was responsible for maintaining and programming several of the Navy's new, multi-million dollar IBM computers. These massive, complex, and intimidating machines were designed to communicate and coordinate the entire military operations of our nation's Mediterranean fleet. They operated solely by way of computer punch cards.

The computers were quite fickle and had to be carefully installed on elevated floors and were constantly cooled in a precise, temperature-controlled environment. How these byzantine computers actually functioned was comprehendible only to the most skilled and highly trained technocrat and there were few practical applications for such mysterious technology beyond their use within the narrow confines of the defense industry and global business concerns. Nobody at the time could even conceive that computers would soon become a common household instrument that would forever transform modern life.

When my dad retired from the Navy in 1968, he accepted a job with IBM as a systems analyst in Washington, D.C. Thirteen years later, the company publically introduced its first desktop personal computer (PC). By contemporary standards, the IBM-PC was a cumbersome device, equipped with just a monochrome monitor and two 5.25-inch floppy disk drives. There were no sound cards or any audio-visual capabilities, while its operating system, PC-DOS, was command-driven. Developed by a 25-year old Harvard dropout named Bill Gates, his new company, Microsoft, maintained the copyright to the software and this strategic oversight would allow the company to market the operating system to rival computer manufacturers.

The first PC's were extremely expensive selling for around $1,600. The public demand for this new curiosity was initially limited, but to its credit, *Time* magazine, recognized the burgeoning potential of home computers by declaring the personal computer to be its so-called "Machine of the Year" in January 1983.

At the same time that IBM was developing its PC, an up-start company known as Apple Computers was perfecting its own competing desktop system. In a brilliant marketing ploy, Apple launched a distinctive advertising campaign for its new Macintosh computer during the third quarter of the 1984 Super Bowl game between the Washington Redskins and LA Raiders. The commercial cleverly utilized an Orwellian theme which was aimed directly against arch-rival IBM. According to Bernice Kanner in her excellent book, *The Super Bowl of Advertising*:

> The commercial opens with a stark, futuristic vision. Blue-tinted zombies shuffle in lockstep into a massive assembly hall dominated by a huge screen from which Big Brother orates. 'For today, we celebrate the first glorious anniversary of the Information Purification Directives. We have created for the first time in all history…a garden of pure ideology.' The devolved automatons, their heads shaved and mouths agape, sit transfixed while Big Brother drones on: '… where each worker may bloom secure from the pests of contradictory and confusing truths.'
>
> Suddenly, an athletic blonde in red shorts bearing the new Mac logo charges the screen wielding a sledgehammer, pursued by ominous 'thought police' with face masks. Big Brother's harangue continues: 'We are one people. With one resolve. Our enemies shall talk themselves to death. And we will bury them with their own confusion. We shall prevail!'
>
> After winding up, the woman hurls the sledgehammer. The screen explodes in a blinding flash of light. 'On January 24th, Apple Computer will introduce Macintosh. And you'll see why 1984 won't be like *1984*,' says the announcer.[73]

The clever marketing ploy was an overwhelming success. Apple sold an astonishing 72,000 Macintosh computers over the ensuing few weeks and demand for home computers sored nationwide. The ensuing rivalry between Apple and Microsoft operating systems became intense and bitter but the competition had a positive outcome since it served as a catalyst for future innovation.

My own personal platform loyalties rested with IBM since the company was my dad's employer. He helped me get my first PC through a deeply discounted employee purchase program. Dad hoped that this new computer would help me with my teaching career, but it did far more than that—it forever transformed me as an educator. I was determined to make the most of this miraculous technology and wanted to use it to improve student learning. On a purely practical level, my lesson plans and handouts instantaneously improved since I was able to use the system's proprietary word processing software to scan my files for errors and misspellings. I was also able to acquire my first DOS-based grading program, which allowed me to enter all of my class grades quickly and efficiently. The software was also able to calculate student averages instantaneously and I regularly generated detailed printouts and graphs for the students to provide them with detailed information about their academic progress. All of these things convinced me that through the effective use of technology, it was possible to transform American education and enhance student learning.

I soon upgraded my system by adding a hard drive and a dial-up modem. This communication device allowed me to use the PC to connect to a global information network through my home telephone's land-line. Access to these resources was made possible through an hourly subscription service offered by a telecommunications company known as CompuServe.

The information resources available online were impressive but this was by not by any means the sophisticated, modern Internet. There were no websites, graphics or audio-visual resources available and everything remained entirely text-driven. Still, there was no doubt that this was a revolutionary advancement in modern communications with enormous potential providing quick and easy access to information.

At the time I got my modem, I was teaching a unit in my Contemporary Issues classes on the growing epidemic of world terrorism. This present-day plague of barbarism posed a serious threat to our contemporary society and it was important for my students to gain a better understanding of its dangers. The primary goal of terrorists is to instill maximum fear and to intimidate their perceived enemies. An ancient Chinese proverb once stated, "To kill one is to scare 10,000," but with today's advanced communications, the truth of this statement has increased exponentially—to kill one is to scare one billion. Terrorism ultimately hopes to destabilize civilized society.

To illustrate just how widespread the problem of global terrorism had become, I decided to use my new computer access to search a current news database for all stories about terrorist attacks that occurred throughout the world. Inevitably, each night there were reports of over two dozen such incidents, so I would carefully collect and copy the digital headlines and print them out on my dot-matrix printer. The next morning, I would post the printout on the bulletin board so that when the students entered the classroom, they would first read the list. Then, they were to investigate and discuss the reported incidents and organize them into ethnic, religious, nationalistic, and political categories. To identify the location of these terrorist occurrences, they would insert a small colored pin into a world map. By the end of the unit, our classroom map had distinct, large concentrations of pins which effectively illustrated the extent of global terrorism as well as the countries most impacted.

The students also conducted research on various terrorist attacks, extremist movements, and political assassinations through history. They began by looking at the French Revolution and the "Reign of Terror," and continued their inquiries up to the modern day.[74] I also had the students look at the newspaper and magazine accounts of a specific incident, the hijacking of a TWA airliner in June 1985. Two Islamic terrorists seized control of the plane shortly after takeoff while en route from Athens to Rome. For the next two weeks with its 153 passengers and crew held hostage, the entire world's attention was riveted on the news as the airplane crisscrossed the Mediterranean Sea. The plane landed periodically at the Algiers and Beirut airports to refuel and it was during one of these stops that a 23-year old Navy Seabee, Master Chief Robert Stethem, was executed by the terrorists after haven been brutally beaten.[75] His body was then callously discarded from the airplane where it remained on the tarmac for several hours in order to maximize the visual and psychological impact.

During the long and terrifying ordeal, the flight's purser, Uli Derickson, performed heroically and would be later credited by many of the passengers with saving their lives. Her incredible story was dramatized in a made-for-television movie entitled *The Taking of Flight 847* starring the actress, Lindsay Wagner.[76]

We watched the film together as a class and I offered my students extra credit for writing to Uli through the TWA offices in St. Louis. A few weeks later, she responded with an incredibly profound letter which I immediately shared with all of my classes. (See Appendix A) She began:

> It is now almost 5 years since the fateful day of June 14, 1985, when TWA flight 847 was hijacked out of Athens, Greece. I am moved and deeply honored that you and your students have taken the time and effort to write to me... It is my belief, that any one of your students in the years to come could just as easily be handed a similar surprise or maybe even a worse one than what was handed to me on June 14, 1985—a surprise incidentally, I would rather not have been given, but we can't always be choosy about what life decides to schedule for us.[77]

Uli explained her own personal background. She was born in Nazi-occupied Czechoslovakia during World War II and later lived in communist East Germany. Eventually she was able to immigrate to the United States and began her career as a flight attendant. Her letter went on to explain to the students the ultimate lesson she had learned from her experiences onboard TWA 847:

> I appreciate freedom, too—more than I ever thought possible. Because, I tell you, you can't believe what it feels like to be held captive, under someone's total control—until it happens to you. And to have your mind terrorized and held captive, too. When that happens, you realize how precious freedom is. And that doesn't mean freedom to ignore others. That's a kind of terrorism all in itself. No, freedom implies a

responsibility to others—which is liberation of your ability to make a difference. I know now, as a result of my experience, that when you are responsible for someone else other than yourself, it intensifies the fighting instinct in you. And the ability to act is the greatest freedom of all.[78]

The TWA hijackers were affiliated with the radical groups Hezbollah and Islamic Jihad. But there were hundreds of similar radical sects worldwide. Their individual motivations differed but they were all united in their common goal of inflicting the utmost harm while generating maximum publicity for their cause. This fidelity to violence was the most difficult for westerners to comprehend.

Despite the advent of the computer revolution, there was still very little good educational software available for use in social studies classes. One summer when I was working at the Governor's School for the Gifted at Virginia Tech, two of my colleagues introduced me to a home computer game entitled, *President Elect*. It was published by Strategic Simulations Inc. (SSI) and was being marketed to the general public to coincide with the 1984 presidential campaign. The programmers had conceived and written the software for entertainment and did not envision its use in a classroom setting. In the game, one player would direct Ronald Reagan's re-election campaign while his opponent would manage that of former Vice President Walter Mondale. Over the course of a simulated nine-week period, the two players would strategically determine where to allocate their limited financial resources and how to best spend their allotted advertising dollars. Likewise, they would determine which electoral-rich states were most advantageous for their candidates to campaign in.

The game itself was a modest commercial success but since its computer algorithms had been skillfully and accurately constructed to reflect the actual demographics of the nation in 1984, the simulated results inevitably mirrored those of the real election. That year, President Reagan won the election in an epic landslide, carrying 49 of the 50 states and winning the popular vote by a staggering 58.8% to 40.6% margin.[79] It was virtually impossible for Mondale to win in the simulation and this greatly limited the game's popular appeal. SSI reissued the game 1988 presidential contest but the Bush/Dukakis matchup proved not to be very competitive either, so the company allowed the program to die a quiet death.

It was almost an afterthought but the software designers at SSI had included a few historical scenarios on the program's floppy disk, including the 1960 campaign between Senator John F. Kennedy and Vice President Richard Nixon. This was an ideal presidential contest to teach about modern electoral politics and contemporary American history. Indeed, it was one of the closest elections in the country's history, with Kennedy winning by a plurality of just 112,827 votes.[80] I was also fortunate to have access to the classic documentary film, *The Making of a President 1960*, which was based upon Theodore White's bestselling book.[81] But to effectively use the simulation with my classes, I needed to make several adaptations and modifications. First and foremost, I had to figure out how to rig the library's Apple IIe computer to a television monitor so that the entire class could see the screen as the polls, electoral maps, and voting results were revealed. Most importantly, I had to write specifically designed lessons that would convey the course content and actively involve the students. I required the campaigns to conduct primary source research, produce campaign materials, develop political position papers, write

Students at Bethesda-Chevy Chase High School play "President Elect" in class. The computer simulation ran on an Apple IIe computer and was used to dramatically recreate the 1960 presidential election. (Philip Bigler)

Using technology effectively in the classroom can both increase student motivation and enhance learning. (Philip Bigler)

pamphlets, hold mock presidential debates, and make speeches. The students were also expected to know about the major issues involved in the campaign such as the status of Quemoy and Matsu, the validity of the alleged missile gap, the status of U.S./Soviet relations as a result of the U-2 affair, the dangers of Fidel Castro's Cuban revolution, and an assessment of the Eisenhower administration.

The simulation quickly became one of the most anticipated activities in my course and was a powerful student-centered learning experience. All of the students were engaged and involved. I took a great deal of personal satisfaction watching them carefully study and analyze the computer generated electoral map and then make strategic adjustments to their campaign tactics predicated upon the computer generated political polls and projections. The highlight of the simulation came on our mythical election night, "November 5, 1960." The campaigning was finally finished and all of the states would cast their votes. It was entirely plausible for the Nixon campaign team to win in this classroom scenario and thereby rewrite history.[82]

The tension in the classroom was palatable as everyone anxiously awaited the returns. As each state finally projected, often late into the simulated evening, the students would either shout with delight or cry in anguish. Other teachers on our hallway would often look out of their classroom doors, perplexed by the commotion, but what they were actually witnessing was authentic, content-rich learning.

For several years, journalist and noted television commentator, Chris Matthews, would come and talk with my classes. He was an engaging and compelling speaker who has an encyclopedic knowledge of contemporary American politics with a particular fascination with John F. Kennedy. Chris had authored an excellent book entitled *Kennedy & Nixon: The Rivalry That Shaped Postwar America* and it contained a chapter on the 1960 presidential election. During one of his visits, my class had just finished our *President Elect* simulation and Chris casually asked my students who was Richard Nixon's vice presidential running mate in 1960.[83] In truth, very few adult Americans would be able to answer this question but immediately one of my students eagerly raised his hand and responded correctly that it was Henry Cabot Lodge. He then went on to elaborate in exhaustive detail that Lodge was, in fact, a terrible political choice. Indeed, he had lost his bid for election to the United States Senate some eight years earlier to none other than a young John F. Kennedy. Furthermore, since Lodge was from Massachusetts, he added no electoral advantage to the GOP ticket, since Kennedy would assuredly carry his own home state. My well-informed student proceeded to explain that it was Kennedy's choice of Lyndon Johnson as his running mate that proved far more astute since LBJ provided both a philosophical and geographic "ticket balance." Indeed, in the election Johnson successfully ensured that the Democrats carried the state of Texas with its crucial 24 electoral votes. This was a critical factor in Kennedy's ultimate narrow electoral victory over Richard Nixon.[84] Chris was astonished that a 16-year old high school student could be so knowledgeable about a distant historical event but as I explained to him, this is what is truly possible when students are emotionally vested in your class and when you use modern technology effectively to enhance learning.

As much as I loved teaching at B-CC, I was enthusiastic about my impending transfer to McLean High School for the 1991-1992 school year. I like change and firmly believe that it is healthy for teachers to regularly transfer to other schools. It forces you to adapt to new teaching environments and helps ensure that you maintain a fresh perspective. Going to a new school also requires a teacher to re-establish his reputation with students.[85] I have found that the best teachers never rest upon their laurels but are always seeking new challenges.

My new job at McLean offered an opportunity to further explore the potential of using modern computer technology with my students. For my yearbook class, I insisted that we incorporate the latest computer hardware and software so that we could make a successful transition to full desktop publishing. This meant that we had to replace all of our publication's rudimentary computers, which were little more than glorified word processors and had become obsolete.

Over the summer, I attended several teacher workshops in order to learn all that I could about yearbook publishing, and spent hours working to master the latest software programs. I also devoted a good deal of my time to renegotiating all of McLean's publishing and photographic contracts. I insisted that the companies we would hire would be committed to supporting my instructional efforts and that they would assist us in meeting and maintaining our technology needs.[86] As the school's yearbook advisor, I was responsible for managing and accounting for a forty thousand dollar-plus annual budget. I had to supervise my editors' and staff's efforts to promote, market, and sell the book to the McLean student body so that we could earn enough money to cover all of our printing expenses. Moreover, we were expected to work together as a team to meet all of our publisher's stringent deadlines,

Yearbook staff member, Nadine Pryke, consults the yearbook deadline board at McLean High School. Students learned desktop publishing, editing, and other important skills while producing the school's annual. (Philip Bigler)

and were collectively accountable for all of the yearbooks editorial and photographic content.[87] It was a huge responsibility but it was also rewarding since we were producing, in essence, the McLean High School official history as well as its informal resume.

I had inherited an excellent group of student editors from the previous advisor, but I wanted yearbook to be an inclusive activity, free from the cliques that often plague high school groups and clubs. I began to augment the staff by recruiting several other talented students. I implemented a new policy with my principal's full support whereby the students could earn varsity letters just like our school's athletes. Indeed, the yearbook's staff's commitment and contributions to the school's culture was comparable to any sports activity and needed to be appropriately recognized.

I hired a new yearbook publisher over the summer. The company, Herff Jones, had the added advantage of being located in Gettysburg, so my editors and staff could actually visit the plant and witness firsthand the process of printing and producing a book. Likewise, through our negotiated contract agreement, we were able to purchase three brand new computers, a state-of-the-art laser printer, and a site license for Adobe PageMaker software. The students were able now to digitally design their own page proofs and this gave them complete creative control over their layouts. More importantly, they were acquiring important, real-life skills that would help them in their other classes as well as in their future academic endeavors.

I was extremely proud of all of my yearbook students. They were amazing, selfless young people who were committed to producing a quality publication for the school. They devoted countless hours working to meet our publishing deadlines, and the staff even volunteered to devote an entire week of their precious summer vacation to attend yearbook camp in order to improve their design and editing skills. It wasn't long before McLean's *Clan* yearbook was earning statewide and national recognition for journalistic excellence.[88]

Our 1995 edition of the yearbook celebrated the 40th anniversary of the school's founding. My two editors-in-chief were Stephanie Clark and Emily Wu, and they had developed the perfect theme for this special commemorative issue, "Forever Plaid." It celebrated McLean's proud Scottish traditions as well as the school's distinguished history of academic excellence.[18] By April, we had submitted all of our final page proofs and corrections to the publisher, so the staff was rewarded with a brief respite before the book's scheduled delivery in late May. It was a relaxing time and we were all enjoying the warm spring weather while recuperating from the months of stress, pressure and late night deadlines.

One morning, the assistant principal interrupted my third period Civ class and quietly informed me that our school's custodians had just discovered that the yearbook room had been broken into and vandalized overnight. All of our computers had been stolen. It seemed that all of the years of hard work and effort trying to modernize our publi-

Editors-in-Chief for Forever Plaid, *Stephanie Clark and Emily Wu.* (Philip Bigler)

cation had been destroyed. I took the sacking of the yearbook office as a personal insult and I was angry and frustrated. This was, without question, the lowest point in my entire teaching career.

I was now forced to spend much of my day meeting with the Fairfax County police who were investigating the crime. It was quickly discovered that the computers had been abandoned and discarded by the thieves in the school's trash dumpsters, but not before they had been pillaged of their RAM memory, hard drives and sound cards. The machines were rendered useless and the stolen components were untraceable. It was immediately apparent, though, that the felons had a strong knowledge of computer technology and were well-acquainted with our publishing operations. This was not a random act—they knew exactly what they were looking for.

Despite the fact that the police had gathered a considerable amount of incriminating evidence, it was obvious to me that no one would ever be arrested or prosecuted for the crime. This only added to my growing sense of outrage and disillusionment. All of the resulting stress and personal anxiety was impacting me negatively as a teacher and it was interfering with my job performance. During one lunch period, Elizabeth came down to the yearbook office to talk with me about all that had recently transpired. She told me that she could understand my sense of indignation but that I could not continue to dwell on the past. It was time to accept what had happened and to let it go. To be a good teacher, Elizabeth said, you have to be an optimist; you have to have faith in your students and believe that things will eventually work out for the best. These thoughtful and profound words forever transformed me as a teacher and would hence forth be my guiding principles.

All of the students at McLean were outraged and they, too, felt violated. It was, after all, *their* yearbook and everyone was impacted by the theft. Several representatives of the school's student organizations came by my classroom and offered to contribute funds to help us in our efforts to recover. Simultaneously, Elizabeth was conducting her own quiet, effective lobbying campaign with county officials to secure additional funding to replace our destroyed machines. The following September when we returned to school, there was a full complement of new computers waiting, which allowed us to resume work with minimal interruption.

I loved McLean High School and it was there that I received my first public recognition for my work as a classroom teacher. On two occasions, the school's graduating senior class selected me as their "most influential teacher." I was deeply honored by this award since it was predicated upon what I taught them, not personal popularity. Indeed, far too many teachers are more than willing to sacrifice their academic integrity in order to gain the approval and "friendship" of their students. Their classes may have a reputation for being fun but they are typically devoid of substance and lack any seriousness. I wanted instead to be remembered as a teacher who cared for his students and who earned their respect by challenging them to learn. I also hoped that I would serve as a positive role model.

As part of the award, the seniors invited me to be their faculty keynote speaker during their school-wide convocation ceremony. I didn't want to waste this precious opportunity by delivering the routine end of the year speech full of platitudes and meaningless slogans. Instead, I approached the occasion as if it were my last lesson.

The convocation was held in the school's gymnasium. A temporary stage was set up at the end of the basketball court and all of the seniors proudly wore their cap and gowns as they processed into the assembly. The underclassmen were assigned seating in the bleachers and watched enviously.

I began my address by recalling my early impressions of the Class of 1995 when I first met them as freshmen in my World Civilization classes:

> I was impressed by your eagerness to learn. You, as a class, were still free from cynicism and blessed with the innocence of youth—you were honest and uninhibited learners, a true joy to teach...I still have countless fond memories of your freshman year. I will never forget how you learned to make camel sounds, honking and snorting at all the appropriate times during *Lawrence of Arabia* and how you all cheered, or in some cases, bemoaned, your Greek fate which was seemingly imposed upon your *polis* by an arbitrary, random god. I was pleased when you spoke intelligently and thoughtfully about the very essence of mankind and contemplated the meaning of life as solitary, reflective medieval monks. We shared many special moments...

I had many of the students again during their junior year in U.S./Virginia history and as seniors in Advanced Placement American Government. I was impressed by how they had matured over the years and by their academic progress. I continued my address:

> As seniors...I have been exceedingly impressed by the scope of your intellectual growth and your acquired knowledge—

this is, after all, what high school is all about. But instead of being involved in manors, polis's, samurai clans, and gens, I have watched in awe as [you portrayed attorneys arguing before the Supreme Court and] delivered an impassioned and brilliant defense of the 1st Amendment, arguing eloquently for the rights of the rap group, Too Live Crew, to make and produce a parody of the song, "Pretty Woman." I have read some of the most outstanding research papers of my career, thoroughly researched, well-documented, and fully developed...Yes, there is so much good about the Class of 1995.

My primary focus, though, was the growing educational and societal crises that were threatening the very mission our nation's schools. Mass mediocrity and foolishness had become commonplace and it was incumbent upon our students to resist the many temptations of modern life and live a significant and meaningful life:

But I would be less than honest if I do not also express some of my concerns. Over the past decade or so, I have seen the insidious growth of apathy in our society and this has, sadly, infiltrated into our schools. Far too often in today's American classrooms there is a climate hostile to learning and a total loss of any sense of personal responsibility. Our nation is now in the midst of an intellectual crisis very much as real as the perils of World War II or of Cold War nuclear annihilation and we, as a people, collectively seem to be oblivious to this threat. We are, instead, rapidly developing a caste system as real as those social, economic, and political divisions that separated Romans into plebeians and patricians; Russians into *boyars* and *moujik*; medieval man into noble and serf. But unlike these previous systems based upon the accident of birth or the circumstance of wealth, ours is self-imposed and avoidable, for our society is becoming unconsciously divided into the educated and the uneducated.

One of the very real causes of this lamentable situation has been the steadfast refusal of our citizens to accept personal responsibility or any consequences for their actions. How many of our students want an "A" without any work or quality? How many exhibit disruptive behavior that directly interferes with the rights of others to learn? How often are the serious academic accomplishments of our students deprecated by others out of sheer jealousy?

My friends, life is fundamentally about choices—not excuses. You, and you alone, are responsible for your own actions and you cannot consign blame to others or to some cosmic forces beyond your control. Ultimately, you must face the consequences for your own existence…

I freely admit that it is not an easy time to be young and growing up in America. Indeed, you are daily bombarded with all sorts of contradictory messages that seem to condone every sort of perversion imaginable and which advocate all types of socially aberrant behavior. Television beams into our homes the world of situational ethics where there are no absolute values, no truth, no justice. From OJ to Geraldo, we are given the false impression that this is a nihilistic world; but if that were truly the case how can civilization ever exist? How different are we in the 20th Century than our Roman ancestors who barbarically cheered at the coliseum as lions devoured Christian martyrs, or those spectators who watched with glee during the French Revolution as the shinning blade of the guillotine did its work until finally dulled and caked with the blood of intellectual, dissident, and priest?

…All of you have been exceedingly blessed to have been educated at a school that remains committed to noble principles—complete with a serious honor code and an innovative ethics day. As importantly, those significant lessons delineating right from wrong and good from evil are reinforced daily in each and every classroom by a dedicated, committed faculty. These remarkable teachers, despite a callous and uncaring society which often deprecates their labor, somehow find the courage and commitment each day to come here to McLean with a renewed sense of hope, selflessly dedicated to your personal intellectual enlightenment. It has often been said that teachers sow seeds of harvest unseen. The greatest reward, the most meaningful tribute you can give to us, your teachers, is your future success.[90]

I was pleased with the overall reception of my speech, and Elizabeth had it copied and distributed to all of the parents at the subsequent graduation ceremonies. Personally, it was hard for me to say farewell to the Class of 1995. They were collectively one of the best groups of students I had ever taught. But the cycle of public education is relentless and the next September, we welcomed an entire new group of eager freshmen to McLean. I was teaching my usual allotment of World Civ, American history, government, and yearbook (Photojournalism) classes.

Every spring, McLean had a tradition of selecting its own "teacher of the year." The procedure called for circulating an initial ballot with the names of the entire faculty. From this extensive list of over 100 names, the teachers voted to cull it down to just five finalists. These names were then submitted for a final vote and the winner was announced over the school's public address system in late April. I had been a finalist before, but in 1996, I was selected to be McLean High School's "Teacher of the Year."

I was humbled and honored to receive this professional acknowledgement by my peers. I really didn't think that my colleagues were aware of how hard I was working at the school, since I spent the vast majority of my day helping my students. I had always been careful to stay out of the teachers' lounge and did my utmost to avoid the nefarious cliques and petty gossip that are part of all large institutions.

A few weeks later, I received an invitation to attend an elegant dinner hosted by the McLean Chamber of Commerce in my honor. During the festivities, I was presented with a beautiful plaque which recognized my "outstanding accomplishments and dedication to excellence in education." It was also a valuable opportunity for me to represent my profession to the greater business community. There was, though, little time for celebration or reflection, since the very next morning, I had to distribute our new edition of the new yearbook, *Beam Me Up, Scottie*, to our student body.

As the school year was gradually grinding to a close, I was once again getting restless and I desired a new professional challenge. The catalyst had been Elizabeth's unexpected retirement at mid-year and the uncertainty it caused. There was a good deal of angst among the faculty since everyone knew that it would be exceedingly difficult to replace her as an academic leader. Elizabeth had an enormous influence on me as an educator and as a classroom teacher. I would be forever grateful but it was impossible for me to envision McLean High School without her.

My wife was teaching Spanish at Thomas Jefferson High School for Science and Technology (TJHSST) and she heard that there was an opening in the school's history/humanities department. Linda urged me to apply for the position since she knew it would give me the opportunity to pursue my strong interest in using educational technology in the classroom.

Jefferson is a regional magnet school for northern Virginia and is application-based. It had been established by Governor Chuck Robb with the avowed mission of operating as an innovative lab school where both students and teachers would be encouraged to experiment, try new things, and learn together. Project-based learning was emphasized and the school's academic curriculum was incredibly challenging. Although TJ's physical structure was old and decrepit, the high school did have on-site its own state-of-the-art super computer and the building had been hard wired for students and teachers to access the Internet.[91]

I decided to apply for the job and interviewed with the principal, Geoff Jones. He soon offered me the position and I formally transferred to TJ for the 1996-1997 school year. It was a move that came with considerable regrets. My five years at McLean had been wonderful and I would always miss the students there, but I knew that in my heart I would remain "forever plaid."

My initial schedule at TJ consisted of four Humanities I (World History and Literature) and two Humanities II (US History and Literature) classes. It was an incredibly difficult teaching day made even more so due to the fact that I was paired with three different English teachers. It was practically impossible to arrange for joint planning time, but I was fortunate that all of my partners were skilled and experienced teachers so we were able to work well together. My students were impressive, serious, and intelligent, but what I enjoyed the most was the fact that they were eager and voracious readers. You would always find the students at lunch or between classes sitting in the hallways immersed in a good book. In many ways, it reminded me of what it must have been like on the ancient Greek agora—a hallowed sanctuary away from the distractions of daily life and a place where intellectual pursuits were cherished and venerated.

One of my first technology goals at TJ was to learn how to write and develop an effective class webpage. To do so, I had to learn how to write html code, but I found it to be a relatively logical and it was easy to understand. I particularly enjoyed the creative process of creating my own unique, content-based class homepage complete with a detailed daily course calendar and an up-to-date list of class assignments. The ability to access course material online greatly improved

Technology can be a wonderful teaching tool when used effectively in the classroom. The computer and the Internet have made available incredible resources for students to study history, but students need to become critical users. (Ashwin Kharidehal Abhirama/Dreamstime)

my communication with parents as well, since they had the ability to monitor their child's education. The parents knew exactly what was being taught in class and were kept well-informed about course requirements, critical due dates, and assigned projects. They also had easy access to the lists of books that we were teaching in class.

The class webpage provided crucial links to dozens of pre-screened, high quality history websites which the students were able to use to supplement regular classroom instruction as well as to conduct additional research. This ensured that they were accessing reputable material rather than conducting dangerous blind Internet searches.

I regularly tried to incorporate the latest technology into my lesson plans and my instruction. I found that this helped keep my students focused and motivated, but my ultimate goal was not to showcase high tech computers or the latest software or some other digital fad; it was to better teach history and to enhance my students' learning.

During back-to-school night, rather than bore the parents with the usual ten minute monologue explaining the litany of classroom procedures and policies (all of which were posted online), I instead designed a highly visual PowerPoint slide show which incorporated digital photographs of classroom activities, and synchronized all of it to music. The parents could actually see their children actively engaged and involved and they inevitably left with a far better un-derstanding of what we were studying in our humanities classes.[92]

Still, despite these students' incredible intellects, they were also present-day teenagers and were vulnerable to the same lapses in judgment that were commonplace in more traditional schools. It was incumbent upon us, their teachers, to provide these students not only with an outstanding content-based education but also with a solid moral foundation and strong ethical direction. Indeed, I have found that gifted students are especially prone towards hubris, and when smart people make mistakes, there are usually profound and have lasting consequences.

The Jefferson students had a naïve faith in scientific advancement and technological innovation. They were willing to embrace each and every new craze and did so often without ever critically questioning its potential ethical, moral, or philosophical implications.[93] Since technology was such an important part of the overall culture at TJHSST, my teaching partner, Sheri Maeda, and I decided to begin our Hum II (American history and literature) course with an extensive unit on the Columbian Exposition of 1893. This amazing world's fair was held in Chicago as part of the nation's commemorations of the 400th anniversary of Columbus' first voyage to the new world.[94] It was seen by its organizers as an opportunity to showcase the incredible amount of human progress that had been achieved due to the nation's rapid industrialization and urbanization. It had, in fact, produced an unprecedented improvement in the living conditions and the quality of life for the vast majority of Americans. The resulting inventions and many modern marvels made mankind's continued progress seem inevitable.

Millions of visitors traveled from all across the United States to visit the fair and were dazzled by such technological wonders as electric lights, massive dynamos, sewing machines, electric ovens, telephones, and phonographs. They feasted upon such delectable treats as Cracker Jack, popcorn, ice cream, Juicy Fruit gum, Hersey's chocolate, and Quaker Oats before taking an obligatory ride on the fair's signature attraction, the steel-structured Ferris wheel. From one of its massive 36 cars, it was possible to enjoy a breath-taking panoramic view of the fair and of the recently rebuilt Chicago.[95] For those sightseers with more prosaic interests, there was ample entertainment along the exposition's famed Midway, which featured

The Columbian Exposition in Chicago, 1893 was a celebration of technology and human progress. Just a few years later, the same technology would be used to unleash unprecidented death and destruction. (Library of Congress)

anthropological exhibits from Algeria and Tunisia, China, Japan, Java, Turkey, and Egypt. Everywhere you looked there were new, exotic wonders which included snake charmers, sword swallowers, camels, lions, and parrots. The most popular attraction, though, was understandably, the titillating and provocative hootchy-kootchy dance performed by the exotic "Little Egypt" on the Streets of Cairo.

The fair proved to be an economic and political success. It was estimated that over 27 million people attended the exposition and it confirmed the widely held view that it was a wondrous and exciting time to be alive. As one visitor to the fair observed, "Those who saw this…declared that the nineteenth century is indeed the century of progress and enlightenment."[96]

But just a few blocks from all of the glitz and glamour of the exposition, there was a nefarious side to the city of Chicago. Dr. Henry Howard Holmes, a pharmacist and sadistic serial killer, was using the Columbian Exposition as an opportunity to lure gullible young women to his boarding house-hotel located conveniently at the corner of S. Wallace and 63rd Street. There he brutally murdered and butchered the women, eventually confessing to 27 homicides.[97] It would be, ironically, H.H. Holmes, the remorseless psychopath, who would serve as a far better metaphor of what was to come in the not too distant future.

After the Columbian Exposition closed, its structures were unceremoniously demolished. Most had been constructed out of cheap plaster. The entire façade had been, in essence, an American Potemkin Village—a fraud. Just two decades later, the very same technology and innovation that was so glorified and celebrated in Chicago was metamorphosed into new and horrible weapons of mass destruction. During the "Great War" (1914-1918), the same nations that had proudly exhibited in Chicago used their technological prowess to develop tanks, machine guns, poison gas, dirigibles, and airplanes. These implements of war unleashed unprecedented destruction upon the European continent, and when combined with pestilence, disease, and starvation, the death toll was conservatively placed at over 37.5 million people.

After the armistice was mercifully declared at 11 o'clock, November 11, 1918, there would be only a brief respite before the outbreak of World War II. Another 60 million people would perish during the global conflagration culminating with the nuclear annihilation of two Japanese cities—Hiroshima and Nagasaki. Modern technology had made the extinction of civilization possible and it is a fate that can only be avoided only through the education of a wise and vigilant populace.[98]

Thankfully, the misuse of modern technology has not yet resulted in the same catastrophic consequences in our public schools, but it is a substantial and increasing problem. Teachers, administrators, and parents need to be informed and proactive in order to provide children with detailed and clear parameters for the appropriate use of digital resources both at home and in school. This will ensure that students are fully aware of the school's academic expectations as well as their own personal responsibility.

One of the growing abuses in today's classrooms is rampant plagiarism. In our cut and paste culture, it has become easy to copy reams of material from various Internet sources (including many of questionable credibility) and seamlessly insert this stolen information into papers, reports, and projects without the appropriate citation. Many students who are guilty of such transgressions commit this academic misconduct out of ignorance rather than with intentional malice, but their intent does not excuse or condone the behavior. Plagiarism is a serious violation of both intellectual property rights and an individual's personal integrity. It simply cannot be tolerated.

Part of the problem is cultural. The ongoing digital revolution and our rapidly changing society pose serious and unprecedented ethical challenges for our schools. Indeed, the conventional distinctions between right and wrong have been effectively blurred by an increasingly amoral culture which justifies all sorts of aberrant behaviors and which has effectively eliminated the traditional deterrents of shame and guilt. The consequences for a civil society are devastating.

The proliferation of an infinite number of satellite tv channels along the widespread accessibility of streaming video has led the entertainment industry to producing cheap "reality" shows in an effort to meet the public's insatiable demand for amusement. *Sans* professional actors and skilled script writers, modern programs glorify the most barbaric behavior, and these shows are edited, produced, and aired with little or no concern for the noxious aftermath. These programs place a premium on contestants who successfully scheme, plot, and lie. Uninhibited, obnoxious and loathsome pseudo-stars are more than willing to perform for the omnipresent cameras by drinking, cursing, and fighting. [99] In return, they are generously compensated with unjustified fame and fortune. The entertainment industry's overall message to our nation's impressionable school children is that there are no adverse consequences for duplicitous behavior. Anything and everything is now acceptable—go ahead and lie, steal, and cheat so long as you don't get caught. It is this nihilistic world view that is having a deleterious effect on our schools.

On the popular website, YouTube, there are dozens of amateur videos that elaborate on the latest techniques for cheating in school. Unscrupulous students are instructed on how to deceive their teachers by using cell phones, scientific calculators, digital readers, and mp3 players, and other portable devices. One typical video was entitled, "How to Cheat on any Test," and was part of a multi-episode series that had been viewed by an astonishing seven million people. Likewise, there has been a proliferation of websites which provide additional support for this unethical behavior. Run by anonymous and mysterious webmasters, these uncensored sites are impenitent, as illustrated by one administrator's boast that: "I have cheated on tests, homework, projects and other assignments...It's something I take pride in. I feel very good about myself when I cheat on a major test and get away with it." [100]

New technologies do have an enormous potential to improve student learning, but they can also be easily abused. Many teenagers are wasting their time by endlessly texting their friends, gossiping on Facebook, or just idly surfing the Internet.[101] Even worse are the graphic video games that are marketed specifically to juveniles (particularly boys). The narcotic games encourage them to live in an imaginary universe where they engage in endless, epic battles against mythical monsters, demons, and Nazis. The educational consequences of these diversions have been an epidemic of hyper-active students with shortened attention spans and a general lack of personal discipline. With adolescents daily gorging themselves on the digital equivalent of Aldous Huxley's fictional hypnotic drug, soma, their minds have been numbed and anesthetized with: "...the result [is] that [they] could now sit, serenely not listening, thinking of nothing at all."[102]

With a readily available and endless source of intoxicating entertainment and addicting amusements available, too many young people have forsaken books as a source of knowledge. In one survey, it was estimated that the average high school student currently spends just 49 minutes per week reading traditional print materials.[103] The impact this has had on core content knowledge has been substantial, with many students lacking basic proficiency in literature and history. Despite their abysmal knowledge of the past, our nation's less informed younger generation has become increasingly self-absorbed and egotistical. Social networking encourages them to publish their random and uncensored (and frequently unwelcomed) ramblings without consideration of the potential harmful consequences. Likewise, many imprudent minors routinely distribute risqué digital photographs of themselves or their friends over the Internet or on cell phones. Once private, intimate, and embarrassing moments can be circulated worldwide in just a matter of seconds and once so disseminated, the postings are easily available to perverts and predators. It is ironic that the catastrophic perils predicted of an Orwellian future where Big Brother surveillance is all pervasive has been willingly embraced by the contemporary generation that seems impervious to the consequences concerning their loss of personal privacy.

The Internet is convenient, fast, and efficient. It allows for effortless retrieval of an infinite amount of factual data and as such, has essentially replaced libraries as the primary research tool for students. Facts are no longer a major problem for students but large amounts of raw information is little more than trivia when viewed out of proper context. The challenge for students, is to convert vast amounts of random information into substantive knowledge in order to better understand complex historical topics.

I discovered just how important this is during my Hum I (World History and Literature) course at TJ. As part of our course curriculum, we had the students read portions of James Michener's historical novel, *The Source*. The book is a fascinating, albeit verbose, chronicle of the history of the Jews from pre-historic times through the creation of the modern day state of Israel in 1949. As with all of Michener's works, the book is rich with historical detail and is filled with vigorous, memorable characters. Still, despite his admirable research, it remains a work of fiction and it is important for those readers to be able to distinguish between actual historical truth and the imaginary stories that were formulated wholly out of Michener's vibrant imagination. This requires a considerable level of skill and academic sophistication when dealing with a novelist as skilled and gifted as James Michener.

In truth, we have all been guilty of accepting literary accounts of the past as accurate portrayals of historical events and personages. Fiction writers are not constrained or limited by extant documents, archival materials, and known sources, so they are free to speculate, consign motives, create dialogue, and enhance historical circumstances to build drama and excitement. William Shakespeare's

Reading is still the most important skill that a student needs for success in school. Nothing replaces the experience of reading a book. (Used with permission "Back to School" Mike Keefe)

14 "history plays" for example, are masterpieces of literature and have shaped much of our historical memory. It is Shakespeare's account of the assassination of Julius Caesar (*Et tu, Brute?*) that most people remember today, not the factual account by the emperor's contemporary chronicler, Gaius Suetonius Tranquillus. Similarly, the "Feast of Crispin" speech delivered before the impending battle of Agincourt in 1415 by the English warrior/king in *Henry V* has rightfully become a fundamental part of our literary canon and a fundamental part of our rich western heritage, but it has no basis in fact.[104] And even the most stolid historians can respect and admire Robert Bolt's classic play, *A Man for All Seasons*, as a semi-biographical account of the life of Sir Thomas More. The work dramatizes the climactic feud with King Henry VIII and effectively personalizes the Reformation while providing valuable

moral lessons on the importance of personal integrity and a commitment to one's essential beliefs. Even though these interpretations of historical events are relatively benign, they must still be balanced with historical truth.[105] So after my students had finished reading the assigned chapter, "The Saintly Men of Safed," in Michener's *The Source*, I had them re-examine the following passage:

> In 1492, after more than seven hundred years faithful service to Spain, the Jews were expelled from that state. They fled to Portugal, where they were scourged, forcibly baptized and later exiled. In Italy and Germany they were forced into inhuman quarters where they wore inhuman costumes. At almost rhythmic intervals they were charged with murdering Gentile children for blood to be used at Passover. They were accused of poisoning wells, of spreading cholera, of knowing how to infect rats with the plague to decimate Christian communities; and they were particularly accused of posing as Catholics, accepting the holy wafer of communion and hiding it slyly under their tongues until they could produce it for blasphemous black masses. In an age of growing freedom they were constantly restricted as to where they could move, what they could wear and especially what occupations they could engage in.[106]

Although Spain has been traditionally considered to be the epicenter of medieval anti-Semitism, such prejudice was widespread throughout Europe. This is common historical knowledge, but was Michener's chapter in *The Source* an accurate portrayal of Jewish persecutions in Europe? The book is close to 1,000 pages long, but it does not contain any footnotes or a bibliography. It is this absence of documentation that should be a critical concern to all would-be historians.

To help my students develop their critical reading skills, I designed an extensive research project to guide them in their investigation and analysis of Michener's novel. The first part of the project required the students to spend a class period in our school's library for background research, but as soon as the class arrived, the students sprinted past the stacks of historical materials in order to stake their claim on a coveted computer terminal. They began hastily searching the Internet for all the information they could find on anti-Semitism, the Inquisition, and Jewish persecution. It was a simple task to find encyclopedic material on famous personages such as Tomás de Torquemada but there was nothing specifically on Michener's book or any relevant or substantive information pertaining to the "The Saintly Men of Safed." I let the students continue for a few minutes until they were collectively frustrated, since it was important that they experience the limitations of technology when conducting scholarly research. I finally called the class back together and with the assistance of our school's librarian, showed them the stacks of excellent books and pertinent historical atlases where they could more efficiently find the answers to many of their questions. Indeed, the library was filled with well-sourced and scholarly materials that had been specifically acquired to support our instruction and to assist the students with difficult research topics. I explained to them that books remain the most significant resources for the acquisition of knowledge.

A few days later, after the student had successfully completed their projects, they came to a general consensus that although many of Michener's characters and locations were fabricated, *The Source* was overall an accurate historical account. Of course, it was the primary reason that I had assigned the book to the students in the first place.

Endnotes

72 Aeschylus, "Prometheus Bound," excerpted in Bernard Knox, ed. (1993) *The Norton Book of Classical Literature*. New York: W.W. Norton, pp. 304-305.

73 Bernice Kanner. (2004) *The Super Bowl of Advertising: How the Commercials Won the Game*. Princeton: Bloomberg Press, pp. 25, 27. A copy of the original Apple 1984 commercial is available on Youtube at http://www.youtube.com/watch?v=HhsWzJo2sN4.

74 The word "terrorist" was first used in reference to the Reign of Terror (1793-1794).

75 Robert Stethem was buried at Arlington National Cemetery in Section 59, which became unofficially designated as a section for victims of terrorist attacks.

76 *The Taking of Flight 847: The Uli Derickson Story* (1988) is available only on VHS tape and has been retitled *The Flight*.

77 Letter from Uli Derickson in the author's personal collection.

78 *Ibid.*

79 In 1984 Walter Mondale only carried his home state, Minnesota, with a plurality of just 3,761 votes. He also carried the District of Columbia, which was allotted electoral votes by virtue of the XXIII Amendment to the Constitution. The final tally in the Electoral College was Ronald Reagan 525, Walter Mondale 13.

80 Kennedy's popular vote total was just .17% more than that of Richard Nixon. Almost 69 million votes were cast in the election. Hawaii was decided by just 115 votes; Alaska by 1,144; Illinois by 8,858; Missouri by 9,980.

81 *The Making of the President 1960* is now available on DVD at MediaOutlet. com for under $10.00. Also available now are the Kennedy/Nixon debates as well as actual election night news coverage.

82 At the Republican Convention in Chicago, Vice President Nixon pledged a 50-state campaign. At the time, this seemed to be an astute political move since Alaska and Hawaii had just been admitted to the union. Unfortunately, Nixon got sick during the campaign and was forced to miss two critical weeks of campaigning. The weekend before the election, Nixon was forced to spend an entire day flying to Anchorage, Alaska to fulfill his foolish pledge while John F. Kennedy spent the time campaigning in New York. Nixon easily carried Alaska with its 3 electoral votes but lost New York and its 45 electoral votes by less than 400,000 votes. The other critical factor in the election was the televised debates. It is widely believed that Nixon's poor physical appearance during the first debate (he refused to use makeup) hurt him with the electorate.

83 Today, many students question why they need to know factual information when they can use Google or some other search engines to quickly get an answer. The simple explanation is that facts are meaningless without appropriate context.

84 There were many allegations of voter fraud in the 1960 election, particularly in Illinois and Texas. Mayor Richard Daley reported assured Kennedy that: "With a bit of luck and the help of a few close friends, you're going to carry Illinois." Kennedy's plurality in the city of Chicago was a staggering 456,312 votes. It was estimated that fully 10% of the people on the city's voter lists were dead or had moved away. Nixon lost Illinois by just 8,858 votes. In Texas, Kennedy won the state by just 46,267 votes. Many people urged Richard Nixon to contest the results of the election but the Vice President steadfastly refused. According to David Pietrusa, "In Fannin County, 4,895 registered voters cast 6,138 ballots. In Angela County's Twenty–seventh Precinct, 86 individuals voted—Kennedy won 147 to 24." See David Pietrusza (2008), *1960: LBJ vs. JFK vs. Nixon: The Epic Campaign that Forged Three Presidencies*. New York: Union Square Press, pp. 403-405. Despite the urging of many of his campaign supporters, Richard Nixon refused to contest the election results. To his credit, Nixon conferred the stamp of legitimacy on the election by visiting the president-elect in Palm Beach, Florida.

85 During my 23 year teaching career, I taught at five different schools: Oakton High School—1975-1980; W.T. Woodson High School—1980-1982; Bethesda-Chevy Chase High School—1985-1991; McLean High School—1991-1996; and Thomas Jefferson High School for Science and Technology—1996-2001.

86 Photography contracts are big business in high school. A company receives permission to photograph and sell portrait packages to students in return for a large financial commitment to the school. They are also required to provide "mug shots" of all the students and faculty to the yearbook. It is important that publication advisors regularly bid these lucrative contracts to maximize a company's financial commitment to the school.

87 One of the most tedious parts of producing a yearbook is going through hundreds of student "mug shots." I insisted that the students verify each and every name because I believed that it was important to spell all of them correctly and to list the students accurately. This was something personal for me since I go by my middle name, Philip. For my four years in high school, though, I was always listed in our yearbooks by my first name, "Bernard." I always hated when the yearbooks came out and felt slighted that the editors never checked to see if this was my preferred name. We certainly made our own mistakes at McLean, but we always made an effort to be accurate.

88 McLean High School has a strong Scottish tradition. The school even has its own bagpipers who perform with the marching band.

89 During my five years at McLean, our yearbook themes were "Never Before, Never Again," "Rock Solid," "We've Got It," "Forever Plaid," and "Beam Me Up, Scottie."

90 This is an excerpt from the speech I gave to the entire student body at McLean High School's senior convocation which was held on June 9, 1995.

91 I worked on a pilot program over the summer of 1995 at McLean to develop Internet-based lesson plans. I was given a copy of the new browser, Netscape Navigator, and prepared a series of projects for the upcoming presidential campaign. Unfortunately, the vast majority of students still did not have Internet access, so the lessons had to be altered and modified to reflect that reality.

92 Country singer, Lee Ann Womack's song, "Dance," was very popular.

93 To their credit, the TJ English teachers assigned Mary Shelley's *Frankenstein* to the freshmen. It is an incredible novel which poses serious ethical and moral questions about the use of technology.

94 The fair was a year late. It is interesting for students to compare the nation's commemorations in 1893 to those one hundred years later. In 1992, many people were protesting Columbus as a genocidal murderer who brought death and disease to the American Indians. According to Tony Horwitz in his book, *A Voyage Long and Strange*, "...progress was out, postcolonialism in. Columbus was dug up again, this time to be damned as the first in a long line of Europeans to exploit and exterminate Native Americans. The Indian activist Russell Means set the tone for the 1992 remembrance by pouring blood on a Columbus statue and declaring that the discoverer 'made Hitler look like a juvenile delinquent.'" p. 48.

95 In 1871, the Chicago fire had destroyed almost 1/3 of the city. The world's fair was, in many ways, a celebration of the city's rebirth.

96 There are many outstanding books on the Columbian Exposition. Much of this information comes from Norman Bolotin and Christine Laing's book, *The World's Columbian Exposition*. The University of Virginia also maintains an excellent website which is ideal for students to explore the fair. It is available at: http://xroads.virginia.edu/~ma96/wce/introduction.html.

97 Erik Larson's *The Devil and the White City and* Theodore Dreiser's *Sister Carrie* are great outside readings for this unit.

98 A very good book to use with students is Alfred Heller's *World's Fairs and the End of Progress*.

99 Universities were once bastions of advanced learning, but these esteemed institutions have become totally corrupt and complicit in lowering our cultural standards. In 2011, the "Jersey Shore's" self-proclaimed Italian-American princess, "Snooki" was paid $32,000 to appear before students at Rutgers University. Her insightful advice to the attending audience was, "Study hard, but party harder." According to an account in New Jersey's *Real-Time News*, her final words to her admiring audience were "I love you, bitches." Article available at: http://www. nj.com/news/index.ssf/2011/03/snookis_advice_to_rutgers_stud.html. The Rutgers University's annual tuition and board for in-state students is $24,017; for out-of-state students the fees total $36,679. In fairness to Rutgers, this is hardly an isolated incident. In 2010, Snooki appeared at several colleges including both the University of Virginia and James Madison University. Perez Hilton reported on his website that while visiting JMU, Snooki appeared before a sold out student audience in Wilson Hall and: "entertain[ed] the students and hilarity ensued including a fist-pump tutorial, a back flip and an abs contest!" She later tweeted: "JMU you guys are awesome! Had soooo much fun, thank you!! Def gonna remember you guys for a long time!!!" See Perez Hilton's website at: http://perezhilton. com/2010-03-04-snooki-at-james-madison-university#.T1usrDGwx_g. The best novel on the perils of contemporary college life is Tom Wolfe's *I am Charlotte Simmons*.

100 Because of the nature of this topic, I have intentionally chosen not to provide the link to this source. The name of this individual's personal webpage is "How to Cheat in School."

101 It is estimated that the average teenager sends 2,272 text messages per month. Carr, p. 86.

102 Aldous Huxley in *Brave New World* available at: http://www.huxley.net/soma/somaquote.html.

103 Carr, p. 15.

104 Kenneth Branagh's rendition of the Crispin speech in *Henry V* is available on DVD and is magnificent.

105 One of the best ways to teach history is by looking at historical myths and their evolution. These stories are significant because they often reveal a society's fundamental values.

106 James A. Michener. (1989) "The Saintly Men of Safed," *The Source*. Norwalk: Easton Press, p. 638

CHAPTER VIII

A Crusade Against Ignorance

I am quite conscious of my ignorance...I am wiser...[in]that I do not think I know what I do not know.

Socrates, quoted in Plato's *Apology*

During my first several weeks at TJ, I felt overwhelmed by the vast amount of daily preparation that was required for me to teach my six humanities classes effectively.[107] I was also inundated by a seemingly infinite number of lengthy papers which had to be individually read and graded.[108] Coupled with the usual array of faculty meetings, routine committee assignments, and regular parent conferences, it was a hectic pace. I added to this already demanding schedule by voluntarily agreeing to sponsor the incoming freshmen class (Class of 2000). So instead of using my precious weekends to catch up on work, I was spending my time helping a group of enthusiastic 14-year olds construct a float out of two-by-fours, chicken wire, and tissue paper for their upcoming homecoming parade.

The weeks were frantic but fun when in late October a student

My Humanities students Sarah Bowman, Sandi Lin, and Irene Paz with me at Thomas Jefferson High School for Science and Technology in Fairfax County.
(Mary Jo LoBianco)

assistant interrupted my class to deliver an urgent message from the main office. It was from McLean's interim principal, Paul Jones, and he needed to speak to me immediately. Despite the exigent tone of his message, it was impossible for me to return the call until after classes had adjourned for the day.

When I was finally able to reach Paul by phone later that afternoon, and he said that he wanted to check on my progress in completing my application for Fairfax County Teacher of the Year. I was totally perplexed since I had absolutely no idea what he was talking about. I had always assumed that my congratulatory dinner with the chamber of commerce the previous April had been the highlight of my selection as McLean's Teacher of the Year, but apparently that was not the case. I should have received a packet of materials to complete and to submit to the Fairfax County leadership team for consideration for the annual county-wide teacher of the year honor.

These mysterious forms, however, apparently got lost or misplaced in the confusion resulting from my summer transfer to Jefferson. The missing packet was now due at the county offices in just a matter of few days and this deadline was strictly enforced. Paul said that he would dispatch a courier over to TJ with the required materials and he insisted that I put in the time to complete the required paperwork on schedule.

When the county forms arrived the next morning, I was dejected. The formal application process required an updated professional resume and a detailed philosophy of education, along with several expository essays. It would take, at a minimum, several hours to complete and I was now in mid-semester mode. I didn't have any spare time for such things but I still felt an obligation to McLean, so I resolved that I would put forth my best effort in composing my responses within the short amount of time that was still allotted.

Writing is hard work and composing the essays proved to be excruciating. At the same time, though, I found the process of seriously reflecting on my career to be surprisingly therapeutic. I had become comfortable, even complacent, with my instruction and content knowledge. I had a great rapport with my students and was popular, but it had literally been years since I had taken the time to analyze and evaluate my beliefs as an educator. I knew intrinsically that my overall philosophy of education had evolved and matured since my college days, so this was an ideal opportunity to revisit my teaching ideology. I vowed, though, that if the process was going to be at all worthwhile, I had to be honest and forthright regardless of the ultimate consequences. I would not write or say anything that would compromise my own personal beliefs in an effort to please some anonymous selection committee.

My first essential tenet of teaching was the importance of establishing a climate of academic rigor in class. In a perfect world, our public schools would be intellectual sanctuaries where all of our students are challenged and taught by skilled, well-trained teachers. It is critical that we ensure that students are engaged in substantive, meaningful learning while at school.

When I was still a young, novice teacher at Oakton High School, a good friend and colleague of mine, Mike Dobson, shared with me an article that had been written by James Michener for publication in *Reader's Digest*.[109] Entitled "When Does Education Stop," it was based upon a chance encounter he had with a puerile college student who was upset about having to write a short term paper about one of Michener's many books. Michener, who could be admittedly a bit of a curmudgeon, had no patience for intellectual lethargy and he strongly rebuked the young man for his complaining. The aging author told the student that he should be grateful to be engaged in an academically challenging assignment. Michener went on to explain:

> Young people, especially those in college who should know better, frequently fail to realize that men and women who wish to accomplish anything must apply themselves to tasks of tremendous magnitude. A new vaccine may take years to perfect. A Broadway play is never written, cast and produced in a week. A foreign policy is never evolved in a brief time by diplomats relaxing in Washington, London or Geneva.
>
> The good work of the world is accomplished principally by people who dedicate themselves unstintingly to the big

job at hand. Weeks, months, years pass, but the good work-man knows that he is gambling on an ultimate achievement which cannot be measured in time spent. Responsible men and women leap to the challenge of jobs that require enor-mous dedication and years to fulfill, and are happiest when they are so involved.

This means that men and women who hope to make a real contribution to American life must prepare themselves to tackle big jobs, and the interesting fact is that no college or university in the world can give anyone the specific edu-cation he will ultimately need. Adults who are unwilling to reeducate themselves periodically are doomed to mediocrity.

…we learn only those things at which we have to work very hard. It's ridiculous to give a bright fellow like you a three-thousand-word term paper. It ought to be fifteen thou-sand words - or thirty. Tackle a real job. Then, when you're through, you're on the way to facing big jobs in adult life.[110]

The essay had a profound and lasting influence on my outlook as a teacher and I would often assign it to my own students to read. I completely agreed with Michener's assertion that a meaningful education requires discipline and hard work, but I also believed that qualified, capable teachers can make their courses inspiring, stimu-lating, and liberating.

As I continued to write, I felt that it was important that I address the growing problem of academic hooliganism in our schools. This despotic orthodoxy of thought (i.e., political correctness) encroach-es on our fundamental intellectual and political freedoms, and con-tinues to plague our schools and our society. Indeed, this rigidity in political ideology and group thinking poses a lethal threat to a teacher's essential mission to be an objective seeker of truth and apostle of enlightenment.

My role as a history and humanities teacher was to create a classroom environment that was conducive to a free, open, and unobstructed inquiry into the great ideas of human civilization as well as to offer a serious discussion of philosophical matters. This quest for ultimate truth has challenged and motivated thoughtful people throughout the course of human history. On my classroom wall, I prominently displayed a plaque with a quote from Thomas Jefferson that encapsulated his goals in establishing the University of Virginia in 1819. It read: "Here we are not afraid to pursue truth wherever it may lead nor to tolerate any error so long as reason is left free to combat it."

It is important, of course, that we expose students to new ideas and provide them with a valid historical perspective, but this can only occur when students and teachers feel free and safe to express themselves honestly without fear of retribution or censure. Social studies and humanities classes, in particular, must provide a safe classroom environment which encourages civil discourse and open debate. This will help the students understand that in our society, well-meaning and honorable people can fundamentally disagree with one another about controversial topics. It is part of an energetic, democratic education and students must be encouraged to think for themselves and be able to adjust their thinking appropriately when confronted by superior logic, ideas and arguments.

In order to preserve my objectivity with my classes, I scrupulously chose never to reveal my own personal political beliefs. I did not want to unfairly influence my students' thinking and wanted them to develop the confidence to form their own fact-based opinions. This can only occur when they are free from intellectual coercion. My ultimate goal for them was that they would see their personal education as a continuous life-long process which would enable them to lead productive, meaningful lives. As the wise Socrates once stated "The unexamined life is not worth living."[111]

I spent several nights cloistered in my own personal purgatory working on the essays and agonizing over every word, syllable, and punctuation mark. I finally declared the packet finished. It was an enormous relief to put it in the mail. I could now focus on teaching my classes, since there was nothing left to do but to await my fate which was now in the hands of the selection committee. I wasn't overly optimistic about my chances. I knew that I was a good teacher, but there were over 11,000 educators in Fairfax County. Each of the system's 200-plus elementary, middle, and high schools had selected their own teacher of the year, so the "competition" would be formidable. I was content, though, that I had done my best and was resigned to accept whatever the future might hold.

The normal routine of the school year quickly returned and the ensuing months passed by quickly, punctuated by the Thanksgiving and Christmas holidays. There was no further news, so with the advent of the New Year, I had pretty much given up on the possibility of becoming Fairfax County's Teacher of the Year. But shortly after we returned to school from the holidays, I was surprised to receive a confidential letter from the superintendent's office informing me that the selection committee had met and deliberated and that I had been selected as one of five finalists for the county-wide honor.

A few days later, a peer evaluation team consisting of several previous Fairfax County honorees arrived at Jefferson and observed my classroom instruction. Two weeks later, on February 11, I was provided with a full-day substitute so that I could meet with the county's leadership team at the Burkholder Administrative Center for the formal interview.

The Superintendent's Conference room where the interview panel met was an intimidating space. These high ranking county administrators and division superintendents were seated in a semi-circular configuration. It reminded me of a Congressional hearing room *sans* the bright lights and press cameras. They were polite but relentless in their inquisition as they queried me about my views on a wide range of topics, including my teaching philosophy. It was tense and a bit uncomfortable, but I was well prepared and answered all of their many questions.

After this initial surge of activity, the entire process seemed to grind to a halt once again. We were anxiously awaiting a final decision, but weeks passed with no further news. Then one morning in April, Geoff Jones, TJ's principal, announced over the PA that there was a mandatory faculty meeting immediately after school. This was not uncommon so there was no reason to suspect anything unusual.

After my last class had departed for the day, I began to pack up my papers and clear my desk in order to get to the meeting on time. Sheri Maeda, my Hum II partner, stopped by the room and seemed intent upon chatting. It was obvious that she was in no hurry to get to the faculty meeting, which I found a bit weird since we both had a reputation for being punctual. When I glanced at the clock, I knew

Dr. Robert Spillane announces my selection as Fairfax County Teacher of the Year. My wife, Linda, taught Spanish at TJHSST as well.
(Philip Bigler)

Being interviewed shortly after the announcement of my selection. With me is a good friend and collegue, Charlotte Bruce, the librarian at McLean High School. Charlotte was also one of my nominators for Teacher of the Year.
(Philip Bigler)

that we were precariously close to being late, but Sheri continued to delay. Finally, she agreed to walk down to the library with me and we arrived uncomfortably close to the scheduled start of the meeting.

Upon entering the room, it was apparent to me that Sheri had been sent to delay me since this was not a faculty meeting at all. Interspersed among the TJ faculty were many of my friends and colleagues from McLean High School. I also spotted my wife's parents, Leroy and Eva Belle Mimms, as well as my sister-in-law, Rebecca Mimms. I was greeted with applause and by the Fairfax County school superintendent, Robert "Bud" Spillane. He shook my hand and informed me that I had been selected as the 1997 Fairfax County Teacher of the Year. I was deeply humbled by the honor. I had been a classroom teacher for over 19 years and had come a long way since those challenging early days at Oakton High School.

In his prepared remarks for the occasion, Dr. Spillane publically announced my selection as the county's new teacher of the year and went on to explain: "We wanted someone who has contributed a lot not just to the school community, but to the world as well. Phil Bigler is what we want to typify as a teacher." He would later write to me:

> Your nomination materials speak to the tremendous respect and admiration that administrators, parents, students, and colleagues expressed for you. Most notable were their comments about your enthusiasm and commitment to developing a program tailored to meet the needs of students so they will be successful.

A building administrator talking with students shared the

following: 'Mr. Bigler has demonstrated the characteristics of excellence, hard work, and leadership. He is an innovative and charismatic teacher who inspires the students he works with. One student remarked, *Mr. Bigler is one of the best teachers I've had.* Another student, hearing this, responded, *Yeah, he really gets into the zone.* They refer to his fervent efforts to make history come alive.'

…I congratulate you on having been selected Teacher of the Year. I am proud of you and your many accomplishments. You exemplify the finest qualities of a professional educator, and you are an outstanding representative of Fairfax County Public Schools.[112]

The next day, the *Washington Post* ran a nice article about me in its local Metro section. It was a pleasant surprise since rarely does the mainstream media write anything positive about public education. Indeed, contemporary journalists prefer the salacious and sensational, so it is the titillating bad news stories about schools and teachers (Columbine, Mary Kay Letourneau, sexual abuse, etc.) that are reported and repeated so that they become entrenched in the general public's collective memory. [113] These aberrations and atypical stories create a serious misconception about what is actually occurring in our schools, and teachers are collectively disparaged and slandered. The routine good work of teachers goes unnoticed, unacknowledged and uncelebrated. I was becoming increasingly aware that with my new title, I had a unique forum which I could use to advocate for my profession and to celebrate exemplary teaching.

The remaining weeks of the 1996-1997 school year quickly became a blur of community events, speeches, press interviews, class projects, research papers and final exams. One of the more memorable highlights, though, was a special reception held at the *Washington Post* headquarters in Washington, D.C. for myself and 17 other metro area educators.[114] We were presented with a stunning Steuben crystal apple along with a check for $3,000 by the paper's publisher, Donald Graham. Also in attendance that evening were journalists Ben Bradlee and Bob Woodward, who had gained widespread acclaim for the tenacity of their coverage of the Watergate scandal during the Nixon administration.

During this hectic spring, I also received an invitation to address the Fairfax County School Board. It was even more meaningful for me since my widower father was able to fly up from Tampa to attend the function. My dad was extremely proud of me and all of my accomplishments, but everything I had achieved professionally was due to my parents' support and guidance. Indeed, my brother, Bob, and I had grown up during the tempestuous sixties. Those were morally challenging times and many of our friends and peers had willingly succumbed to a period of prolonged drug abuse, personal irresponsibility, and individual recklessness. But Bob and I had been immune from the worst excesses of the era and we credited this to the strong ethical and family values of our parents. We both were blessed with wonderful wives and went on to have distinguished careers. After finishing high school in 1968, Bob went to Texas A&M University where he completed his undergraduate studies. He served a stint in the Merchant Marines, but after a few years at sea and as a stevedore at the port of Houston, he returned to college at age 30 to pursue a medical degree. It took a decade of hard work, study, sacrifice, and night-time bartending, but Bob became a board-certified OBGYN and my mother was so proud. She always loved to boast about her doctor-son.[115] My mother died in 1989—she was just 68 years old and did not live to see my ultimate success as a teacher. This pained me greatly.

I spent a good deal of time preparing my remarks to the school board. I wanted to use the occasion to stress the importance of good teachers in maintaining high quality public schools. "Our schools," I explained, "are just empty, impersonal places. It is the principals, the teachers, and the students who bring them to life and give them an identity. For a brief moment in time, these people create a living, vibrant community of learners. Fairfax County's greatest asset is its teachers—respect them, cherish them—for this county is blessed." I concluded my address that evening by reminding the audience that "...the fate of our schools will depend upon the choices and decisions that we all make. It is imperative that these are made free from politics and partisanship with the welfare of our children our only agenda. Only then will we choose wisely."

That summer, my ever expanding portfolio of teacher of the year materials was automatically forwarded by the county to the Virginia Department of Education for consideration for the Commonwealth's state teacher of the year honors. Yet another committee would convene in Richmond to assess and evaluate my credentials and qualifications along with those of other teachers representing the state's 128 individual school divisions. For administrative purposes, each school system was grouped and categorized into one of eight geographical sub-regions (Regions I through VIII).[116]

I was relieved that there was nothing additional for me to do. I had accepted a consulting job that summer to work with several

Department of Defense (DODea) teachers in Aviano, Italy, in incorporating the latest technology into their classroom instruction. It was an exotic venue, and each day, I conducted my workshops at a school which was within the secured barbed-wired perimeter of the NATO Air Force base.

The actual town of Aviano is a quaint Italian village situated at the base of the magnificent Dolomite Mountains. Known primarily for its excellent skiing, the town also boasts an ancient castle along with a picturesque central piazza. The town also had the added advantage of being in close proximity to Venice, so on my off weekends, I was able to spend time enjoying that city's magnificent artworks, splendid canals, rich history, and delectable cuisine.

After the summer in-service concluded in mid-August, I flew

Aviano, Italy in the summer, 1997. For several years, I worked with Department of Defense teachers in Europe on incorporating technology effectively in their classrooms.
(Philip Bigler)

down to Rome where I rendezvoused with my dad. He had always wanted to make a personal pilgrimage to the "eternal city," so I was glad to have this opportunity to serve as his official tour guide. We were able to share some cherished father/son moments that week as we hiked through the city's ancient ruins and visited its splendid monuments, museums, galleries, and basilicas.

I called home regularly that summer and one evening while I was still in Rome, my wife, Linda, informed me that I had received an official looking letter from the Virginia Department of Education. Since it was probably something important, I asked her to open and read it to me over the phone. The letter was from the Assistant Superintendent for Compliance, Thomas Elliott, and was to inform and congratulate me on being selected as the new Region IV Teacher of the Year. This meant that I was one of eight finalists for state's 1998 Teacher of the Year honors. His letter went on to explain that I was to report to the state capital in Richmond on October 3rd, where I would be interviewed by a distinguished 12-member selection panel which "represent[ed] teachers, principals, central office administrators, school board members, parents, institutions of higher education, and the business community." After they completed their interviews with the candidates and had time to deliberate, their decision would be formally announced at a gala banquet scheduled for later that night at the Omni Hotel.

By now, I had lost much of my trepidation about appearing before so-called "distinguished panels of educational experts." I had already been fortunate to receive an enormous amount of recognition for my classroom teaching and I was mindful about how rare this was in our profession. Indeed, very few of my colleagues had ever been publically acknowledged despite their own efforts, skill, and dedication. I was extremely fortunate regardless of whatever transpired in the future.

Thomas had given us instructions to prepare a concise statement about our views on the state's new educational initiative, the Standards of Learning (SOL's), for the panel. These academic and grade-level guidelines had recently been adopted by the legislature and were causing a good deal of angst. As with most top-down education reform movements, teachers were skeptical about the overall effectiveness that the legislation would have in actually improving the schools. Many teachers were understandably cynical since historically most politically motivated measures rarely endured beyond the next election cycle. The required course content, particularly in the social studies, was controversial and led to complaints from a wide variety of interest groups. Likewise, many parents objected to the potential consequences for their children of the required high-stakes testing, especially since the tests utilized low cost and easily graded multiple choice questions.

There was, of course, no way to gauge whether or not there was any consensus among the various panel members about the efficacy of the SOL's. In truth it was irrelevant since I was expected to express my own opinions based upon my professional judgment. I had no intention of altering or modifying my views in an effort to placate anyone.

I began my presentation to the selection committee by providing a short synopsis about the uneven history of public education

Shortly after completing my interview with the Virginia Teacher of the Year selection panel in Richmond, October 3, 1997.
(Philip Bigler)

in Virginia. During the colonial period, there was no government-supported public education in the south and much of the region's population was functionally illiterate. I explained:

> The debate over the nature and role of public education in Virginia has been a long and bitter one. In the 17th Century, the royal governor of the colony, William Berkeley, wrote, 'I thank God, there are no free schools nor printing (in Virginia), and I hope we shall not have these [for a] hundred years, for learning has brought disobedience, and heresy... into the world ... and libels against the best government. God keep us from both.'

With the adoption of the United States Constitution, however, attitudes slowly began to change. Most of the founding fathers believed that a well-educated and knowledgeable citizenry was vital to the preservation of the rights and liberty that had been recently won during the American Revolution. One of the staunchest and most eloquent advocates for a system of universal public education was Thomas Jefferson, and his views mirrored many of my own. I continued:

> Fortunately, a century later another Virginian saw things quite differently. Thomas Jefferson, the sage of Monticello and arguably the greatest man of the millennium, urged the state legislature to adopt a bill for free, universal education. Moreover, he wrote to his good friend and mentor, George Wythe, to '… preach a crusade against ignorance … [since] no other sure foundation can be devised for the preservation of freedom and happiness.' It is Jefferson's vision that I sincerely hope still motivates us and our state legislators in the quest to achieve a truly quality education for all of our students.

I did believe, though, that it was important for our schools to have a coherent, focused curriculum with a common core of knowledge that all students need to master as part of their graduation requirements. Unfortunately, a distinct but significant minority of teachers were engaged in "freelance teaching" and taught whatever they wanted regardless of pacing guidelines and mandated course requirements. They were oblivious to the fact that they had been hired, contracted and obligated to teach a specific curriculum. These ineffectual teachers were in effect guilty of educational malpractice and their students ultimately suffered. Over the years I personally witnessed some teachers wasting weeks of valuable classroom time on meaningless tangents and digressions. Some would spend hours discussing battlefield tactics during the Civil War while completely ignoring the important political, economic, and social significance of the conflict as well as other important aspects of the curriculum.

Others spent months studying China but neglected the course material concerning Japan, India, Africa, and South America. Even worse were the inept educators who would send their students to the school's computer lab without any direction or purpose.

There definitely was a content problem in our schools that needed attention. But the bad teachers were now using the newly mandated state guidelines as an excuse to justify their own ineptitude. They bored their students with pointless classwork and handed out endless reams of useless worksheets. These so-called "assignments" consisted of long and meaningless lists of terms and definitions which they required their students to memorize and regurgitate. The offending teachers defended their uninspired lessons by claiming that it was necessary because the material would be on the state tests and as such, there was no longer any room for flexibility or creativity. This, of course, was nonsense, and was never the intent of the SOL's, nor was it effective teaching. Any course content is essentially useless unless it is placed in appropriate context. Successful teachers can make the required material interesting and compelling and they always have clearly defined learning objectives and strong content standards. As I explained:

> The recent adoption of the Virginia Standards of Learning has been controversial and has caused a considerable degree of uncertainty and apprehension among students, educators, principals, parents, and the community. In principle, these standards promote the idea that there is a common body of knowledge that all students should have mastered upon graduation from high school. I whole heartedly support this ideal, for I firmly believe that all good instruction is content-based and substance driven. I know of no good educator who is afraid of accountability.

It is certainly possible and commendable to establish a core of knowledge in any given subject area. Most local jurisdictions, including Fairfax County, have already done so through detailed programs of study which clearly establish content, skills, and objectives for courses, and certainly meet those set forth in the new standards. In high school, I believe that all of our students should study the Declaration of Independence, the Constitution, and the Bill of Rights, along with the other great documents in American history. Likewise, they should read Homer, Voltaire, Twain, and Shakespeare for these important literary luminaries and their historical tracts represent the cumulative efforts of over 3,000 years of human civilization. It was no mere coincidence that as a boy living on the remote frontier, Abraham Lincoln read Thucydides' *History of the Peloponnesian War*. Later, as president, when he faced a similar dramatic struggle, Lincoln could recall that the great Pericles had once stood before the dead of Athens and there, justified his city-state's bloody struggle with Sparta as a holy crusade to preserve Hellenic Culture. So, too, in 1863, Lincoln would stand at Gettysburg at the new national cemetery and in 272 carefully crafted words, poetically explain the Union cause and the necessity of continued sacrifice so that '... government of the people, by the people, and for the people shall not perish from the earth.' As Harry Truman once so accurately observed 'The only thing new in life is the history that you don't know.'

It is foolish to believe that any law or legislative fiat can miraculously mandate quality schools. This only occurs when there is a staff of committed teachers and principals working together to make student learning their top priority. Effective schools also require students to take a personal responsibility for their own learning. I concluded my remarks by emphasizing that:

The United States is not the Balkans; we are not a hopelessly divided and fragmented people. As a nation, we share a wonderfully rich and diverse history and literature that our students should both know and cherish. The Standards of Learning can help achieve a framework for this study and can easily provide new teachers with a strong content focus. But we must ensure that testing for such standards emphasizes higher order thinking skills, comprehension, and understanding rather than just a bland recitation of facts and trivia.

The Virginia taxpayers have invested heavily in education and they are entitled to a quality school system. At the same time, our schools must never lose their focus, for public education continues to represent the finest and most cherished ideals of American democracy. We teachers, as a profession, are totally committed to educating each and every child regardless of income, race, ethnicity, mental or physical impairment, or any other pre-existing condition. To do this, our schools must maintain their academic rigor by firmly establishing a set of high expectations and goals. Our students must leave school as life-long learners, for in today's information-rich society, there will always be more to learn and new things to know. The truly educated person is never bored, never content, for the miracle of life provides a constant source of wonderment and inquiry. If the SOL's prove successful in this noble mission, then they surely will have accomplished their goals.

After finishing what amounted to my own brief epistle on the merits of the SOL's, I answered questions for another 30 minutes from the panel. When my allotted time had expired, I was content and pleased with my overall performance. I was now liberated to enjoy the remainder of a beautiful fall day with Linda and my father. We had a leisurely lunch at the Tobacco Company in Richmond's historic Shockoe Slip area before touring Hollywood Cemetery while awaiting the start of the evening's festivities.

The banquet began at 6:30 PM in the James River Ballroom at the Omni. Each of the finalists had been allotted a table for eight, so I was able to invite my former McLean principal, Elizabeth Lodal, and my teaching partner, Sheri Maeda. The official program was hosted by Dr. Elliott, and featured live musical performances by students from Chesterfield County. There was also a montage of videos, and several speeches including remarks by the state superintendent, Richard LaPointe.[117] As with most such events, the banquet ran late and it was already 9:30 PM when they were ready to make the announcement of the state's new Teacher of the Year. Each of the eight finalists was re-introduced and we took an assigned seat at a long table that had been set up on a dais at the front of the ballroom. We waited nervously as Dr. LaPointe slowly opened the sealed envelope which contained the selection committee's decision. Finally, pausing for maximum effect, he announced that the new 1998 Virginia Teacher of the Year was "A.......Philip Bigler." It took a moment for me to react since he had gotten my first initial ("B") wrong, but I recovered and approached the podium where I received a crystal apple along with a check for $1,000.[118] I was invited to make some brief remarks, but it wasn't a particularly memorable speech or my best effort since I hadn't really prepared anything for this outcome.

And then, it was over. I was enveloped by well-wishers, and several representatives from various education organizations handed me their business cards along with invitations me to speak at some future function. It was a blur of faces and a jumble of brief conversa-

*Linda (left) and my former McLean High School principal celebrating my an-
nouncement as the 1998 Virginia Teacher of the Year.* (Philip Bigler)

Speaking at the Teacher of the Year banquet at the Omni Hotel in Richmond.
(Philip Bigler)

tions but one individual did command my full attention—Jon Quam, the director of the National Teacher of the Year (NTOY) program. He explained that now as the new Virginia Teacher of the Year, I was expected to be at an important three day conference in Dallas, Texas. It was scheduled to be held from January 22nd through the 25th, and all of the other state teachers would also be there. From the elite group, a new National Teacher of the Year would be selected.

After returning home to Fairfax, life again returned to some degree of normality and I finally had the opportunity to do some additional research on the National Teacher of the Year program. I was vaguely aware of the program, but had never followed it closely. I discovered online that there were several of organizations, groups, and businesses that funded their own teacher recognition programs in the United States, but these varied dramatically in terms of scope, prestige, and competitiveness. The NTOY program was considered to be the nation's preeminent honor and was sponsored by the Council of Chief State School Officers (CCSSO), a national "...nonpartisan, and nonprofit [organization that consisted of] the top education leaders from every state in the nation." [119] The first national teacher, Geraldine Jones, was selected for the honor in 1952. Gerry taught first grade teacher at the Hope School in Santa Barbara, California and was recognized for her accomplishments at a White House ceremony hosted by President Harry Truman. At the time, the National Teacher program was funded by *McCall's* magazine to elevate the prestige of the profession in an ongoing effort to offset the severe teacher shortage caused by the post-war baby boom. Since Gerry, there had been 46 other national teachers but only one had been from Virginia—Mary Bicouvaris (1989), a government teacher at

The Commonwealth of Virginia's 1998 Teacher of the Year
(Philip Bigler)

Bethel High School in Hampton.[120] The NTOY program continued to increase in its stature and prestige over the years and it periodically changed financial partners. Its current financial benefactor was *Scholastic* magazine.

The national selection committee for the Teacher of the Year consisted of representatives from 14 major of the nation's foremost education associations, including the National Congress of Parents and Teachers, the National School Boards Association, the National Education Association, and the Association for Supervision and Curriculum Development.[121] The committee would initially review all of the portfolios and resumes of the state teachers and then select four finalists. Ultimately one "winner" who would be chosen and that individual would be granted a year's sabbatical to "… serve as a spokesperson for the entire teaching profession to colleagues, the business community, government officials, parents, and students at forums and meetings across the country."[122]

Shortly after the Christmas holidays, Thomas Elliott called me at TJ with some very exciting news. He had just heard from Jon Quam at the CCSSO and was informed that I had been selected as one of the four finalists for the National Teacher of the Year honors. The other teachers were from Iowa, Kansas, and New Mexico, and we would all be together for the first time in Dallas.[123]

On January 22nd, I flew into Texas on American Airlines flight 1881. Jon was patiently waiting for me in the baggage claim area, and after we retrieved my luggage, we drove together over to the nearby Doubletree Hotel where the NSTOY conference was scheduled to convene later that evening. On the brief trip over, Jon offered an abbreviated overview of what would occur during the ensuing weeks as the selection process for the new national teacher proceeded.

After arriving at the Doubletree, I was given a few minutes to check into my room and freshen up before coming back downstairs for a casual lunch with the other finalists. It was a welcomed opportunity for all of us to get acquainted and we were glad to finally be able to associate an actual face with their resume. My colleagues were exemplary educators and regardless of what ultimately transpired, we felt privileged to be representing our individual states and the teaching profession.

After our lunch, Jon arranged for us to meet privately with the current national teacher, Sharon Draper. She openly shared with us many of her most memorable experiences as NTOY and talked frankly about some of the travails and pitfalls of the endless travel. The hardest part, Sharon explained, was the occasional prolonged absence away from home, family, and friends. Still the opportunity to advocate for the teaching profession would far outweigh any of the negatives. During this confidential, off-the-record meeting, we were encouraged to articulate some of our concerns and reservations and could do so without any fear of repercussions or adverse consequences.

During the course of our first day in Dallas, we learned that as finalists for the National Teacher of the Year, we would meet again in Washington, D.C. in early March. There, we would undergo three days of interviews, press conferences, and other activities which would be monitored and assessed by the NTOY selection panel. My fellow finalists were, of course, thrilled about the prospect of visiting our nation's capital, but I was disappointed. For me, the March meeting would constitute little more than a 45-minute subway ride into the city; I would have far preferred Los Angeles, Chicago, Honolulu, or New York as a venue.

We were told that once the selection panel had time to deliberate and come to a final decision, each of us would be informed privately of the outcome, but this information was strictly confidential. The news would be embargoed for weeks and during this period, we were instructed not to tell any of our friends or co-workers about the results. The official announcement of the selection of the new national teacher would come from the Office of the President and would be issued in conjunction with a special recognition ceremony held in the White House Rose Garden. All of the other state teachers would be in attendance and would likewise be acknowledged for their professional accomplishments.

Our afternoon session finally concluded. It had been an exhaustive orientation filled with an incredible amount of information, much of which had been impossible to absorb in one sitting. I was pleased to finally meet the other state teachers at the evening's casual buffet dinner. It proved to be a welcomed opportunity for all of us to mingle and relax before the onset of the business portion of the conference which was scheduled to begin early the next morning.

To be surrounded by many of our country's finest educators was a terrific experience, but it was difficult to generalize about the group as a whole. Certainly most of the teachers were experienced, mid-career educators, but they taught every conceivable grade level and subject matter. Moreover, they came from a wide-variety of teaching environments and held differing teaching philosophies and divergent political beliefs. The one common characteristic I discovered about these teachers, though, was their overall positive outlook. They did not whine or complain; they were proud of their profession and took joy in the accomplishments of their students.

The next morning, the workshops and presentations began. During these sessions, we were told that we needed to accept our rec-

With the Kentucky Teacher of the Year, Susan Stucker, at the Dallas Conference in January, 1998.
(Philip Bigler)

ognition unapologetically and that we should use this unique opportunity to develop our own individualized message about teaching. Although I was still formulating my thoughts on this, I knew that I wanted to emphasize the need for high academic standards in our schools as well as the importance of content knowledge.

One of the more evocative sessions that day focused on media relations. Most teachers have limited experience in dealing with the press and the news media, so it was vital that we understood that now all of our statements would be carefully scrutinized and a single careless word or an unintentional remark could have serious and lasting consequences. Likewise, it was imperative that we present ourselves in a dignified, professional manner.

During the entire NSTOY conference, everyone was conscious of the ominous political news emanating from Washington. A new Internet blogger, Matt Drudge, had broken a scandalous story about an alleged illicit affair between President Bill Clinton and a young White House intern. Each day, there was an onslaught of new disclosures. The President angrily denied the charges but by Saturday evening, there were rumors that the FBI had in its possession incriminating audio tapes that could escalate the scandal from marital infidelity to criminal wrong doing, including obstruction of justice and, potentially, perjury. The Clinton presidency could well be in peril.

We were all depressed and dismayed. It seemed that our White House ceremony in April could be jeopardy. For most of us, this would be our only opportunity to meet an American president and we hoped that the National Teacher of the Year event would not be cancelled. It was a bit of a damper for the gala dinner that evening but it still had been a wonderful few days and we all left Dallas reinvigorated and inspired.

There were a few weeks before the Washington interviews, so I thought I had plenty of time to prepare. However, on January 28th (the 12th anniversary of the *Challenger* disaster), my father-in-law, Leroy Mimms, died from a massive stroke. Although he had been in declining health for the past few months, it was nevertheless a shock.

Leroy had enlisted in the Army Air Corps during World War II and spent much of the war in Great Britain. He eventually retired from the Air Force Reserves as a major, and was thus eligible for burial at Arlington National Cemetery. I contacted one of my friends at the cemetery and he graciously helped make the funeral arrangements but because of the increased demands for burial services caused by the aging World War II generation, it took two weeks before we could schedule a full honors funeral.

On a cold, icy afternoon in mid-February, Leroy's flagged-draped casket was conveyed to Section 7 on a horse-drawn caisson accompanied by an Air Force band and military honor guard. As the haunting notes of "Taps" faded away, it began to sleet as we stood at the gravesite. Nearby were the graves of George C. Marshall, Matthew Ridgeway, Bedell Smith, Pappy Boyington, Joe Louis, Lee Marvin, and my mother, Bernice Bigler.

Endnotes

107 The TJ contract called for all teachers to have one more class or activity period than a regular school. As a result, we were paid 7% more than other teachers in the county.

108 For all of my history classes, I assigned a thesis-driven, sourced-based research paper. These papers generally ran from 10 to 15 pages in length. With 150 students, adequately grading these papers took countless hours of time. I finally devised a lottery system where the students drew due dates for the papers during the first week of school. The dates were staggered over the third quarter, which meant that for that entire nine weeks, I would receive four student papers per day. I could grade them overnight and return them promptly to the students while retaining my sanity.

109 Mike Dobson and I worked together at Oakton and then again later at TJ where he served as the school's athletic director. In 1979, we ran the Boston Marathon together.

110 James Michener, "When Does Education Stop," available at: http://www.asahi-net.or.jp/~xs3d-bull/michener.html.

111 Plato. (2000) *The Apology*. Translated by Hugh Tredennick and Harold Tarant. *The Last Days of Socrates*. Norwalk, CT: Easton Press, p. 63.

112 Robert "Bud" Spillane. Personal letter to Philip Bigler, March 7, 1997.

113 Mary Kay Letourneau was the big education story during my teacher of the year tenure. She was an elementary school teacher in Washington State when she began an "affair" with one of her students. Letourneau was sentenced to jail for two counts of child rape. Undeterred by her jail sentence and being branded as a Level 2 sex offender, she had two children by the boy and eventually married him. According to one account, Letourneau and her former student have hosted several "Hot for Teacher" nights at a Seattle night club.

114 We were all being recognized as recipients of the Agnes Meyer Outstanding Teacher Award. The Fairfax County Teacher of the Year automatically receives this honor, while some of the other school jurisdictions select their representative independently. Named for the mother of *Washington Post* publisher, Katherine Graham, the award "honor(s) 18 teachers—one representing the private schools and 17 representing the public school systems in the Washington metropolitan community. These teachers exemplify the excellence in education for which Mrs. Meyer worked so hard and embody the qualities which assure that our children receive a quality education."

115 My mother got very sick just before Bob graduated from medical school and she was unable to attend his graduation ceremonies at Baylor. Bob flew to Tampa the very next day to be with her and to show her his medical degree.

116 Virginia has participated in the National Teacher of the Year program since 1964.

117 I had taught our state superintendent's daughter, Katie, while at McLean High School. She went to Brigham Young University and received her teaching license and later became a history teacher in Fairfax County.

118 The check was provided courtesy of the renowned Richmond law firm: Allen, Allen, Allen, and Allen.

119 See the Council of Chief State School Officers website at: http://www.ccsso.org.

120 Mary and I became good friends that year. She had taught social studies in Tidewater at the time of her selection and had gone on to become a professor at Christopher Newport University in Hampton Roads. Sadly, Mary died prematurely a few years later. The demographics for the National Teacher program in 1998 were as follows: 14 National Teachers were elementary school teachers (30%); three taught middle school (7%); and 30 were high school teachers (64%). There were 30 female and 17 male national teachers. The youngest National Teacher was Tracey Bailey (1993) who received his award at age 29.

121 The complete list of the selection panel was: American Association of Colleges for Teacher Education, American Association of School Administrators American Federation of Teachers, Association for Childhood Education International, Association for Supervision and Curriculum Development, Association of Teacher Educators, National Association Elementary School Principals, National Association of Secondary School Principals, National Association of State Boards of Education, National Congress of Parents and Teachers, National Education Association, National Middle Schools Association, National School Boards Association, and National School Public Relations Association.

122 See http://www.ccsso.org/ntoy.html.

123 The finalists were Ruth Ann Gaines, a drama teacher at East High School in Des Moines, Iowa; Darla Mallein, a middle school social studies teacher at Emporia Middle School in Emporia, Kansas; and Carolyn Foster, a board certified elementary school teacher at James Elementary School in Portales, New Mexico.

CHAPTER IX

Lessons That Will Last a Lifetime

If we work upon marble, it will perish. If we work upon brass, time will efface it. If we rear temples, they will crumble into dust. But if we work upon immortal minds, we engrave on those tablets something that will brighten to all eternity.

Daniel Webster

I didn't have to take the subway to the NTOY interviews after all. Jon had instead sent a chauffeured town car to my home in Fairfax on Sunday, March 1, 1998, to pick me up and drive me into Washington where I would be staying at the luxurious Washington Court Hotel on Capitol Hill. The other finalists had arrived earlier and we had a nice reunion dinner that evening. We were in agreement that the next few days were going to be memorable, intense, and stressful.

I had spent a few days preparing for the selection process by reviewing the latest educational literature and relevant policy initiatives that were currently being advocated by the U.S. Department of Education and President Clinton. Although the United States Constitution clearly delegates educational authority to the individual states, Washington's influence had steadily grown over the previous decades, mostly due to the coercive power of federal grants and funding.[124] As such, more and more politicians were anxious to make education a political issue.

Although the current scope of federal involvement is debatable, most of the U.S. Department of Education's goals were well-intentioned and even commendable. They included such things as achieving student reading proficiency by the end of third grade, reaching general competency in mathematics, and providing students with a drug-free environment. The Clinton administration was simultaneously proposing new legislation that would provide aggressive federal funding to the states to help wire all of the nation's public school classrooms to the Internet by the year 2000. This would, the President argued, give all students equal access to the world's growing digital resources. I was in philosophical agreement with all of these things, but the proposal that I found particularly relevant was the one that claimed to ensure that "there will be a talented, dedicated and well-prepared teacher in every classroom."[125]

Teacher quality is undeniably the single most important factor in maintaining quality schools. Indeed, several research studies have confirmed this statistically, proving that an outstanding teacher has a long-lasting influence and a positive correlation on student progress. Everything else in education is secondary—all of the computer technology, the latest software gimmickry, the best textbooks, and the most up-to-date facilities are essentially worthless unless skilled teachers are in the classroom engaged in serious content-based instruction. The entire purpose of the NTOY program was based upon this premise and I was committed to making teacher quality my own personal platform.

After returning to the hotel from our reunion dinner, it was late and I knew that it was imperative that I get a good night sleep. But I decided to relax a bit by reading from Marcus Aurelius' *Meditations*. I had recently rediscovered Stoic philosophy after reading Admiral James Stockdale's book, *Thoughts of a Philosophical Fighter Pilot*.[126] Stockdale claimed that it was his study at Stanford of the classics and, in particular, the Greek philosopher, Epictetus, which enabled him to persevere during his eight year captivity in a North Vietnamese prison camp. Stockdale survived daily torture, intense pain, and physical isolation because in his words, "my 'secret weapon' was the security I felt in anchoring my resolve to those selected portions of philosophic thought that emphasized human dignity and self-respect. Epictetus certainly taught me that."[127] The Roman Emperor, Marcus Aurelius, had similarly been influenced by the teachings of Epictetus, albeit 1,900 years earlier. Aurelius and the stoics believed that all intelligent individuals should lead a productive, self-reflective life and his *Meditations* was, in essence, a compendium of the emperor's thoughts and observations which he compiled over several years. His musings remain pertinent even in our contemporary times. For instance, Marcus Aurelius observed that it was important to live only in the present; this was the only portion of your life that was in your control. Furthermore, he wrote that:

> If you do the job in a principled way, with diligence, energy and patience, if you keep yourself free of distractions...[if you] can find fulfillment in what you're doing now...your life will be happy. No one can prevent that.[128]

So I resolved that rather than fear some unpredictable, adverse result, I would enjoy the entire interview process. The worst outcome for me would be that I wouldn't be selected as the National Teacher of the Year. That would be personally disappointing but it would hardly alter who I was or what I believed in.

Early the next morning, my jam-packed agenda began with a taping of a simulated television interview. A member of the CC-SSO's public relations staff was assigned to conduct the session in a conference room that had been modified to mimic an actual TV studio, complete with bright klieg lights and boom microphones. During the taping, I was asked to respond to a variety of impromptu questions and I was expected to answer quickly and competently. Ultimately, the selection team would independently view and judge the video tapes as part of their overall evaluation.

There were other meetings and discussions throughout the day at the CCSSO offices on Massachusetts Avenue. The culminating event was an elegant, private dinner with the entire selection committee at an exclusive downtown restaurant. Jon Quam had carefully choreographed the occasion so that each of us would have ample time to mingle and converse informally with the various educational representatives. The dinner served to lessen our anxiety somewhat while giving the committee the benefit of seeing how each one of us interacted and performed in an unfamiliar social setting.

The next day had been reserved for the formal interviews before the selection panel. I was fortunate since the venue was similar to what I had experienced in both Fairfax County and Richmond, so it was not overly intimidating. The process started when the committee chairman welcomed me and asked that I begin with my prepared remarks.

I had recycled some of the ideas and themes from my Virginia speech, but I expanded and modified my message to include the importance of education in maintaining a civil society. I explained:

> Today, we teachers proudly stand firm as the caretakers of civilization, the last true bastion against the onslaught of barbarism and tyranny. Education remains the greatest gift that any society can bestow upon its people, for knowledge provides judgment in time of crisis; solace in periods of despair; perspective on occasions of joy; and in daily life—contentment. Moreover, no government, no economic condition, no person can ever deprive an educated person of their mind or of what they know.[129]

I also talked about Uli Derickson and James Stockdale; Thomas Jefferson and Abraham Lincoln; history and teaching. I concluded with:

> The word "school" is derived from the Greek root meaning "leisure." Some 2,500 years ago, for a brief moment in time, the center of civilization was anchored on the shores of the Aegean. There, a remarkable group of people established a society where learning was seen as a virtue and where knowledge was a daily pursuit. To be a teacher is to be forever an optimist, and I believe that our own American golden age is still before us. It will be created and nurtured by a new generation of students dedicated to their own personal enlightenment and to the advancement of mankind.

My speech essentially encapsulated everything that I fundamentally believed as a high school history teacher. I was then ready to answer the follow-up questions that were posed by the other members of the committee. It was intense and inquisitorial, but after a reasonable interval of time, the panel seemed satisfied and the chairman concluded the interview. Before leaving, I thanked the entire group for their generous support of the National Teacher program. It was a high quality program and we felt personally validated and energized by this special recognition. It had served to reaffirm our commitment to our students, made us proud to be teachers, and elevated the dignity of our profession.

I left the conference room and had to wait for some time while the other finalists finished their own individual interviews. When everyone was finished, we had one final task—a joint press conference.

An elevated stage had been set up in a large ballroom and the audience consisted primarily of staff and employees of the CC-SSO and, of course, the selection committee. We were asked to respond individually to two questions and Jon had urged us earlier to try to speak in succinct but memorable sound bites.

The first question was an uncomfortable hypothetical:

- "If you had the power to make one major change in American schools, what would it be and why?"

The second question was more straight forward and I felt easier:

- "In what ways can the National Teacher of the Year help attract talented students to become teachers?"

In truth, the entire press conference seemed a bit artificial and anti-climactic. I really can't remember much of what I said. I was emotionally drained and then it was over. The other finalists left to go to the airport while I got into my awaiting town car for the short drive home.

Now the waiting game began and for the next two weeks, there was no news of any decision. During this time, my heart skipped a beat every time the phone rang until finally, on the eve of my annual class field trip to Gettysburg, I received a call from Wilbert Bryant, the Virginia Secretary of Education. He informed me that I had been selected as the new 1998 National Teacher of the Year.

It was hard to comprehend—the whole process had begun over two years ago when the faculty had chosen me to be the McLean High School Teacher of the Year. Never in my wildest dreams had I imagined that it would eventually lead to this amazing honor.

March 23rd was Senior Switch day at TJ. Several of my students took turns "teaching" my classes and that evening, Jon took Linda and me to dinner at Morton's Steakhouse in Tyson's Corner. It was a semi-working dinner, where Jon explained and elaborated on all of the responsibilities that I would have as the National Teacher of the Year. There were many details that I needed to address before "Washington Week," which had now been officially scheduled for April 20-24. First, I needed to provide Jon with a list of my frequent flier numbers. I also had to prepare an official guest list for the White House ceremonies, and since I was local, I would be allowed to bring five of my students with me to the major events.

Over the next few weeks, Jon and I would have various meetings with my school superintendent and key individuals from the Virginia Department of Education. He would handle the negotiations that would be required to arrange for my one year sabbatical, including the delicate matter of funding my teacher salary and health benefits. Jon would likewise make arrangements for Fairfax County to loan me a laptop computer which I could use while traveling. Once again, he reiterated the need for absolute secrecy; the news of my selection could be shared only with those who had a direct need to know.

Between the savory steaks and cocktails at dinner, Jon informed me that as NTOY I would be visiting Japan in September as an official guest of the government and the Baba Foundation (a Japanese educational exchange organization). I would also address the National Education Association convention in New Orleans in July and join the other state teachers of the year at Space Camp in Huntsville, Alabama during the first week in August. I carefully jotted down each new engagement in my Franklin Planner.

The next week, Jon arranged for me to meet privately with an actor from the Shakespeare Theatre in Washington. Ed Gero was hired to help me with my so-called "stage presence." Although I felt fairly comfortable with public speaking, whenever I spoke to large groups or over a microphone I was still inclined to write out all of my remarks. But with the number of appearances and speeches I would be making as National Teacher, it would be impractical to continue to do this, so clearly I needed to adapt my speaking style.

Ed said that he had watched the tapes of my earlier CCSSO television interview and felt that I did reasonably well. I was relaxed and natural on camera, so he was wondering why I felt the compulsion to be so formal when delivering a prepared speech. I justified myself on the grounds that I didn't want to make an embarrassing mistake or a serious misstatement when speaking before an audience. He dismissed this rationale and told me that I should treat my speaking engagements like I would my own classroom. As the National Teacher, he explained, the audience wanted to know about me and to hear my personal and professional story. They were not there to listen to me read pages of prepared remarks or to pontificate about educational policy. It was a major epiphany for me. Ed helped me gain the confidence to speak to groups from notes containing just a few bulleted points.

Of course, during all of this I was still teaching full time and my classes had to be my top priority. There were grades that had to be calculated for the 3rd quarter, new lesson plans to be created, and dozens of scholarship letters to be written. The students and staff at Jefferson were still clueless about the outcome of the NTOY interviews and whenever I was queried about the results, I replied that I didn't know anything and that the announcement would be forthcoming sometime in late April.

I still had the difficult task of selecting the students I wanted to invite to the National Teacher of the Year festivities. It was a hard choice since I taught many outstanding students, but I knew that I definitely wanted to include Amanda Neville. Mandy had graduated three years earlier from McLean High School but she was studying at nearby Georgetown University. While she was at McLean, Mandy had been one of my all-time favorite students and she had written one of my nomination letters. (See Appendix B) The other students I chose were from my current Hum II (US History and Literature) classes: Sandi Lin, Leon Scott, Katelyn Shearer, and Emily Spengler. They were exemplary young people and I knew that they would be the perfect representatives of both our school and of Fairfax County Public Schools.

Washington Week finally began with the arrival of the State Teachers of the Year on April 20th. My good friend, Kay Long (Oklahoma STOY) and her husband, Mark, arranged to arrive a little early, so I was able to give them a special tour of Arlington National Cemetery. Kay and the other state teachers were staying at a hotel in Crystal City in Arlington but Jon had arranged for Linda and me to stay at a different location, the Henley Park Hotel near DuPont Circle. He wanted to limit my distractions so as to allow time for me to focus on finishing my remarks for the

A sign at Thomas Jefferson High School for Science and Technology announcing my selection as the 1998 National Teacher of the Year. (Philip Bigler)

Rose Garden ceremony. I also had to prepare for the various media interviews that would take place over the course of the week.

On Wednesday evening, the formal announcement of my selection was released to the media. The official press release read:

EMBARGOED FOR RELEASE 4/23/98

Contact: Jon Quam, Director

VIRGINIA HISTORIAN/EDUCATOR NAMED
1998 NATIONAL TEACHER OF THE YEAR

Fairfax County, Virginia High School Humanities/History Teacher

Honored at the White House

Washington, D.C. --- April 23, 1998. For almost twenty years the students in Philip Bigler's classes have been awakened to the excitement of learning through history. On Friday, April 24, he will be named 1998 National Teacher of the Year by President Clinton in a ceremony at the White House that also honors the 1998 State Teachers of the Year. At the conclusion of the 1997-98 school term Mr. Bigler begins a year as spokesperson for education to the nation and the world.

The National Teacher of the Year Program is the oldest and most prestigious awards program to focus public attention on excellence in teaching. Now in its 47th year, the program is sponsored by the Council of Chief State School Officers and Scholastic Inc. The National Teacher of the Year is chosen from among the Teachers of the Year from the 50 states, five extra-state jurisdictions, the District of Columbia, and the Department of Defense Education Activity by a committee of the 14 leading education organizations in the nation.

'In naming a National Teacher of the Year, America honors all teachers who demonstrate daily their dedication and love for the profession,' said Gordon Ambach, Executive Director of the Council of Chief State School Officers. 'At a time when the nation is focusing on the content of education, Philip Bigler exemplifies teachers who are both historians and great mentors,' said Ambach.

Although it was in college that Bigler began seriously considering a teaching career, two extraordinary teachers had a profound impact on his life. In the 8th grade Sister Mary Josephine at Sacred Heart School, Jacksonville, Florida taught him a love of learning that has inspired him forever. In high school, a battle-hardened Marine fresh from Vietnam, Colonel Ralph Sullivan, showed him the rigor of academics and the reality that there would always be more to know and another book to read. 'To follow in their footsteps and to help young people in the same ways that my teachers had helped me is both a privilege and an honor,' says Bigler.

In Bigler's classroom history is made relevant and exciting for his students. Interactive historical simulations are the basis of his courses. His students have become members of a Greek *polis* and have made a sacred pilgrimage (the *hajji*) to Mecca. They have argued the intricacies of Constitutional law before a mock Supreme Court, recreated the court-martial trial of Lt. William Calley and waged a fierce computer campaign for the 1960 presidency. Bigler's students find real history in interviewing residents of the Soldiers' and Airmen's Home, where the students conducted oral history interviews with elderly and disabled veterans as to their experiences in the World Wars. 'My greatest satisfaction as a teacher has been helping young people learn to love history and instilling in them a personal desire to seek knowledge,' says Bigler. 'My students soon appreciate that civilization rests upon the foundations of the past and realize they are inheritors of a rich, intellectual legacy,' says Bigler.

'In Phil's classroom learning is real,' said Dr. Ernest Fleishman, Senior Vice President of Education at Scholastic Inc. 'Phil's students come to love learning on their own terms and that skill will last them a lifetime,' said Fleishman. 'Scholastic is proud to sponsor the National Teacher of the Year Program because we recognize how vital the role of teaching is to our nation's future.'

Bigler's own love of history led him to take a break from teaching to serve as the historian at Arlington National Cemetery. Even with that high profile job Bigler realized that he had no greater nor nobler vocation than laboring to enlighten young minds. After two years he returned to the classroom a wiser and better educator.

Bigler holds his Bachelor of Arts in History and Masters of Secondary Education/History from James Madison University and a Masters of American Studies from The College of William and Mary. He is the author of four books including *Hostile Fire: the Life and Death of Lt. Sharon Ann Lane* and *In Honored Glory, Arlington National Cemetery, the Final Post*.

Widely recognized, Bigler has received the *Washington Post* Agnes Meyer Outstanding Teacher Award, the Hodgson Award for Outstanding Teaching of Social Studies, and has twice been honored with the Norma Dektor Award for Most Influential Teacher from the students of McLean High School, and the United States Capitol Historical Society: Outstanding Teacher Historian Award.

Bigler's teaching career has been in the greater Washington, D.C. area, beginning at Oakton High School—his alma mater; then at the Governor's School for the Gifted; Bethesda-Chevy Chase High School; McLean High School and now at Thomas Jefferson High School for Science and Technology in Alexandria, Virginia. He is married to an educator, Linda, who teaches Spanish at Thomas Jefferson.[130]

That same evening, we had a gala black tie dinner in the Hall of States at the CCSSO's headquarters building. It was a special night to celebrate teachers. Linda and I were seated in the front of the room at the head table with the CCSSO executive director, Gordon Ambach, and the Secretary of Education, Richard Riley. My dad, brother, and sister-in-law were assigned a nearby table as were our friends, Phil and Wende Walsh, Jeff Dunson, Elizabeth Lodal, and Sheri Maeda.

I was thrilled that my five students were able to attend and that they looked so stylish and sophisticated in their formal attire. The various state teachers were gracious and thoughtful and they made a point to talk with my students throughout the evening so that they would feel special and comfortable.

Jon Quam had a meticulous sense of style and the dinner was elegantly organized around three separate courses. The first was appropriately "Virginia" blue crab salad and it was followed by an entrée of rack of venison. For dessert, the caterers provided an exotic concoction called "Ruby Grapefruit & Chocolate Tart under a Sugar Dome." Between each of the various dinner courses, there was a speaker who offered brief remarks and during the evening festivities, Jon made sure to introduce all of the state teachers, the "Class of 1998."

My former student and one of my nominators from McLean High School, Amanda Neville, is introduced to Secretary of Education, Richard Riley. (Philip Bigler)

My students: Leon Scott, Amanda Neville, Emily Spengler, Sandi Lin, and Katelyn Shearer at the National Teacher of the Year banquet. (Philip Bigler)

While the waiters were clearing the tables and serving coffee, I was invited to give the keynote address to the group. It was a very important speech for me since it was before my distinguished peers and colleagues. I wanted to use the occasion to acknowledge our collective commitment to education and to talk about my own personal teaching odyssey.

I began by explaining that when I started college, I was still uncertain about what I wanted to do with my life. I was directionless, so I decided to become a history major because I loved the subject even though I realized that it offered "no obvious practicality or immediate benefit."

In fact, my reasoning proved sound since I discovered that college should be a sanctuary to learn and to study:

> I was fascinated by the lives of great men and women and I loved to read and study about past generations, and to analyze those climactic events that had molded and transformed civilization. I guess it was one of those rare moments of epiphany in my life, for I finally understood that college was a place where you went to become educated, not to get a job. For the next four years, I would have the unique opportunity to explore unknown realms of knowledge free from the mundane, daily responsibilities of life.

At Madison College, I slowly began to realize that a teaching career would provide me with the opportunity to share my love of history with literally thousands of students. It would also allow me to make a significant difference in the world.

I recounted that I started taking my first education classes during my junior year. In an era before video tape or DVD's, one of my professors took our class to a local Harrisonburg movie theater to see the new teacher film, *Conrack*. The movie starred Jon Voight and was based upon a novel written by Pat Conroy. It was essentially a semi-autobiographical memoir about Conroy's first (and only) year as a teacher on Daufuskie Island (referred to as Yamacraw Island in the book), South Carolina. The entire school consisted of just two multi-age classrooms and there Conroy saw the intolerable situation of children suffering the daily humiliation of ignorance. In the film, Conroy teaches the children to read and exposes them to the joys of learning. It is an inspiring story and the message I derived from the film was that all teachers must to be missionaries of learning and apostles of excellence.

Another film that I liked was *Stand and Deliver*. It is the true story of Jaime Escalante and chronicles his efforts to teach content-based mathematics at Garfield High School in southern California. As I explained in my remarks, "[Escalante] taught AP calculus in the poverty-ridden *barrios* of Los Angeles and through sheer hard work and determination, his Latino students learned the most difficult math on this planet and thereby received their passport out of poverty, despair, and ignorance." Still, despite Escalante's herculean efforts, his success would have been impossible without the support of his innovative principal, Henry Gradillas.[131] Henry refused to tolerate or excuse educational mediocrity and he provided the type of dynamic leadership that is essential for successful schools. From *Stand and Deliver* I learned that all teachers must have faith that their students can learn and it is our responsibility to ensure that they do.

My all-time favorite movie, though, was *Mr. Holland's Opus*. I watch it at the beginning of every school year for renewed inspiration and encouragement. Produced in 1996, the film is the transformative story of music teacher Glenn Holland as he struggles to become a successful educator. I could personally relate to the film and told the audience:

> [*Mr. Holland's Opus*] is a beautiful film, though, and covers the entire career of a high school music teacher and orchestra conductor. I see a lot of myself in this film. Thank GOD I am not the teacher that I was in 1975. My first year, I was dedicated, hardworking, naïve, and terrified. Each night, I would go home to my new, modest apartment and wrestle with the fundamental issues of what to teach and how to provide meaningful instruction. I would literally spend hours hovered over my small, portable typewriter; carefully composing dittos and lessons. The next day, I would watch in utter horror as my previous evening's work and preparation evaporated within the first 20 minutes of class. I don't think time ever passes more slowly than when you are forced to stand defenseless before a group of hormonal 9th graders with absolutely nothing left to say.

> No, I wasn't a great teacher in 1975 but neither was Mr. Holland. But both of us had the 'right stuff' because we had the will and desire to become good teachers. And so each year, I gradually improved, I evolved, and I learned. I was motivated by a single philosophy, 'Always do what is best for students and you can't go wrong.'

> Each year was new and different—one of the great things about teaching is that we have the opportunity to start over. I changed the way I taught and I adapted to the changing student population. One of the greatest tragedies in education today is seeing those few teachers who have stagnated—who have

refused to innovate or to learn more. What kind of life is that?

Mr. Holland was a humble man and a great teacher. In the movie, at the end of his career, he is packing up his life's work with only his son and wife present. As I said, I won't spoil the end of the film for you but suffice it to say that what I learned from this wonderful film was that 'Teachers sow seeds of harvest unseen.' Each day we touch the lives of so many students and we often never know how much of an impact we have--but we do make a difference.

It was very important to me that I individually recognize each of my students during the dinner. I was very proud of them and was honored that they were in attendance. I introduced Sandi Lin first. She was one of the most brilliant students I had taught during my entire career. Also an award-winning cellist, I considered Sandi to be the epitome of a modern Renaissance individual.

Next I had Leon Scott stand to be recognized. He was the type of student who made coming to school each day a pleasure. Leon took pride in his work and I will always remember his dramatic reading of Jonathan Edwards' jeremiad, "Sinners in the Hands of an Angry God." After he finished, the entire class was silent and trembling as he "made all of us contemplate our humanity and seek forgiveness."

Katelyn Shearer had been in two of my humanities classes at Jefferson. She had an incredible mind and an insatiable desire for knowledge. On Veterans Day, our class put on a special assembly for the residents of the Soldiers and Airmen's Home and Katelyn produced a 12-minute video that effectively encapsulated the entire history of World War II. "It was a work of brilliance," I explained, "and by the time it concluded, virtually every student, teacher, and veteran in the audience had tears in their eyes."

The last TJ student I introduced was Emily Spengler. I could always depend upon Emily to assume a critical role in our historical simulations. She could be trusted to do a magnificent job and that year she memorably portrayed John Adams during the critical election of 1800.

Finally, I introduced Mandy. I recalled that she had been one of the first students I met after I transferred to McLean in 1991. I eventually had her in several of my classes including World Civ, AP American Government, and Photojournalism. Mandy always impressed me with her intellect, her long term goals, and her high ethical standards. She also had a delightful sense of humor so that night, I shared with the teachers a story about what happened during Mandy's freshmen year at McLean:

> In my Civ I class, I was teaching a unit on the medieval period and Mandy said something to me that no other student had ever said. I was stunned and shocked when she casually remarked, 'My mother is younger than you.' Now, this was another moment of epiphany for me in my career—I thought I was teaching a unit on the Middle Ages but instead I was now being callously informed by a student that I had reached middle age! I always assumed that parents were OLDER than me but that apparently was no longer true. For her penance, I had Mandy sit in front of the classroom for the entire period shrouded in a monk's robe. I have since forgiven her for this transgression but woe to the first student who says to me, 'You taught my mother!'

In so many ways, these remarkable young people were the embodiment of the thousands of students that I had taught over the course of my career.

I concluded my speech at the banquet by recalling what Thomas Jefferson had prophetically said in 1818: "If children are untaught, their ignorance and vices will in future life cost us much dearer in their consequences than it would have done in their correction by a good education." Our ultimate challenge as America's teachers and our most important priority is to provide our students with a first-rate education.

With that, the dinner concluded and all of the state teachers were asked to assemble on the ballroom's stairway for some pictures. An ABC television camera crew was there to film our group and they asked me to deliver a special greeting from the group which would

"The Class of 1998" poses for pictures at the conclusion of the National Teacher of the Year banquet. (Philip Bigler)

be aired on the following morning during a broadcast of "Good Morning, America."

Once the pictures and filming were done, my family got into our awaiting limousine and we returned to the Henley Park Hotel. With all of the day's excitement, I found it difficult to sleep and at precisely 6:30 AM the next morning, the first of my scheduled news interviews began. There was also an appearance on "Good Morning, America" which was taped locally at the ABC studios in Washington. Then throughout the day, I appeared on CNN, National Public Radio, WRC Channel 4 News, as well as several other television and radio programs.

The STOYs spent their day at the U.S. Department of Education, where they participated in a forum and a series of discussions about current educational policies and trends. I was able to join the group periodically sandwiched in between my many media interviews. That afternoon, I delivered yet another speech, this time before the DOE's staff as well as my Teacher of the Year colleagues.

Finally, there was a private meeting with Secretary of Education, Richard Riley arranged for late afternoon. Before his cabinet appointment by President Clinton, Riley had served as the governor of South Carolina and he was well-respected for his personal integrity and his honest commitment to improving the quality of schools. He was seen as the "class act" of the Clinton advisors and received bipartisan acclaim for his dedication to our nation's children.

Secretary Riley's office on Independence Avenue offered an impressive vista of the U.S. Capitol, and there we chatted for about 30

With Secretary of Education Richard Riley in his offices at the United States Department of Education. (DOE Photo)

minutes, conversing on a variety of topics including my teaching philosophy and techniques. I discovered that the Secretary and I shared a mutual admiration of novelist Pat Conroy, who happened to be an adoptive son of South Carolina and one of Riley's personal friends. During our meeting, we were joined by two other National Teachers of the Year, Terry Dozier (NTOY 1985 South Carolina) and Mary Beth Blegen (NTOY 1996 Minnesota). They were both working at the Department of Education and during my tenure, they would become my good friends and would offer helpful and supportive advice.

At the conclusion of our meeting, I was mysteriously escorted to a nearby conference room at the DOE. There, a television monitor had been tuned to the local WUSA9 evening news. I sat down and watched as the anchor, Mike Buchanan, began a report in which he announced my selection as the new National Teacher of the Year. He went on to explain that I taught locally at Thomas Jefferson High School for Science and Technology and that one of my most important influences had been a Catholic nun named Sister Mary Josephine. At that instant, a film of Sister Josephine appeared on screen at Sacred Heart, where she was now the school's principal. She was surrounded, of course, by a group of enthusiastic young students and Mike went on to explain that he had Sister Josephine live on the telephone. Sister relayed some of her decades-old memories of me as an eighth grader and told Buchanan about how much I loved history and the social studies. She said that she was very proud of my many accomplishments and especially of my decision to become a teacher. It was an emotional moment for me and will be one that I will treasure forever.

The next morning was an ideal spring day in Washington. Although the city's famed cherry trees had blossomed two weeks earlier, the tulips were in full bloom and the mild temperatures were a welcome harbinger of summer. The Rose Garden ceremony was scheduled for early afternoon so I had a little down time to rehearse my speech. Jon came by my hotel room and went over the details of the day's itinerary and he briefed me on White House protocol. I was grateful that he never once asked to see a copy of my speech or tried to edit my remarks. He had faith in me to use the occasion appropriately and I intended to use it as an opportunity to celebrate excellence in education.

Once again, Jon had arranged for a limousine to pick Linda and me up and it took only a few minutes to get to the northwest gate of the White House. We first had to clear security and pass through the magnetometers before entering the grounds and the famed West Wing. The state teachers were already in the Roosevelt Room and had been lined up alphabetically by state beginning with Alabama and ending with Wyoming.[132] At the appropriate time, each teacher was individually escorted across the hall and into the Oval Office for a brief meeting and photograph with President Clinton and Secretary Riley.

Jon Quam, the Director of the National Teacher of the Year program. (Philip Bigler)

As the national teacher, I was situated last in line and thus slightly out of the prearranged alphabetical order. I was able to bring my entire family with me into the Oval Office and President Clinton was warm and gracious. Our Congressman, Tom Davis, was also there. Tom had actually gone to middle school in Arlington with my wife and was a friend as well as a TJ parent. Likewise, one of our state's senators, Chuck Robb, was in the Oval Office. I had taught Senator Robb's daughter, Jennifer, while at McLean and was pleased to learn that she was studying to become a math teacher. Senator Robb noticed that I was wearing a red Marine Corps tie and complimented me on it. Robb had served in the Marine Corps during the Vietnam War and I told him that I was wearing the tie in honor of M/SGT Fred Fisher. [133] Fred had honorably served two tours of duty in Vietnam and he received the

Purple Heart for wounds he sustained near Chu Lai in 1967. The previous September, Fred died unexpectedly at the age of 50 and I intended to give his teenage son the tie after the ceremony.

After we posed for a series of photographs, my family was escorted out to their seats in the Rose Garden. As the President and I waited for the ceremony to begin, he graciously showed me some

Congressman Tom Davis, President Bill Clinton, Sec. of Education Richard Riley, Philip Bigler, Linda Bigler, and Senator Chuck Robb in the Oval Office prior to the National Teacher of the Year Rose Garden Ceremony. (White House Photo)

of his prized artifacts including a collection of military challenge coins. He also pointed out some of the original artwork in the Oval Office, including Childe Hassam's famous impressionist painting "Avenue in the Rain."

Then someone opened the doors and indicated that they

were ready to begin. Over the public address system I heard the announcement, "the President of the United States" and together we walked out to a podium which had been set up on the office steps.

It was an impressive, historic setting. All of the state teachers and their families were seated and there were several other guests standing around the perimeter. In the back, a platform had been erected for television cameras, photographers, and reporters. In the crowd, I spotted ABC news correspondent Sam Donaldson.

It was a momentous occasion and a great opportunity to pause to celebrate teaching. I remembered, though, that several years earlier, presidential speech writer, Peggy Noonan, had claimed that many cynics denigrated these types of events as meaningless "Rose Garden rubbish," but that was not how President Clinton treated the occasion.[134] For him, it was important and it was obvious that he was totally engaged and was having a wonderful time.

After being introduced by Senator Robb, the President addressed the group:

> You know, this is the Rose Garden, and from these steps we have, at various times, paid tribute to our bravest soldiers, our pioneering astronauts, our greatest athletes. Americans who, in offering up their personal best made our spirits soar, and sometimes changed the course of history, and in so doing, earned the title of "hero." But nothing could be more fitting than to celebrate the men and women whose great deeds are too often unsung, but who, in offering up their personal best every day, help to create those other heroes. For every soldier, every astronaut, every scientist, every athlete, every artist can thank in no small measure a teacher, or more than one, for what he or she ultimately was able to become. [135]

President Bill Clinton delivering his remarks at the Rose Garden Ceremony for the National Teacher of the Year. (White House Photo)

The President spoke eloquently about the important role that teachers have in American society. He then talked about my teaching and career:

> Our national honoree, Philip Bigler, brings all these gifts to his history classes at, appropriately, Thomas Jefferson High School for Science and Technology in Virginia. For more than 20 years, his students haven't just studied history, they have lived it. He's transformed his classroom into a virtual time machine, challenging students to debate each other as members of rival ancient Greek city states; as lawyers before the Supreme Court; as presidential candidates named Thomas Jefferson and John Adams.
>
> Through these historic simulations, his students have learned lessons about democracy and the meaning of citizenship, lessons that will last a lifetime -- lessons we want every American to know.
>
> We need more teachers like Philip Bigler and all our other honorees in every classroom in America today. For it is they who can make our schools the best in the world. It is they who can guarantee that America will have another American Century in the 21st century…Now, I close with these words, so that we can give our honoree the last word: The great Daniel Webster once said, "If we work upon marble, it will perish. If we work upon brass, time will efface it. If we rear temples, they will crumble into dust. But if we work upon immortal minds, we engrave on those tablets something that will brighten to all eternity."
>
> Thank you, Philip Bigler, for brightening those minds to all eternity. (See Appendix E for entire transcript)

President Clinton presented me with a crystal apple and then invited me to speak. Since I was a good deal shorter than him, he had covertly pulled out with his foot a hidden step in the podium so that I would appear taller.

I began my remarks by acknowledging the VIP guests, my fellow teachers, and my students. As I gazed out over the audience, it was a surrealistic experience. I could see Linda, smiling and beautiful, in the front row sitting next to my dad, brother, and sister-in-law. It would have been perfect if only my mother could have lived to see me on this incredible occasion. I continued:

> When I began my teaching career some 23 years ago at Oakton High School, I never dreamed that one day I would be invited to the White House and to be recognized by the President of the United States for my work as a classroom teacher. But my mother and father could, because they, like all parents, wanted the best for their children and they had the highest aspiration for us. The parents and teachers of this nation represent a powerful coalition for quality public schools, and we, working together, can assure educational excellence.

My father, Charles; sister-in-law, Regina; wife, Linda; and brother, Bob in the White House Rose Garden. (Jeff Dunson)

My former principal in McLean High School who is also present today, Elizabeth Lodal -- Elizabeth, please stand -- (applause) -- once imparted these words of wisdom to me. "To be a teacher," she said, "is to be forever an optimist." Each day, we teachers are privileged to glimpse the future, and I believe that our American Golden Age is still before us, and it will be a time when learning is cherished and scholars are revered.

Thank you, Mr. President, for inviting us here today and for all you're doing to support our public schools. Thank you.

The President returned to the podium and said, "Class dismissed." He then immediately walked into the crowd to shake hands with the invited guests. President Clinton made a point to arrange for a group picture with all of my students and I will always be indebted to him

Delivering my speech as National Teacher of the Year with President Bill Clinton, Secretary Richard Riley, and Senator Chuck Robb. (White House Photo)

for this singular act of kindness. It was something that these young people would remember for the rest of their lives.

On the way out of the White House grounds, I looked once again at my schedule. The last line read, "The saga continues…" Indeed, it would.

The President with my students as well as TJ Principal, Geoff Jones, and my teaching partner, Sheri Maeda. (White House Photo)

Endnotes

124 The role of the federal government increased incrementally after the Soviet's launched *Sputnik* in 1957. Seen as a national security issue, Congress passed the National Defense Act in 1958. Its emphasis was primarily on math and science. In 1965, Lyndon Johnson's "Great Society" programs had several federal education initiatives including the Elementary and Secondary Education Act which was designed to address the inequity in schools caused by poverty. The "No Child Left Behind Act" was, in fact, a 2002 reauthorization of this legislation.

125 The Clinton era initiatives were posted online at the Department of Education's website: http://www.doe.gov. There were several programs design to implement each proposal.

- All students will read independently and well by the end of the 3rd grade.

- All students will master challenging mathematics, including the foundations of algebra and geometry, by the end of 8th grade.

- By 18 years of age, all students will be prepared for and able to afford college.

- All states and schools will have challenging and clear standards of achievement and accountability for all children, and effective strategies for reaching those standards.

- There will be a talented, dedicated and well-prepared teacher in every classroom.

- Every classroom will be connected to the Internet by the year 2000 and all students will be technologically literate.

- Every school will be strong, safe, drug-free and disciplined.

126 James Stockdale was Ross Perot's choice for Vice President in 1992. Stockdale was not a skilled politician and his performance during the Vice Presidential debates with Dan Quayle and Al Gore was widely mocked. In truth, he was the far superior intellect but that intelligence could not be reduced to a mere sound-bite. Despite his poor performance, the Perot-Stockdale third party ticket garnished 19% of the popular national vote and almost assuredly ensured Bill Clinton's election to the presidency.

127 Jim Stockdale. (1995) *Thoughts of a Philosophical Fighter Pilot.* Stanford, CA.: Hoover Press, p. 23

128 Marcus Aurelius. (2002) *Mediations.* trans. Gregory Hays. Norwalk, CT: Easton Press, p. 33.

129 See Appendix D for the entire speech.

130 Press Release dated April 23, 1998 from the Council of Chief State School Officers.

131 I had the opportunity to meet Henry Gradillas during one of our in-services at Bethesda-Chevy Chase High School. I interviewed him for my book, *Failing Grades.* In the book, Gradillas explained the importance of teaching content: "Gradillas made instruction a priority. With only 10 percent of the school's graduates pursuing any form of higher education, it was clear that major changes in the curriculum were vital. He ordered the counselors to encourage all students to accept the academic challenge of higher mathematics to improve their chances of going on to college or obtaining a well-paying job, but there was strong resistance. After a year of little progress, Gradillas 'personally got a marker, a highlighter, and wiped out 12 classes that were scheduled to be remedial math-basic classes. I said, by the power vested in me, these 12 classes we are programming for next year are gone. They don't exist. And I penciled in Algebra. The guidance counselors died. Twelve sections of Algebra replacing 12 sections of basic nothing...and so they said, You're nuts! You are not going to do that. And I said, Yes, it is done. By the power vested in me. It is arbitrary and unilateral. This is not negotiable. This is it.'" See Philip Bigler and Karen Lockard. (1992) *Failing Grades: A Teacher's Report Card on Education in America.* St. Petersburg, Florida: Vandamere Press, p. 37.

132 The Roosevelt Room is an interior meeting room with no windows. It has portraits of both Theodore and Franklin Roosevelt. On the mantel piece is Theodore Roosevelt's Nobel Peace Prize which he was awarded for mediating an end of the Russo-Japanese War (1904-1905).

133 Chuck Robb was President Lyndon Johnson's son-in-law.

134 The first speech that Peggy Noonan wrote for President Ronald Reagan was for the Rose Garden ceremony honoring the 1984 National Teacher of the Year, Sherleen S. Sisney. See Peggy Noonan. (1990) *What I Saw at the Revolution: A Political Life in the Reagan Era*. New York: Random House, pp. 57-59.

135 CSPAN has a video of the entire 1998 Rose Garden ceremony online at http://www.c-spanvideo.org/program/Teachero. Also see http://www.philipbigler.com for additional information.

CHAPTER X
Mr. Bigler's Grand Adventure

*Certainly civilization cannot advance without freedom of inquiry. This fact is
self-evident. What seems equally self-evident is that in the process of history
certain immutable truths have been revealed and discovered and that their value
is not subject to the limitations of time and space...*

William F. Buckley

The following Monday, after all of the excitement of Washington Week, I was back at work. Sheri and I had arranged for our Humanities classes to take our annual field trip to the United States Soldiers' and Airmen's Home (USSAH) in Northeast Washington on that day. Gail Russell Chaddock, a reporter with the *Christian Science Monitor* had asked to accompany us, since she planned on doing a story about my selection as the National Teacher of the Year.

We had always begun this particular field trip with stops at the Korean and Vietnam War Memorials.[136] We felt that it was important for our students to understand memorial architecture since the way a nation chooses to honor and remember its past tells a lot about a society's values and beliefs. Moreover, the students needed to appreciate the human consequences of war—36,516 dead in Korea and 58,209 during the Vietnam War. The elderly soldiers that our students would be meeting on that day had once been young men and had personally sacrificed much to serve their country's call in its time of need.

We required the students to dress professionally and I was very pleased on how they interacted with the veterans. They were polite, sensitive, and inquisitive while they carefully recorded their conversations so that they could accurately transcribe and write oral histories when they returned to school. These types of field trips are incredibly rich in content and provide students with a unique learning opportunity that is difficult to replicate in the classroom.

Gail's article came out in the May 5th edition of the *Monitor* and was entitled, "America's Top Teacher Gets Teens Out of Their Seats and Into History." It was an excellent piece, reflecting the time and effort that was required to be thorough and accurate. In the article, she wrote about how important reading was in my history classes:

> '[Bigler says that students]   are bombarded by visuals. That's why teachers need to talk about books all the time and why they're exciting'...One way to make books come alive is to link them to personal stories and experiences, he says. Student Katelyn Shearer recalls reading Russian history on her own all last summer because of a story Bigler told in class about Rasputin, notorious adviser to the last czar of Russia. 'My dinner conversations have gotten a lot better since taking his class,' she quips.[137]

Gail had spent a good deal of time with my classes and made a point to interview several of my current students. In her piece, she kindly wrote:

Students from Thomas Jefferson High School for Science and Technology at the United States Soldiers' and Airmen's Home in Washington, D.C. (Philip Bigler)

The students meeting with World War II veterans. Each group was responsible for conducting an oral history interview which they later transcribed and used to write original plays. (Philip Bigler)

Philip Bigler's students aren't surprised that their history teacher was just named National Teacher of the Year. 'He's incredible,' says Samuel Davies, an 11th grader at Thomas Jefferson High School for Science and Technology. 'We just love to hear Mr. Bigler speak. He has such a passion for everything.'

Bigler is a master storyteller, and an even better listener. It shows in how he focuses on his students as they make a point, or lights up when a class speaker recounts an interesting experience...Christiana Dee [recounts] 'How could you not love a teacher who gets you so involved.'[138]

Although my official tenure as National Teacher of the Year would not begin until after I had completed the school year, I still had several local appearances and obligations scheduled. I was also receiving numerous inquiries from various groups asking me to speak at future events and conferences. On Monday, May 4th, though, I was shocked to receive a phone call from one of the producers of "The Late Show with David Letterman" program. She said that David wanted to extend an invitation to me to appear as one of his featured guests on that Wednesday night's program.

I was shocked and a bit apprehensive. Letterman had a well-deserved reputation for his caustic wit and sarcastic sense of humor and I was not a professional entertainer, a comedian, or a celebrity. I was a high school history teacher and could not afford to be made fun of or mocked just for amusement's sake. The producer, though, assured me that Letterman would be respectful, and claimed that he had seen me during one of my earlier television appearances and thought that I would make an interesting guest for his show. So cautiously reassured, I agreed and the very next day I received a Federal Express envelope containing a round trip airline ticket to New York City.

On Wednesday morning, I took the day off from school and drove to Reagan National Airport. There I caught the hourly Delta Shuttle to LaGuardia. It was a relatively easy, short 50-minute flight especially since I didn't have to travel with any luggage. I arrived in New York around noon and my schedule called for me to tape the show at 5:30 PM and to return to DC on a later shuttle. I would be home in time to watch the actual broadcast of the program later that night.

I walked out of the airline terminal to discover that the show had sent a stretch limousine to pick me up. On the window was a sign in bold letters with my name and the words "The Late Show with David Letterman." For the first time in my life, I felt like a movie star. The chauffeur explained as we were driving into Manhattan that he was taking me to the Riga Hotel, where a suite had been reserved for me. This was a bit perplexing since I was not going to be spending the night, but the driver said that it was a routine precaution. The show's producers wanted to know where their guests were at all times and thus ensure that I would be on time for the taping.

When we arrived at the Riga Hotel, I immediately checked in with the desk clerk and went upstairs to my room. There were still a few hours before I needed to leave for the show but it seemed to be an eternity. I was anxious and uneasy, uncertain about what to expect from Mr. Letterman. I couldn't concentrate enough to read anything serious so I tried to pass the time by watching daytime television. That experience proved more horrifying than relaxing.

Finally, at precisely five o'clock, I came back downstairs and there I found my driver waiting. I got back into the limo and we literally drove around the block onto Broadway and slowly passed the famous Ed Sullivan Theater. Its marquee featured the CBS logo and "The Late Show" in large yellow block letters. There was a large crowd of people waiting patiently in line and I couldn't help but smile at the irony—just a few weeks ago, I wouldn't have been able to get a ticket to the show and somehow, by virtue of my new title, I was miraculously going to be on the program as David Letterman's guest.

Things soon got progressively weirder when we turned the corner

The marquee for the Late Show *at the Ed Sullivan Theater in New York City.*
(Rorem/Dreamstime.com)

and approached the stage door entrance. There were a number of New York policemen lining the street and a large crowd had gathered behind several strategically positioned barricades. The people were clearly enjoying themselves and the excitement was palatable. They were shouting and cheering while many fans were taking pictures and others had autograph pads. My driver adroitly navigated a maze of orange traffic cones and pulled into a special area that had been carefully cordoned off. By now, the crowd noise had become thunderous and someone quickly opened the car door for me. As soon as I got out, the crowd became eerily silent, since obviously no one had any idea who I was.

I was whisked inside the building and taken upstairs to the second floor where a dressing room had been reserved for me. On one side of the hall, there was a large entourage of people who were with country music singer Lyle Lovett. Likewise, there were several other people congregating around the opposite dressing room which was occupied by academy award winning actress Sally Field. I was suddenly beginning to feel very isolated.

About fifteen minutes later, the program's producer entered my dressing room and accompanied me downstairs to the makeup room. There were several closed circuit television monitors strategically positioned around the room, which enabled me to watch Letterman as he began his opening monologue. And then Sally Field walked into the room and I was totally enchanted. She was charming, beautiful and gracious and she was talking to me.

Sally Field was one of my earliest teenage television crushes when she portrayed Gidget on the short-lived ABC sitcom in the 1960's. I also appreciated her character, Sister Bertrille, in the iconic, albeit absurd, series *The Flying Nun*.[139] I was thoroughly enjoying my interaction with Sally while Letterman was continuing his initial monologue. Then she abruptly stopped talking and pointed to the television monitors and said, "He's talking about you."

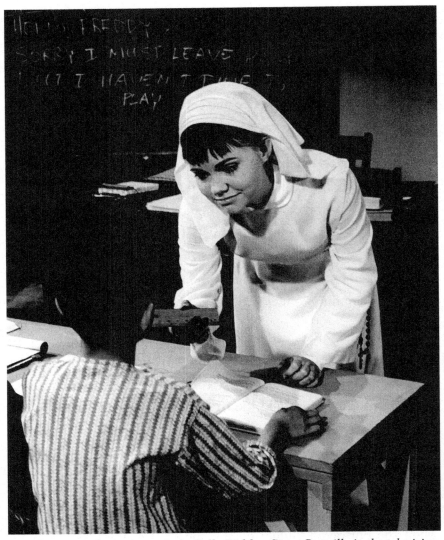

Academy award-winning actress, Sally Field as Sister Bertrille in the television series, The Flying Nun. *Sally was one of the guests on the* Late Show *with me in May, 1998.* (Getty Images)

"Oh, this is pretty good ladies and gentlemen," Letterman said. "This is one of the heroes, there aren't that many heroes left in the world today and we have a hero with us tonight. The man's name is Philip Bigler and he is the National Teacher of the Year. Mr. Bigler will be out here." That was quite an introduction and I felt a bit relieved. Maybe this interview wasn't going to be so difficult after all. With that, Sally Field said goodbye and left the room in order to get ready for her appearance. Meanwhile, I was escorted back to my dressing room to await my own "curtain call."

I watched the show, which included a mildly amusing spoof on mother's day cards followed by Letterman's signature Top Ten List. Tonight's topic was the "Top Ten Least Popular Summer Jobs" which included: "#10 Taco Bell Cook in Charge of Deep-frying the Chihuahuas" and "#4 U.N. Weapons Inspector Assigned to Digging through Saddam Hussein's Undershirts." It wasn't one of his better efforts but then Sally Field was introduced and she was wonderful and appeared in two segments. I was flattered when at one point, she and Letterman discussed my forthcoming appearance.

Mid-way through the program, the producer took me back downstairs and into the actual recording studio. I was instructed to stand just offstage and await my cue. The set was brilliantly lit and the overhead spotlights were so bright that the studio audience was completely invisible to me. The room temperature was extremely cool to counteract the perspiring effects of the hot lights. I was personally able to watch Dave finish his interview with Sally Field and then go to a commercial break. Sally came offstage and I told her how much I enjoyed meeting her before saying goodbye. Then, Paul Shaffer's band began to play "To Sir with Love" and someone with headphones told me to "GO!" and I walked out onto the stage to polite applause. Letterman came over and shook my hand and then directed me to a seat next to his desk. I was suddenly conscious of the reality that there would soon be millions of people watching throughout the country.

Letterman began the interview by claiming that all he ever hears about schools "is one horror story after another...It can give you the impression that we have lost the fight." Unfortunately, his conception of education, as well as that of the general public, is predicated more by the 24-hour news cycle than by reality. Indeed, the media prefers the outrageous to the routine, so that the regular work being done in our nation's classrooms goes unnoticed. I explained to David that as teachers, we had to be optimists and that we had to have faith in our children's futures.

I then tried to redirect the topic by recounting the story about our recent oral history project at the Soldiers' and Airmen's Home. I explained that these aging veterans had been very much impressed by my students and their experience with these wonderful young people had renewed their faith in our country's ultimate destiny. The students had studied World War II extensively before their visit, so I joked, "that if a World War II veteran was talking about the Battle of the Bulge, the students didn't think the he was talking about a middle age weight problem." There was a momentary pause while the studio audience digested this information and then they erupted into laughter. History humor takes a little while to comprehend but David smiled and laughed as well. With that the entire tenor of the interview shifted and it became great fun.

We talked about the importance of reading skills, of parent involvement, and of the need to become lifelong learners. Throughout, Letterman was glib, humorous, and at his good-natured best.

At one point during the interview, he asked me about classroom discipline, "Do you ever have to toss a kid out? Ever boot him? Ever give the kid the boot?" I laughed and told him that "my feeling is that I would rather have my kids fear my disappointment than my anger. So I hope that's going to be the case." Letterman warmly responded "And that works!" to which I replied, "It does work."

As my eight minutes of fame were drawing to a close, David posed one final question, "Were the students thrilled for you when you got the honor?"

In truth, the TJ students were far more excited about my appearance on "The Late Show" than they were about the White House recognition so I replied, "Well, David, there about 1,600 students from Thomas Jefferson watching at this very moment since they were so excited about me being on David Letterman."

Hearing that, David turned, looked directly into the camera, and with impeccable timing commanded, "You kids go to bed. You shouldn't be up this late!" We shook hands and he concluded with, "Congratulations. Enjoy your year. Philip Bigler, National Teacher of the Year."

It was all over and I was hurriedly escorted off of the stage but had the opportunity to shake Lyle Lovett's hand before being taken out of the studio to my awaiting limousine. Within three hours, I was back at my home in Fairfax and, of course, Linda wanted to know all of the details. It had been such a surrealistic experience that I was a bit vague and was anxious to see the actual broadcast of the show for myself.

At 11:30 PM after the conclusion of the evening news, "The Late Show" began and it was thrilling to see my name in the credits with Sally Field and Lyle Lovett. After seeing my interview, I was satisfied and felt that it had gone well. Then there was an extensive three minute commercial with advertisements for Honda, UPS, Blockbuster, and KIA. CBS was also running a promo for the "last ever network" showing of the *Wizard of Oz* scheduled for that Friday. Then Letterman returned to the air for a brief 30-second spot. This time was normally reserved for Letterman and Paul Shaffer to engage in a little light banter while announcing the following night's line up of guests. But on this night, Letterman diverted from his routine. David Letterman, a man who has riches and fame, all of the material things you could possibly want in life, looked over to Paul Shaffer and said, "Paul, wouldn't it be nice to know that when you went to work every day, you were making a tangible, positive difference in the world. That's a wonderful thing." At that moment, David Letterman was speaking to every single teacher in America since that is what we have. As educators, we try to make a difference each and every day of our lives. That is not a bad legacy.

As the school year drew to a close, I was invited to speak at three Fairfax County high school commencements including both TJ's and McLean's. These events were very personal to me and I was particular honored to return to McLean. I had always felt a bit guilty about leaving the school, especially now that the surrounding publicity with my selection as National Teacher only mentioned my current appointment at Jefferson. It had been at McLean where I received my first honor, and most of what had occurred subsequently was due to my teaching there. It was nice to be able to return and thank the students and staff, as well as to celebrate the Class of 1998. I had taught many of these graduating seniors in Civ I and in Photojournalism. In my speech, I singled out yearbook staff and editors for their hard work and dedication to the school and I congratulated them on another fine edition of *Clan*, "A Lasting Layer," which had just been published under the able supervision of their new advisor, Susan Sloan.

On the very last day of school, I had the unpleasant task of boxing up all of my classroom files and teaching materials and placing them into temporary storage. Even though I knew that I was about to embark upon a grand adventure, I was still going to miss the daily excitement of teaching history as well as the interaction with my students. Many of them had been deeply disappointed that I was not going to be at TJ for their final year of high school. Although I would not be their senior AP Government teacher, I vowed that I would be available to write all of their college recommendations and reassured them that I could be contacted easily through email.

There would, of course, be no real summer vacation for me this year. I already had numerous NTOY engagements booked, including presenting at the Scholastic Awards at the Kennedy Center, keynoting a North Carolina teacher forum, attending the recognition of the new Presidential Scholars at the White House, and addressing the National Education Association's delegate assembly in New Orleans.[140] There were several other events scheduled throughout Virginia as well as pending trips to Georgia, South Carolina, and Florida for teacher conferences.

Jon would regularly provide me with an up-to-date agenda and this material contained critical information, including a description of the type of event that I would be attending, the intended audience, and the expected content for my remarks. He also provided me with my flight schedules, airline tickets, hotel reservations, and a list of local contacts.

I thoroughly enjoyed the extensive travel and even liked the prolonged airport wait time. It provided me with a degree of solitude and the opportunity to read several novels including Tom Wolfe's *A Man in Full* and Frank McCourt's *Angela's Ashes*. It was fun to visit the various states as well as to meet educators from across the country. I always tried to learn about what was happening in their various school jurisdictions and was interested in discovering new ideas and innovative methods which I could use with my own students.

In late July, I flew to Huntsville, Alabama, where I was scheduled to attend Space Camp with all of the State Teachers of the Year. I was a wonderful reunion and we were joined there by a group of talented international educators. We had earlier been instructed to bring a costume representative of our home state or native country since the program began with an opening parade designed to showcase our group's cultural and global diversity. As a Virginian, I decided to wear a colonial shirt and tri-corner hat to highlight my state's critical role in the struggle for independence during the American Revolution.

Space Camp was an amazing experience for all of us. We visited the nearby Marshall Space Flight Center and were given a VIP behind-the-scenes tour. There we watched and talked with NASA engineers who were actually working on the design and construction of many of the intricate components destined for the International Space Station. Throughout the week we also attended several lectures on

*With my good friend, Kay Long, the 1998 Oklahoma Teacher of the Year at Space Camp. (*Philip Bigler)

the evolution and history of the space program; these presentations were delivered by scientists and experts including shuttle astronaut, Colonel Mike Mullaney. There was even an IMAX theater at Space Camp and we watched several inspiring films including *Hail Columbia* and *Mission to Mir*. Probably our most improbable experience, though, was having the opportunity to learn about the principles of aerodynamics by actually piloting a single-engine airplane.[141]

The major portion of the week involved us undergoing simulated astronaut training. In order to increase the realism, we were issued our own personalized flight suit and then we were divided into various teams. Each group was responsible for conducting two mock shuttle launches which was, in essence, a clever team-building exercise. To be successful, we had to master our individual roles and responsibilities and learn to adapt to unexpected situations. The

Our mission team, Canopus, at Space Camp in Huntsville, Alabama.
(Philip Bigler)

group I was assigned was named CANOPUS, representing the Canadian space agency responsible for studying the aurora borealis. Our team consisted of fifteen members and included international teachers from Mexico, Denmark, Australia, and the Czech Republic.[142] During our simulated shuttle missions, we were responsible for managing the proper ascent and orbit of the shuttle; ensuring the successful completion of all scientific experiments on board the orbiter; deploying a communications satellite within a set timeframe; and effecting the final reentry and safe return of the crew.

Throughout the activity, we were repeatedly challenged by various problems and complications which required an immediate response. These crises were often signaled by bright flashing warning lights and loud alarms which theoretically indicated a serious problem that could jeopardize the success of our mission. To respond effectively, it was imperative that we trusted one another's individual expertise while maintaining a calm, professional demeanor. It was, in fact, providing us with a perfect metaphor for what is necessary in a school to have a truly successful and productive faculty.[143]

August was one of the busiest months for the National Teacher since there were numerous back-to-school events. One of the nicest opportunities I had was to help inaugurate the opening of the new Rachel Carson Middle School in Fairfax County. I had known the school's principal, Gail Womble, for several years and she was someone I greatly admired. An innovative, dynamic educator, she had predictably, assembled a talented group of top-quality teachers for Carson. In the school's sparkling new library, I told the faculty that this was a rare moment when they would have the opportunity to initiate a solid philosophical foundation for the school as well as to create its traditions. I was envious since I never had personally had that chance.

Likewise, I was honored to have been invited back to my alma mater, James Madison University, by President Ron Carrier. I owed much of my teaching success to the high quality education I had received at Madison so it was a privilege to address the professors at the opening meeting of the fall semester. It also provided me with the opportunity to commend the faculty for their commitment to student learning and to publically acknowledge some of my own professors who had influenced my life.

I had recently finished reading Mitch Albom's short book, *Tuesday's with Morrie*. I recommended that the entire JMU faculty read the book before their students returned to classes. It was an inspiring story about personal discovery and the importance of lifelong learning. Albom was a well-known and successful sports writer working out of Detroit when he learned that his former Brandeis professor, Morrie Schwartz, was suffering from the crippling effects of Lou Gehrig's disease. Albom decided that it was time for him to reconnect with his old mentor and over the course of the next several Tuesdays, he once again became Morrie's student. During this time, Albom learned some profound lessons about life. Among them were:

- The young are not wise. Wisdom can only come with age, experience, and education.

- A good education is the only real antidote to poverty.

- Personal wealth alone does not bring happiness or contentment.

- People are too self-absorbed and engaged in frivolous activities that do not matter.

- It is important to live a consequential life.

Professor Morrie Schwartz died from his disease on November 4, 1995. On his tombstone, his family inscribed the epitaph: "A Teacher to the Last." Albom's personal tribute reads: "Have you ever really had a teacher? One who saw you as a raw but precious thing, a jewel that, with wisdom, could be polished to a proud shine? If you are lucky enough to find your way to such teachers, you will always find you way back."[144] It was, hopefully, something to ponder at the start of a new academic year.

Over the summer, I had been periodically working with several of my students on developing a character education program for the opening week at Jefferson. Our presentation was entitled "Character through Time" and utilized a variety of clips from several Hollywood history films to illustrate the importance of resisting peer pressure and of living principled lives. My students chose scenes from such cinematic classics as *A Man for All Seasons*, *Henry V*, *Glory*, and *Gettysburg*. They did an outstanding job incorporating the material into their prepared remarks and explained to the student body the necessity of having academic integrity, intellectual honesty, personal courage, and fidelity to one's personal convictions. It was a powerful and important message which helped start the school year off in a positive direction.

As soon as the assembly was over, I had to rush to catch a plane to Frankfurt. For the next week, I conducted several follow-up in-services for the DODea teachers in Hanau, Germany and worked with individual teachers on using technology in their lessons. I returned home for a few days, which barely gave me enough time to repack and prepare for my impending two week trip to Japan.

I was extremely excited about the prospect of visiting Japan. I had never before been to Asia and my two week itinerary called for me to visit several cities including Tokyo, Naoetsu, Katayamazu Onsen, Hiroshima, Kobe, Koyasan, and Wakanoura. During this time, I would have the opportunity to visit several Japanese schools and meet with teachers and government officials. I was also scheduled to speak at Joetsu University and at the national Japanese PTA conference in Kyoto. I would also due to be interviewed by a news reporter for an article scheduled to be published in the *Asahi Shimbun* newspaper, a Japanese daily with a circulation of over 8 million copies.

Mr. Akio Nakajima at the Baba Foundation had been particularly gracious and generous. He had reserved for me a first class airline ticket on board ANA Flight #1 from Dulles to Tokyo. I had never before been in the exclusive confines of the upper deck in a 747 jetliner and the accommodations were luxurious, especially when contrasted to the pedestrian realities of coach. Rather than the traditional cramped airline seats, the first class cabin chairs resembled spacious La-Z-Boy recliners and were extremely comfortable. Likewise, the service was stellar. The flight attendants greeted each of the passengers as we entered with a deep bow and a glass of sparkling champagne.

The 13-hour marathon flight traversed the great circle route over Alaska and crossed the International Date Line. Despite its length, the trip was relaxed and peaceful and I arrived at Japan's Narita Airport without any of the adverse effects of jetlag. I was met outside of customs by Mr. Makoto Asai and he would accompany me throughout my two week Japanese adventure.

Rather than contend with Tokyo's legendary traffic, Mr. Asai had arranged for us to take an express bus into downtown. I was staying at the Capitol Tokyu Hotel and I had a few hours to shower, freshen up, and relax before I was to attend a special welcoming dinner later that evening.

I was keenly aware of the importance of making a positive impression with my Japanese hosts. I was, in effect, representing both the United States and the teaching profession. I knew that one of my greatest personal challenges was going to be the food since I generally do not like fish and this was the primary cuisine of the Japanese

My business card in Japanese.
(Philip Bigler)

people. I privately vowed that I would eat anything and everything that I was served and would do so without complaint. I never asked, though, what I was being served since many of the delicacies were completely unfathomable. Fortunately, all of the seafood was fresh and healthful, but there were times when I needed to use generous amounts of sake to wash down some of the less palatable portions.

The next day, I had an appointment to meet with the Japanese Minister of Education in his downtown governmental offices. We had an interesting discussion about Japanese and American schools and realized the impossibility of trying to impose one system onto another. Still, the minister hoped that I could help Japanese teachers see the importance of innovation in their classrooms as well as the essential need for students to become more active and involved learners. He also explained to me that one of the serious problems in Japanese schools was that of bullying.

After our meeting concluded, I had the opportunity to do some sightseeing around Tokyo. I was immediately struck by the dichotomy of Japanese society. On one hand, the city was a modern and bustling metropolis; neon signs were ubiquitous, and throughout the downtown area, there were several ultra-modern, vibrant shopping districts. Stores hawked every conceivable electronic gadget, and it seemed that all the pedestrians were using cellphones. I was mesmerized by the crowds of people and the deafening noise emanating from the numerous pachinko parlors.[145] Even the taxi cabs were technological marvels. The passenger doors opened automatically and inside there were monitors broadcasting the latest news, including the steroid-driven homerun duel between Sammy Sosa and Mark McGwire.

At the same time, amidst the energetic atmosphere of modern Japan, there was a reverence for history, tradition, and culture. Many women still wore the customary kimono, and all of the Japanese maintained a strong respect for their elders and venerated the memory of their ancestors. I had the opportunity to visit several ancient pagodas as well as several Shinto shrines where worshippers devoutly prayed and burned incense.

I was quickly discovering the horror of what it meant to be functionally illiterate. I felt completely helpless because I was unable to decipher or decode the simplest of things, including signs, subway maps, and newspapers. Indeed, when I arrived at the train station the following day, I was mystified by the rapidly changing electronic train schedules but was fortunate to have Mr. Asai there to guide me to the proper platform, where we boarded the Super Express Train Asaki #321. It would take us across the country to my next destination, the west coast city of Joetsu.

Joetsu was located on the banks of the Seki River and the Sea of Japan. It was famous for its flowering cherry blossom trees, the feudal Kasugayama Castle, and the magnificent Gochi Kokubun-ji Temple.[146] It was also in relatively close proximity to the city of Nagano, which had recently garnished international attention as the host site for that year's XVIII Winter Olympic games.

Upon my arrival, I was greeted by Dr. Noriko Tokie, an Associate Professor of Music at the university. Having studied for a time at Columbia University in New York, she spoke fluent English and she had graciously consented to serve as my guide and translator during my stay in Joetsu.

I was scheduled to deliver a 90-minute lecture at Joetsu University's College of Education. I had decided, for once, to intentionally ignore Ed Gero's sage advice about speaking only from notes, and had written out my entire speech. This was necessary since I had been asked to provide the text of my remarks to each of the participants in order to help facilitate their understanding of my English.

I began my speech with an overview of the development of public education in the United States. Over the course of our nation's history, I explained, there developed a consensus for the need to have so-called common schools. These modest institutions taught all socio-economic groups and placed a strong emphasis on ba-

Speaking to educators at Joetsu University in Japan and (right) the Takada Castle. (Philip Bigler)

sic literacy skills—the three "R's" of reading, writing, and arithmetic. Throughout the United States, our society came to believe that a good education was a vital for tool needed for individual improvement and economic advancement. It would be the nation's public schools that would ultimately provide a common pathway to success for countless generations of American immigrants.

Over the previous century, I explained, teachers in the United States have been profoundly influenced by the ideas of the famed psychologist, John Dewey. He emphasized the concept of "learn by doing" and that precept continues to be the basic philosophy in American public education. Its most recent metamorphosis exists in the idea of student-centered classrooms as well as project-based learning.

I told the audience that in the United States, students are given an enormous amount of individual and intellectual freedom. Ideally, they are taught to think for themselves and are encouraged to express their personal views. One Japanese educator later told me that "you have so much freedom in America," but explained that in Japan, this would only produce unruly "wolf children".

It was, of course, foolish to try to equate different educational systems. The cultural chasm is completely insurmountable. When I visited classes in Japan, for instance, I was surprised about how large and homogenous they were. Japanese teachers were well-respected and considered to be the omnipotent authority in the classroom. As such, I found that very few Japanese students spoke or participated in class. Still, it was obvious that they were learning despite the lack of technology in instruction or innovative pedagogy.

In most Japanese schools, the students wore identical uniforms and were extremely well-behaved and courteous. When an instructor entered the room, the entire class would stand in unison, bow, and request: "Please teach us, *sensei*." Students even took the initiative to clean the school building after classes had adjourned for the day.

I knew that it would not be a proper forum for me to elaborate on the negatives and problems of American schools. I did, however, feel that it was important to acknowledge that these did exist (lack of academic rigor, student laziness, politicization of curricula, lax standards, poor reading skills, etc.) but explained that one of the greatest strengths of our system was that the vast majority of teachers cared about their students' success and well-being.[147]

Because of my full itinerary, my stay at Joetsu was brief. The next stop on my schedule was Hiroshima. Because of the city's historical significance, it had been the one place that I had specifically requested to visit while in Japan. Sheri and I often began our Hum II classes with the dropping of the atomic bomb. This allowed us to start our American history classes in a unique and unexpected way and would give us adequate time to cover in-depth post-World War II America. The following nine week block we would retrogress to the colonial period and progress chronologically through the remainder of the material.[148].

I particularly like to emphasize in class those singular moments in history when everything fundamentally changes. August 6, 1945 was one of the rare times when you could pinpoint the exact time when an era began. At 8:15 AM, the obliteration of Hiroshima marked the beginning of the nuclear age. The development of atomic weapons would have a profound and lasting psychological effect on the world. The bomb would dictate the course of the Cold War and Americans were forced to adapt to the ghastly idea of Mutual Assured Destruction (MAD). I personally could remember the "duck and cover" drills we conducted while in elementary school during the Eisenhower administration, as well as the proliferation of backyard bomb shelters.[149] I also could vividly recall the country's fear during the Cuban missile crisis when the United States and the Soviet Union came perilously close to nuclear war.[150] And today we are facing the growing threat of nuclear proliferation as several rogue regimes are actively trying to acquire their own nuclear weapons.

In class, I had my students discuss the morality of nuclear weapons and debate whether President Harry Truman was justified in authorizing the twin atomic bombings of Hiroshima and Nagasaki, given the military situation in 1945. It was always an evocative and profound class period and my students frequently reached their own different conclusions.

On September 28th, Mr. Asai and I flew into Hiroshima on a JAL Flight and took a taxi into the city. It was an eerie feeling to actually stand on ground zero, the T-shaped Aioi Bridge which had served as the ideal aiming point for the crew of the B-29 Superfortress, *Enola Gay*. Nearby, on the banks of the Motoyasu River, was the *Genbaku* (Atomic Bomb) Dome memorial, the skeletal remains of the Hiroshima Prefectural Industrial Promotion Hall. It is the only obvious physical remnant of the blast since the modern city of Hiroshima has been completely rebuilt and resurrected, a testament to the resolve and resilience of the Japanese people.

I walked over to the nearby Peace Memorial Park which was built to honor the 66,000 victims of the blast. There is an eternal flame as well as a memorial cenotaph on the grounds. Nearby, was the Hiroshima Peace Memorial Museum that contained numerous exhibits which chronicled the scope and aftermath of the explosion. Virtually everything within a 2 km radius of the blast was obliterated and graphic photographs showed the terrible injuries sustained by the victims as well as the lethal effects of radiation sickness. There were also several display cases filled with children's clothing who had perished in the firestorm.

The Atomic Bomb Dome at Ground Zero in Hiroshima. The city was virtually destroyed on August 6, 1945. (Philip Bigler)

It was perfectly understandable that a museum dedicated to peace should show the horrors of war, but I was disturbed that there was no effort to place the atomic bombing into the proper context of the Pacific War. There was absolutely no mention of pre-war Japanese militarism or of the nation's brutal conquests of China, Southeast Asia, the Philippines, and other Pacific islands. Nor was there any information about rampant Japanese war crimes in Nanking or the Japanese army's brutal occupation policy of "loot all, kill all, burn all."[151] There was nothing about the surprise attack on Pearl Harbor or the kamikaze offensive launched against the United States navy during the 82-day battle of Okinawa, which had resulted in over 72,000 American casualties.[152] Although modern Japan is not the same country, and has renounced its previous militarism, it is a dangerous thing to sanitize the past. That, too, was one of the important lessons I took from my visit to Hiroshima.

The following day, Mr. Asai and I left Hiroshima on board Super Express bullet train Kozomi #6 en route to the city of Kyoto. There I addressed the National Congress of Parents and Teachers Association of Japan. I also had the opportunity to visit several nearby middle and high schools. I was particularly impressed with the strong emphasis on English language instruction. Rather than having the students memorize and recite fixed, unrealistic dialogues, most of

the schools that I visited employed young native speakers from the United States, Great Britain, Canada, or Australia to assist the classroom teacher by engaging in actual conversation with the students. This greatly improved the students' vocabulary and increased their confidence in their ability to communicate.

At Koyodai High School in Osaka, I helped the class practice their English greetings. Each of the students would individually come up to the front of the class and shake my hand while introducing themselves. One particularly ambitious young man even added to his greeting the phrase, "I do not like to study."

An English language class in Osaka. I was impressed by how well Japanese students learned English. (Philip Bigler)

The final stop on my itinerary was a visit to TJ's sister school, Chiben Wakayama High School. I had been asked beforehand to prepare a PowerPoint presentation and to address the students in the school's brand new lecture hall. Many of these young people had already visited Jefferson the previous year as part of our international exchange program organized by our school's Japanese language teacher, Jim Fujita. I was confident in the students' English abilities and actually knew several of them personally. Still, the room was arranged with permanent stadium style seating, which made it a bit awkward and difficult to have any meaningful interaction. Likewise, in this traditional setting, the students refused to speak in class, but as soon as I finished with my lecture, they encircled me and began to ask questions. They were all laughing and joking just like their typical American teenager counterparts. It was great fun and I asked them to tell me what their favorite thing in the United States was. Without hesitation, they shouted in unison, "Taco Bell."

I had to leave Japan on October 6th and returned home via Detroit on Northwest Airlines. I was fighting a bad cold, but there was no time to recuperate since I had to attend a three day teacher forum in Washington beginning the very next day. There were also two upcoming cross country trips to California as well as speaking engagements in Wisconsin, Florida, Georgia, and South Carolina. Likewise, I had several writing deadlines which had to be completed before the Thanksgiving holidays.

As hard as it was to believe, the next selection cycle for the national teacher was well underway. In late October, I was asked to participate on the panel in Virginia to choose its new state teacher. We carefully analyzed and reviewed the resumes and credentials of the eight teacher candidates. Clearly, they were all talented, dedicated and well-qualified but our panel reached a solid consensus that Linda Koutoufas should be our 1999 Virginia Teacher of the Year. She was a dynamic elementary school teacher from Virginia Beach and would represent the Commonwealth well.

On the evening of the formal announcement of Linda's selection, Governor Jim Gilmore hosted an elegant reception for all of the recognized teachers at the Executive Mansion in Richmond. Located on the impressive grounds of the Virginia State Capitol, the antebellum house was built in 1813 and is recognized as one of the most historic structures in the nation. It was an impressive venue to honor and celebrate our state's most outstanding educators.

A few months later, I joined Linda Koutoufas in Dallas and had the opportunity to meet the other State Teachers of the Year. I also had the opportunity to talk with the newly announced finalists and to share with them some of my amazing experiences at National Teacher just as Sharon Draper had done the previous year.

Although January was a relatively light month for travel, I did have an appearance on Dr. Robert Schuller's "Hour of Power" in Garden Grove, California scheduled. My wife, Linda, was able to accompany me on this trip, but since she was enrolled in a graduate course at George Mason University, we weren't able to leave Washington until late Saturday afternoon. Our plans called for us to fly into San Diego and then rent a car and drive to Newport Beach, where we would spend the night at the luxurious Four Seasons Hotel. The taping would take place early the following morning at the Crystal Cathedral.

It seemed to be a straightforward trip. We had a direct flight to California although the plane was due to stop briefly in Dallas before continuing on to San Diego. By now, I was comfortable with travel and could efficiently pack for trips in a matter of minutes. Jon, though, had always insisted that I dress professionally while traveling, as a precaution. If something unexpected happened, I would then still be prepared to speak without having to change clothes. I usually heeded his advice but, in truth, I had become somewhat complacent. I decided that for this long, cross country flight, I would dress comfortably. Instead of wearing my customary blue blazer and chinos, I opted for casual jeans, tennis shoes, and an extremely well-worn sweater.

Everything seemed routine as we made on our final approach into the Dallas/Fort Worth airport. Then the flight attendant announced that due to inclement weather in the Midwest, dozens of aircraft had to be repositioned to accommodate the resulting cancellations. Our plane was one of those that would have to be redirected, so the airline had already rebooked us on an alternative flight to San Diego. The unexpected delay meant that we would not arrive in California until well after midnight. It was inconvenient and frustrating but this was part of the realities of winter airline travel. There was no point in complaining even though upon arrival, Linda and I were still facing an additional two hour drive. It promised to be a long and sleepless night.

Our replacement plane took off a couple of hours later and we arrived in San Diego without further incident. We quickly retrieved Linda's luggage but had to wait while the other bags were slowly disgorged onto the conveyer belt. After about 20 minutes, the baggage claim area was virtually deserted when the belt suddenly came to a stop. My suitcase with my suit and all of my dress clothes was not there.

I went over to an American Airlines agent and implored her to check on the status of my lost luggage. After searching for a few minutes on her computer, she informed me that my bag had been sent to Denver and that the airline could not retrieve it until the following afternoon. It was a disaster, since I was not appropriately dressed for an important television appearance and "The Hour of Power" was internationally syndicated to a global audience of over two million people.[153]

There was nothing left to do at the airport except get our rental car and directions to the nearest Walmart. I still held out hope that I could buy some new clothes but unfortunately, by the time we arrived the store had already closed for the night. We drove up to Newport Beach and arrived at the Four Seasons around 3 AM. I was exhausted but still decided to seek out the hotel's gift shop. It was not due to reopen for another four agonizing hours, so Linda and I went up to our room to try and get a little sleep.

It was a short night and I was up a 6 AM. I used my complementary toiletries to shave before going downstairs where I waited until the gift shop manager opened the store. Most of his inventory was golf attire but at this point, fashion was no longer an issue. I purchased a long sleeve knit shirt, a tie, and a sweater vest and hardly flinched when the bill came to over $400. Still, there was nothing I could do about my jeans and tennis shoes so I called the producer at the Crystal Cathedral and explained my dilemma. She was understanding and reassured me that she could find a sports coat for me to wear. Likewise, she would instruct the cameramen to film me from the waist up so the television audience would not see my blue jeans. Unfortunately, there was nothing to do to disguise my attire from the live congregation in the church itself.

After I changed into my new clothes, Linda and I then drove over to the Crystal Cathedral. Dr. Schuller had begun his ministry in 1955 and originally preached in an old drive-in movie theater. As his congregation expanded, he built the Crystal Cathedral, which was dedicated in 1980 and is an architectural wonder, consisting of over 10,000 individual panes of glass. The grounds also contained the production studio where we met with the program's producer who had procured a 44-long jacket for me. It was way too big but I found that if I crossed my arms, it helped disguise the size problem and didn't look too bad.

The service began with the singing of a few hymns and the playing of Beethoven's "Ode to Joy" on the Cathedral's pipe organ. Dr. Schuller then offered a prayer and introduced me as his special guest to the congregants. To my mortification, he immediately kidded me about my attire. It was an opportunity, though, for me to elaborate on my predicament by telling a humorous anecdote. Bob Hope, I explained, had once gone up to an airline ticket counter and asked to purchase a one way ticket from Los Angeles to New York. He then added that he wanted to have his luggage sent to London. The attending

Linda and I with Dr. Robert Schuller at the Crystal Cathedral. The airline lost my luggage so I was forced to buy clothes in the hotel gift shop. (Philip Bigler)

agent was perplexed and told him that such a thing was impossible to which Hope responded, "Why not, you did it last week!" Dr. Schuller and the congregation laughed and I went on to explain that my suitcase containing all of my dress clothes was currently in Denver.

Unlike most of my other interviews, Dr. Schuller was more interested in discussing the transcendent aspects of teaching. He especially wanted to hear about how Sister Mary Josephine had impacted my life. This was important since the secular media had been relentless in mocking and lampooning the Catholic clergy. These vocal detractors openly denigrated these people's vocations and refused to acknowledge the thousands of dedicated nuns and priests who had labored in American parochial schools for generations. They often worked in modest school buildings with minimal amounts of supplies and taught from graffiti laden textbooks. It was not money or materials that guaranteed a good education, it was these devoted teachers' personal commitment to high standards and substance.

It was certainly true that the parochial schools benefited from a supportive parental community. Indeed, Catholic parents willingly sacrificed and deferred their own personal gratification in order to provide for their children's schooling. This commitment remains a stark contrast to contemporary American society which is plagued by a growing number of perpetual adult adolescents who selfishly avoid any personal accountability and shun individual responsibility.

My mother and father, of course, took my brother, Bob's and my education seriously and it was our family's number one priority. This meant that we never went on exotic vacations and didn't have very many luxuries. In order to afford the tuition that was required to support the parish schools, my father took on a second job delivering hundreds of newspapers for the *Los Angeles Times*. Every morning, he got up at 4:00 AM and drove to the distribution center where he would fold hundreds of newspapers before loading them into the back seat of the family Oldsmobile. He then delivered them to the customers on his route before returning home for a quick breakfast. Afterwards, he went to his regular job at the naval air station and was routinely putting in 12-hour work days. During this time, I never heard him complain. On some weekends, my brother and I would go along with him to help out and our reward was a pre-dawn treat of fresh, hot glazed donuts at the local Winchell's. Although we were unaware of it at the time, Bob and I were actually learning a lot about my father's personal character and integrity. He was working hard so that we received a proper education and would not be academically penalized by the many moves that were necessitated by his naval service.

It was a good message to share and the program seemed to go well despite my wardrobe difficulties. From California, it was on to the national conference for the American Association of School Administrators in New Orleans as then to Columbus State University in Georgia. I loved visiting college campuses since it gave me the opportunity to work with pre-service teachers. It was energizing for me to be around them and I enjoyed their sense of idealism and enthusiasm.[154]

After a few days in Columbus, I flew to Atlanta on February 12th en route to another speaking venue in Chicago. I had a few hours in between planes and was anxious to find a restaurant where I could watch the news. The Senate was preparing to vote on two impeachment charges against President Clinton and I wanted to watch this historic, albeit tragic, event.

The entire sordid Monica Lewinsky scandal had grown progressively worse after my Rose Garden ceremony. The audio tapes and physical evidence were damning and led to the special prosecutor's office issuing a report which alleged serious misconduct on the part of the president. The House of Representatives voted to impeach President Clinton by a 234-200 majority that December. It was only the second time in American history that this had ever happened.[155]

Regardless of the nefarious motives of some, the scandal was humiliating and embarrassing. It was appalling that Bill Clinton, a man of considerable charm and talent, would forever damage his historical legacy by such a terrible lapse in judgment. Indeed, the President had always claimed that he was an avid student of history, so he should have been well aware that the pages of antiquity were littered with the political corpses of those individuals who could not resist the triumvirate of vices—power, money, and sex. Thucydides had written in his *History of the Peloponnesian War* that among the essential traits of the ideal politician were "to know what must be done and to be able to explain it; to love one's country and *be incorruptible*."

I watched with sadness as the votes on the two impeachment charges were tabulated. On the obstruction of justice charge, the Senators were equally divided with 50 votes in favor of conviction and 50 votes against. The second indictment, lying (perjury) under oath to a grand jury, failed to receive even a simple majority with 55 Senators voting "nay." The Founders, in their wisdom, had required in the Constitution a super majority of 2/3 to remove a president from office by impeachment so President Clinton was formally acquitted, although this did not exonerate his behavior. But for now, at least, the country could move forward.

My schedule certainly did, since March proved to be one of my busiest months. It included an extended four day trip to Indiana which had been arranged by Terry Wiedmer, an Associate Professor of Education at Ball State University. Terry had prepared a full and fascinating itinerary for me. It began immediately with the opportunity to speak and interact with her EDAD 600 (Introduction to Educational Leadership) class. Later in the week, I was also able to conduct a distance learning discussion with 42 graduate students who were off campus and who lived throughout the state of Indiana.

With Garfield creator, Jim Davis. (Philip Bigler)

Terry had organized a tour of a juvenile detention facility in New Castle for me where I met and talked with several of the young people who were temporarily incarcerated. All of these teenagers were in varying degrees of crisis and most had serious substance abuse and anger management problems. They had experienced constant failure and frustration while in traditional schools and,

With a group of Indiana educators while visiting PAWS, the studios where Jim Davis produces the Garfield comic strips. (Philp Bigler)

in many ways, were at a personal crossroads. Some were working on their Graduate Equivalency Diplomas (GED) and hoped to reform their lives and improve their behavior. Others, though, remain obstinate and seemed resigned to their ultimate fate. I feared that they would spend the rest of their lives in constant trouble with the law. It was a strong dose of reality and far different experience from what I typically encountered at Jefferson or in Fairfax County.

For fun, I got to visit PAWS, the production studios for Jim

Davis, the creator of the Garfield comic strip.[156] It was a place full of color and creativity where I got to see how the actual comic strip was drawn, produced, and marketed. At one point, I even had the opportunity to meet Jim Davis. He graciously drew my own personal "Garfield" cartoon which he inscribed.

As hard as it was to imagine, my tenure was rapidly drawing to a close. In April, the STOY Class of 1999 gathered in Washington to celebrate the announcement of the new National Teacher of the Year, Andy Baumgartner. Andy was a kindergarten teacher from Augusta, Georgia, and I knew that he would be a great representative of teachers.

On Tuesday, April 20th, while the STOY's were in Washington, the Columbine school shootings occurred. Twelve students and a teacher, Dave Sanders, were killed, while another twenty-three others were wounded. The national press corps immediately descended upon Columbine and in our modern era of instant news coverage continually misreported and misrepresented the story.[157] They unknowingly gave the deceased shooters exactly what they had desired—publicity. As one of them had written in his journal, "i (sic) want to leave a lasting impression on the world."[158] For Andy and the other state teachers, the Columbine tragedy would provide a somber backdrop to their White House ceremonies.

Although I still had a few weeks left before Andy formally assumed his NTOY duties, it was time to begin to refocus my attention to returning to school. It had been a wonderful year, a grand adventure, but it was time to get back to work and to teach history.

Endnotes

136 The World War II Memorial had not been completed at this point.

137 Gail Russell Chaddock. "America's Top Teacher Gets Teens Out of Their Seats and Into History," *Christian Science Monitor*, May 5, 1998, p. B-7.

138 *Ibid.*, p. B-7.

139 During those innocent years, I even had Sally Field's record album "Sally Field: Star of the Flying Nun." Remarkably, the song from the show, "*Felicidad*," is still available for download on iTunes and Amazon.com.

140 At the Kennedy Center awards I had the honor to meet Frank McCourt, the author of *Angela's Ashes*. We were backstage together for over two hours and had an extended conversation about teaching. Frank had taught English at Stuyvesant High School in New York. He would later write about his teaching career in *Teacher Man*.

141 We were individually given about 30 minutes to fly the airplane and even allowed to take off and land under the strict supervision, of course, of a skilled pilot.

142 Team CANOPUS consisted of the following members: Charlie Rossetti (Arkansas STOY), Neil Witikko (Minnesota STOY), Peggy Woods (Arizona STOY), Kim Giesting (Indiana STOY), Roberta Abaday (Guam STOY), Mary Ginley (Massachusetts STOY), Vickie Boutiette (North Dakota STOY), Patricia Randolph (Nebraska STOY), Christine Fisher (South Carolina STOY), Yvonne Ullas (Washington STOY), Philip Bigler (Virginia NTOY) and the International Teachers Peter Sorenson (Denmark), Salvador Ramirez (Mexico), Veronika Nedvedova (Czech Republic), Meg Roche (Australia)

143 This was a very thoughtful team-building experience unlike those teachers are routinely subjected to in schools. I always hated the various ice-breakers, scavenger hunts, and other drivel that were used during back-to-school faculty meetings that were supposedly designed to help us bond as a faculty. I found such activities to be trite and demeaning.

144 Mitch Albom. (1997) *Tuesdays with Morrie: An Old Man, a Young Man, and Life's Great Lesson.* New York: Doubleday.

145 I tried playing the game but I never could understand the goal or purpose.

146 Although I was unaware of it at the time, Joetsu had been the site of an infamous prison-of-war camp where American Olympian and aviator, Louis Zamperini, was held during World War II. His story was told in the bestselling

book, *Unbroken: A World War II Story of Survival, Resilience, and Redemption* by Laura Hillenbrand. Interestingly, Laura was a student at Bethesda-Chevy Chase High School when I was teaching there, although I did not have her in any of my classes. She has become an exceptional writer and her books are highly readable and are perfect for high school history students. According to Laura, "...on the site of the former Naoetsu camp, the peace park was dedicated [in 1995]. The focal point was a pair of statues of angels, flying above a cenotaph." p. 394.

147 I had been given a survey that had been conducted in Japan which compared the attitudes of Japanese and American schools towards their teachers. Interestingly, Japanese students rated their teachers higher than American students in content knowledge but American teachers scored significantly higher on such topics as "Understanding Education," "Motivating Students," "Bringing out a student's Individual Characteristics," and "Being Accessible."

148 In Virginia, students study the colonial period extensively in 4th grade and the American Civil War in middle school. Even though the content in high school is more sophisticated, I felt that it was important to give them exposure to material they had never studied.

149 Many would date the dawn of the nuclear age to July 16, 1945 when the atomic bomb was successfully tested in New Mexico. I have intentionally chosen to use the later bombing of Hiroshima since the initial test was top secret and unknown to the general populace. MediaOutlet.com sells an inexpensive DVD of many of the duck and cover information films that were regularly shown to school children during the 1950s.

150 The Stanley Kubrick film, *Dr. Strangelove*, is a dark comedy about the atomic age. For contemporary students to fully understand the film's humor, though, requires a good deal of background knowledge but it is well worth the effort.

151 Iris Chang's book, *The Rape of Nanking, the Forgotten Holocaust of World War II,* is an excellent source for information about the Japanese conquest of China. It is conservatively estimated that 1.5 million Chinese died directly at the hands of the Japanese army and that an additional 19 million died as a result of starvation.

152 It was estimated by American military planners that if an invasion of the Japanese home islands was required, it would take until 1947 to win the war. In the meantime, the United States armed forces were expected to incur over one million casualties.

153 "The Hour of Power" was seen in all fifty states as well as in New Zealand, Australia, the Philippines, Russia, and Europe.

154 Over the course of the year I visited the University of Virginia, Hollins University, Columbus State University, the University of Wisconsin, Elon University, Trinity College, Norfolk State University, Ball State University, the University of Indiana, James Madison University, and George Mason University.

155 Andrew Johnson had been impeached by the House in 1868 for violation of the Tenure of Office Act. The House Judiciary Committee recommended impeachment charges against Richard Nixon for misdeeds during the Watergate scandal but the President resigned before the House could vote on the committee's recommendations.

156 Interestingly, both Jim Davis and David Letterman are Ball State alumni.

157 Dave Cullen's book, *Columbine*, is the definitive source about the school shooting (It was actually intended to be a bombing but the improvised propane devices failed to detonate). The media quickly decided that this ultimate story was about student bullying and student misfits. This was not true but these stories remain entrenched in the public memory. See Dave Cullen, (2009) *Columbine*. New York: 12 Publishers.

158 *Ibid.*, p. 236.

CHAPTER XI

Panem et Circenses

As wrote the wit Aristophanes, roughly translated: 'Youth ages, immaturity is outgrown, ignorance can be educated and drunkenness sobered—but stupid lasts forever.'

William Hundert from *The Emperor's Club*

I happily returned to my classroom in August 1999 and was once again enjoying teaching my regular allotment of history and humanities classes at Jefferson. My year as National Teacher of the Year had been an incredible experience and I had gained a lot of perspective, both good and bad, about the status of American education. I now realized with clarity that with my public recognition came an enormous responsibility and I wanted to do all I could to help improve the quality of education for all of our nation's students. I was particularly interested in working with pre-service teachers, since many of these young educators were struggling and found it difficult to make the sometimes awkward transition from the theoretical world of academia to the stark realities of the American classroom. The attrition rate for neophyte educators was disgraceful, with fully half of all new teachers leaving the profession within the first five years. As a result, our public schools were hemorrhaging talent and something had to be done to stop this appalling trend.

Along with my normal teaching duties at Jefferson, I continued to have numerous professional obligations outside of school. I was constantly being asked to speak at conferences and to conduct in-service workshops. Likewise, I was serving on a variety of educational commissions. In 2000, Glenda Rooney and Andy Perrine asked me to become an alumni member of a planning committee at JMU to help organize the campus-wide commemorations for the 250th anniversary of James Madison's birth. It was during one of my frequent visits to Harrisonburg that year that I was informed that a search committee had been established to find a new director for the university's fledgling James Madison Center. The Center's original mission had been to serve as a scholarly and academic resource on James Madison, but its focus could easily be modified to include more student interaction as well as expanded to work with public school teachers throughout the state. Both Glenda and Andy urged me to apply for the position.

It was an extremely exciting prospect and it seemed like the ideal job. But I still hesitated since I was content with my current teaching assignment and comfortable professionally. Moreover, I loved working with high school students but I realized that such an opportunity may never come again. So after consulting with my wife, Linda, I decided to go ahead and submit my resume for consideration. It took several weeks, but I was eventually granted an interview with the entire search committee and was asked to make a formal presentation to the university's faculty. After doing all of this, I still had to wait several more weeks while the committee reached its final decision. Although it was frustrating, such a delay was actually quite common, since colleges move at glacial speed when it comes to making important staff decisions. Ultimately, though, I was offered the job and I returned to JMU for the start of the fall 2001 semester. It was the beginning of a new and exciting chapter in my life as a career educator.

One of my first initiatives as the director of the James Madison Center was to create the 1787 Society.[159] This student organization was open to all JMU undergraduates who maintained a minimum 3.0 grade point average and who submitted the required essay and faculty recommendations. The society's primary responsibility was to serve as an advisory panel for me at the Center and to assist with the organizing of our campus-wide activities including the university's annual commemorations of Constitution Day (September 17) and James Madison's birthday (March 16). As a prerequisite for membership, the 1787 students also committed to take my History 316 seminar class, "The Life and Times of James Madison, 1751-1836."

My course chronicled Madison's life and career within the greater context of American history. Madison was born as a British subject in 1751 during the reign of King George II of England. He grew to adulthood during the crises years preceding the American Revolution and would later serve in the Confederation Congress. He played a central role in the drafting of both the United States Constitution and the Bill of Rights and served with distinction as Thomas Jefferson's Secretary of State. Madison was elected to the presidency in 1808, but his tenure was marked by

Members of the 1787 Society at James Madison University during Constitution Day commemorations on the student commons. (Philip Bigler)

Speaking in front of the James Madison statue on the anniversary of Madison's birth, March 16, 2009. (Philip Bigler)

the continuing deterioration in foreign relations with both Britain and France. In 1812, Madison formally requested that Congress declare war against England and during the ensuing conflict, the nation's new capital of Washington, D.C. was sacked and burned by the British army. Despite the physical devastation and national humiliation, Madison's administration successfully negotiated a peace treaty that ended the conflict on honorable terms. What followed was an unprecedented three decades of peace, our *Pax Americana*.

After serving two terms in office, Madison gladly retired from public life in 1817 and returned home to the Virginia Piedmont. He was destined to live another 19 productive years, during which time he was active in the founding of the University of Virginia. In his twilight years, though, Madison witnessed with dismay the continuing growth of sectionalism and the resulting political division caused by the expansion of slavery. He died during the presidency of Andrew Jackson on June 8, 1836 at the age of 85 and was the last of the great founding generation.[160]

Although Madison's historical legacy is often obscured by the more energetic personalities of George Washington, Thomas Jefferson, Alexander Hamilton, and John Adams, his philosophical contributions to the nation continue to have profound consequences. Hence, the central question on my final exam was, "Does James Madison Matter?"[161] I had students with many divergent opinions write substantive, compelling essays that justified their own individual views. They were learning to form their own opinions based upon an accurate assessment of facts.

One of JMU's greatest strengths as a university has been the premium it has traditionally placed on its undergraduate program and quality instruction. Despite the university's ongoing growth and evolution, the College of Education (COE) has remained JMU's premier department. Each year, the COE graduates hundreds of talented and promising teachers, and I was given the opportunity to work with many of these young people by teaching a class section of EDUC 360, "Foundations of American Education."

The "Foundations" course is considered to be a gateway class for prospective teachers and it is required for eventual teacher licensure in Virginia. The course is designed to help interested students decide whether or not a career in public education is right for them. Class topics include such things as school administration, finances, and law as well as current trends in education policy. Likewise, students are given detailed instruction on the history and development of public education in the United States. They also learn about the numerous responsibilities and expectations of teachers, such as course planning, in-service development, classroom discipline, and professional ethics. Ultimately, the students are expected to develop and write their own personal education philosophies, but this comes with the understanding that their perspective could well change as they continue through their own course work and careers.

With my many professional contacts, I was able to invite a variety of guest speakers to campus to talk with my students. These included principals, guidance counselors, police officers (gang task force) as well as Virginia Teachers of the Year and Milken National Educators. One of the course highlights each year was when Virginia's former Superintendent for Public Instruction, Dr. Jo Lynne DeMary, visited the class. The students were thrilled to meet such an important dignitary, and her remarkable professional story served as an inspiration and a validation of the teaching profession.

During the summer while most of the JMU students were on break, I worked as the associate director of the Monticello-Stratford Seminar. This three week professional development program for American history teachers was affectionately known as "Straticello" by the participants, and its primary focus was to help educators assess the pertinent factors that led to Virginia's prominent role in the American Revolution and subsequent Federalist period.

The Straticello seminar program was a perfect forum to promote the legacy of James Madison and it allowed me to disseminate the

Stratford Hall, the home of Thomas Lee, in Westmoreland County, Virginia.
(Philip Bigler)

Center's materials and publications nationally. I also had the opportunity to work with the teachers to develop their own individual lesson plans which they could eventually use with their own classes.

Stratford Hall is located in rural Westmoreland County on Virginia's Northern Neck, a peninsula sandwiched in between the Potomac and Rappahannock Rivers.[162] The Great House was the pre-revolutionary home of Thomas Lee. Lee was the father of eight children, including Richard Henry and Francis Lightfoot, who became the only brothers to sign the Declaration of Independence. For local area residents, though, the plantation is far better known as the birthplace of the Confederate general, Robert E. Lee (1807).[163]

The teachers arrived in late June and during most of the seminar program, lived on the actual grounds of the plantation.[164] Through a generous grant from Mary Tyler Cheek McClenahan, the daughter of the renowned historian, Douglas Southall Freeman, the Cheek guest house was specially constructed to house the seminar participants

Every morning the day began with the teachers walking across the estate to the DuPont Memorial Library. There, they would attend a series of content-rich lectures presented by prominent historians and well-known scholars. We also scheduled frequent field trips throughout the program to important historical sites in Virginia, including Mount Vernon, Montpelier, Monticello, Gunston Hall, Williamsburg, Jamestown, Yorktown, Poplar Forest, and Menokin. The teachers especially enjoyed their "field day" activities at Pope's Creek (George Washington's birthplace) where they had the opportunity to master such colonial skills as sheep shearing, hoeing tobacco fields, and open hearth cooking.

The Lawn at the University of Virginia. The Straticello teachers lived in the Jefferson-designed student dormitories while staying in Charlottesville.
(Philip Bigler)

During the middle week of the program, the seminar was moved to Charlottesville. There, the teachers were granted the extraordinary privilege of living on the Lawn at the University of Virginia.[165] These original student dormitories date from the founding of the university (1819) and were personally designed by Thomas Jefferson. Each room was spartanly furnished with just a student desk, a bed, and a rocking chair, but also had the novelty of having its own working fireplace.[166] Despite Virginia's legendary summer heat, the Lawn rooms were not air conditioned. All of the bathrooms and shower facilities were discretely hidden away in separate, non-descript buildings located in the alleyways behind the rooms. These inconveniences, however, were more than offset by the ambiance of living on the grounds and having the opportunity to attend classes in the university's Rotunda.

Throughout the 28 years of its existence, the Straticello seminar attracted exemplary history teachers from across the country.[167] They were dedicated, motivated, and enthusiastic educators who were willing to give up much of their summer vacations in order

Seminar teachers capture "Augustine," the sheep, during their field day experience at Pope's Creek. (Philip Bigler)

Learning the process of growing tobacco during the Straticello Seminar program. (Philip Bigler)

to improve their content knowledge. The program also provided them with a venue to discuss their classes with their colleagues as well as the opportunity to share their various teaching strategies and ideas. During the program, each group bonded and many became close friends. One year, the seminarians declared that their official motto would be: "I would rather be historically accurate than politically correct." It effectively encapsulated these outstanding educators' desire to pursue an honest interpretation of the past and to defy those who are increasingly using the classroom as a weapon to promote their own ideological agendas. Indeed, many schools in the United States are now engaged in rampant political correctness and this comes at the expense of honest historical scholarship.

Professor Benjamin Ginsberg recounts in his book, *The Fall of the Faculty*, that on college campuses throughout the United States, "...curriculum consisting of a mix of life skills or student life courses and a set of classes and seminars...come perilously close to political indoctrination...[the] goal seems to be the transformation of students' values and beliefs on matters of race, gender, public morality, and environment, and a variety of other political topics."[168] This is hardly confined to our nation's universities, since such courses have permeated the public schools despite the courageous resistance of a few brave teachers. As a result, American students are disengaged from their course work and are oblivious to the adverse consequences resulting from their own historical illiteracy.

Americans naively believe that the United States is impervious to the economic and political turmoil that has ravaged other cultures throughout history. Political tyranny, despotic government, economic collapse, and rampant inflation can easily occur in any society when its citizenry becomes torpid and apathetic. For contemporary Americans, the historic precedent to carefully consider is that of ancient Rome.

For over 1,100 years, the epicenter of western civilization was firmly anchored along the banks of the Tiber River. It was here that a remarkable group of energetic and innovative people built a massive empire that was destined to span the entire Mediterranean basin. Its vast expanse was linked together by over 53,000 miles of paved roads, while massive stone and concrete aqueducts supplied running water to large cities and towns located miles inland. Innovative engineers constructed thousands of architectural marvels, and Roman citizenship was prized and cherished.

But with continuing economic prosperity came political corruption and complacency. Serious societal problems were ignored as devious statesmen learned that the general populace was tolerant of dishonesty and treachery so long as it was placated by full stomachs and gruesome entertainment—*panem et circenses* (bread and circuses). The Emperor Trajan (53-117 AD), for instance, staged 123 days of continuous games at the Coliseum where citizens cheered as 5,000 were slain in the arena. To add to the grisly spectacle, 11,000 animals were slaughtered in various gladiatorial contests. The empire's spiritual malaise led to widespread depravity and contributed to a general loss of civic virtue. Rome became easy prey to the more motivated barbarian hordes, and in 476 AD, the empire's collapse was total, when the once great city was pillaged and burned.

The ruins of ancient Pompei in Italy. Rome civilization collapsed in part due to spiritual decay. (Philip Bigler)

To visit Rome today is, in essence, to walk upon the grave of a lost civilization. Its many ruins provide the casual tourist with only a skeletal glimpse into the once great splendor of the Roman republic. According to an article in *National Geographic* magazine, Frank Bourne, a professor of classics at Princeton University, "...began and ended his course with the words *De nobis fabula narratur—* Their story is our story."[169] His words remain a potent warning to modern America, since far too many people are content to live their lives in utter ignorance of the past.

In 1831, the famed American landscape painter, Thomas Cole, began a series of five evocative paintings entitled, *The Course of Empire*. These canvases graphically depicted the various stages of civilization, chronicling its beginning, rise, flourishing, decline, and fall. As Robert Hughes explains in *American Visions*, "[*The Course of Empire*] were meant as a reflection on the rise and fall of civilizations, and as a warning to America about the dangers of democracy, which (he thought) could so easily degenerate into mob rule at the hands of a demagogue who, in deifying the will of the people without curbing its fickle passions, will become a dictator, an American Caesar...Cole's series was meant to be a visual analogue to Edward Gibbon's *Decline and Fall of the Roman Empire*."[170]

The most profound of Cole's five paintings is entitled *Destruction* (see front cover), which graphically depicts the annihilation of a once great civilization. "Enfeebled by luxury and excess, the imperial city has fallen," explains Hughes. "It is being sacked and pillaged by hordes of unspecified origin—vandals? Other Romans/Americans?—while its colonnades burn. The imperial bridge, which once bore Caesar in triumph, collapses under the weight of struggling armies."[171]

And yet despite the prophetic warnings of Coles and Gibbon, America is today facing a very real education Armageddon. Our students are not being sufficiently challenged in school nor are they being asked to read serious literature. In a modern world where ESPN broadcasts incessantly and the trivial is confused with the significant, contemporary students prefer the iPod to the book and the text-message to the pen. As Aleksandr Solzhenitsyn observed, "We have become hopelessly enmeshed in our slavish worship of all that is pleasant, all that is comfortable, all that is material—we worship things, we worship products."[172] As a result, there is little time left for serious study, long term projects, or deferred gratification.

Our languid culture has placed historical memory at risk and the consequences for our society are profound. As Norm Augustine observed in the *Wall Street Journal*:

> [History is the] subject in which students perform the most poorly…It's the other things that subjects like history impart: critical thinking, research skills, and the ability to communicate clearly and cogently. Such skills are certainly important for those at the top, but in today's economy they are fundamental to performance at nearly every level. A failing grade in history suggests that students are not only failing to comprehend our nation's story and that of our world, but also failing to develop skills that are critical to employment across sectors…Far more than simply conveying the story of a country or civilization, an education in history can create critical thinkers who can digest, analyze and synthesize information and articulate their findings…Now is a time to re-establish history's importance to American education. We

need to take this opportunity to ensure that today's history teachers are teaching in a more enlightened fashion, going beyond rote memorization and requiring students to conduct original research, develop a viewpoint and defend it.[173]

My entire teaching career has been devoted to fighting ignorance and to helping students understand the importance of history. I firmly believe that civilization does begin anew with each child and that is our continuing challenge as public school teachers.

De nobis fabula narratur.

The Roman Forum. (Philip Bigler)

Endnotes

159 The Society's name comes from the fact that the United States Constitution was signed in Philadelphia on September 17, 1787.

160 On March 6, 2009, the 200th anniversary of Madison's inauguration as the nation's fourth president, I published *Liberty & Learning: The Essential James Madison*. The book was intended to make Madison more accessible to contemporary readers and became a primary text for my James Madison class at JMU.

161 Although I hoped that the answer to this question was "Yes," students were free to disagree. You can make a compelling case that in contemporary America, Madison's ideas of limited government and enumerated powers are no longer relevant to a complex, modern society. Many politicians openly disdain Madison's founding principles and have used the commerce clause to justify virtually any Congressional action. Moreover, presidents have used a broad interpretation of their role as commander-in-chief to justify numerous international conflicts without any Congressional declaration of war.

162 The word "Neck" is of Cornish origin and means peninsula. Virginia's Tidewater region has three peninsulas—the lower, middle, and northern neck. Its four major rivers are the James, the York, the Rappahannock, and the Potomac.

163 Stratford openly publicizes its connection to Robert E. Lee with tourists, but Lee lived at Stratford only briefly. Still, the plantation is operated today by the Robert E. Lee Memorial Association and it was this group that was responsible for the preservation of the Great House.

164 The program was organized so that the first week was spent at Stratford and that the second week would be in Charlottesville. After a week on the Lawn at the University of Virginia, the students returned to Stratford for the final week of classes and field trips.

165 To live on the Lawn is the ultimate privilege for a University of Virginia student. There are only 54 rooms available and these are allotted on a merit basis. Some of the more famous residents of the Lawn and the Range have been Woodrow Wilson, Edgar Allen Poe, Katie Couric, Tina Fey, Ralph Sampson, and Tiki Barber.

166 The students often leave hidden messages to future residents and we discovered that in one room, there was a hidden alcove under the floor boards which contained a celebratory bottle of liquor.

167 Sadly, the seminar ended after the 2008 program due to the loss of funding from its endowment.

168 Benjamin Ginsberg. (2011) *The Fall of the Faculty: The Rise of the All-Administrative University and Why It Matters*. New York: Oxford University Press, pp. 125-126.

169 T.R. Reid. "The Making of an Empire," *National Geographic*, July, 1997, p. 12.

170 Thomas Coles' The Course of Empire Series is owned by the New York Historical Society. The five paintings in the series are available at the following web address: http://explorethomascole.org/tour/items/69/series/. Robert Hughes. (1997) *American Visions: The Epic History of Art in America*. New York: Alfred A. Knopf, p. 147.

171 *Ibid.*, p. 150.

172 Aleksandr Solzhenitsyn. (1976) *Warning to the West*. New York: Farrar, Straus and Giroux, pp. 145-146.

173 Norm Augustine. "The Education Our Economy Needs," *Wall Street Journal*, September 21, 2011, p. A17.

Appendix A

oᵢᵢᵢᵢᵢᵢᵢo

Letter from Uli Derickson to Students at Bethesda-Chevy Chase High School

May 7, 1990

Dear Mr. Bigler,

I received your letter dated April 6, 1990 and also letters from eight of your students.

It is now almost 5 years since the fateful day of June 14, 1985, when TWA flight 847 was hijacked out of Athens, Greece. I am moved and deeply honored that you and your students have taken the time and effort to write to me, and I am deeply appreciative of the book, *In Honored Glory.* In view of your kindness I am going to mention a few of the experiences in my lifetime which motivated and gave me the strength during the ordeal on flight 847. Hopefully this will be of some interest to your students.

First, I will explain how I happened to be directly involved. I was the flight purser on flight 847 on June 14, 1985. My native language is German. I am fluent in English and I can speak Arabic. These facts established me as a line of communications be-

tween the hijackers and the passengers and the crew. Neither of
the hijackers spoke English, however one did speak German.

I was born in the Sudetenland and at the end of World War II, my
mother and father and I were forced to flee from Czechoslovakia to
what is now East Germany. And then, my parents determined that
we were going to escape from there into West Germany. And we
did it, by traveling for six nights and hiding for six days. My father watched for weeks before we left. Very carefully, he studied the
changing of the guard. When the guards went for lunch, when they
went for dinner, when there were dogs, when there weren't. When,
in other words, we could safely make it—that is, unless we stepped
on a mine. So we sat out at night and we threaded our way to freedom. I was a five-year old girl then, with a bad cough. And I remember my mother putting her hand over my mouth and throwing me to
the ground when I began to cough, because she was determined that
we would make it. And we did, finally. All those days and nights in
the fields taught me and taught me well: Don't give up, no matter
how bad the situation, no matter how impossible it seems, don't give
up. And I am convinced that experience helped me to make a difference. When those terrible first moments in the airplane arrived,
I had one legacy given to me by the determination of my parents.
I didn't know if I was brave or not. But I knew I wasn't helpless.

When I was the age of your students (16 -18 years old), President John F. Kennedy fired my imagination. In fact he was the
reason I came to America. I idolized him. He represented all that
was hopeful and free to German youth, and that was why, when
I came to America, I applied not for a visitor's visa, but an immigration visa. President Kennedy had so excited my imagination about what freedom was, I was ready to turn that imagination into tangible action, and begin a whole new way of life.

A few years after I came to America I became a flight attendant.
How many of your students I wonder, have sat in a classroom and

said to themselves "I can't imagine what good this course is ever going to be for me. How can it possibly help me? What am I doing here?" I am married to a TWA pilot. Two years after we were married, he was sent to Saudi Arabia to train Saudi Arabian pilots for their National Airline. And, in a flash, I went from being a liberated American woman to being a woman in a Muslem society. After two weeks of this sort of life, I thought to myself, either I am going to go crazy, or I am going to do something productive. So, I went to school and I learned Arabic. Little did I know that 10 years later, it would save my life, and possibly the lives of 147 others.

Originally, there were three hijackers. The only one who could speak English had been bumped in Athens, because the plane was oversold. So when that terrible moment came and these two men charged at us, yelling in Arabic, all of a sudden, my Arabic came rushing back to me, and I screamed back at the hijackers—in Ar-

The grave of Navy Seabee, Robert Stethem at Arlington National Cemetery. Stethem was murdered during the hijacking of TWA Flight 847. (Philip Bigler)

abic. I yelled out—and I can remember every word: "Where are you from? I am from Germany. Can I help you?" And I wish you could have seen the reaction. Here was this western woman, shouting at them in Arabic. They probably thought they were dreaming. After the initial exchange in Arabic, I discovered that one of the hijackers was fluent in German. From that point on, communications with him was in my native language, which I translated to English for my crew members and passengers; - however, I began to think in Arabic. I had to, because I knew that those three short sentences I had spoken had detached me from everyone else, forever, and given me a terrible responsibility, besides. Before that moment, I was just anybody; now I was a line of communication.

It is my belief that any one of your students in the years to come could just as easily be handed a similar surprise or maybe even a worse one than what was handed to me on June 14, 1985—a surprise, incidentally, I would rather not have been given, but we

President Ronald Reagan meets with TWA 847 Captain John Testrake after the release of the hijacked plane's passengers. Uli Derickson served as the plane's purser and her heroic actions were credited with saving the lives of the hostages.
(Ronald Reagan Library)

can't always be choosy about what life decides to schedule for us.

I have thought about it many times since, and I have come to the conclusion that perhaps, in some perverse way, I was fortunate to be thrust into a situation in which my own personal decision became important enough to mean the difference between surviving or not. Not only for me, but for the others too. I believe, for instance, that in order to make a difference, we have to make a difference to ourselves.

And I also believe that deep down, unless there is something very badly damaged in us, we are really all survivors. If we believe we are. And as it was in my case, one person did make a difference— with help from two directions: From the past, and from above. I never prayed so hard in my life as I did during those two and a half days of captivity. They say that there are no atheists in foxholes; there aren't very many in the cabin of a hijacked airliner, either.

I appreciate freedom, too—more than I ever thought possible. Because, I tell you, you can't believe what it feels like to be held captive, under someone's total control—until it happens to you. And to have your mind terrorized and held captive, too. When that happens, you realize how precious freedom is. And that doesn't mean freedom to ignore others. That's a kind of terrorism all in itself. No, freedom implies a responsibility to others— which is liberation of your ability to make a difference. I know now, as a result of my experience, that when you are responsible for someone else other than yourself, it intensifies the fighting instinct in you. And the ability to act is the greatest freedom of all.

I have been honored by the United States Government and the Departments of the Military. So many people in America for all ethnic groups have made a difference in my life. I continue to thank them for being so supportive and for all their prayers during and following the ordeal in June 1985. The outpouring was so overwhelming and so wonderful, and so indicative of all the gifts this country bestows on all of us—not the least of which is making us feel we make a difference.

It is one of the reasons I became an American Citizen in April 1987. I am grateful for that opportunity.

I wish you and all your students success and happiness in your future lives.

God bless you all!

Uli Derickson

Uli Derickson died of cancer at the age of 60 in 1990.

Appendix B

ᵒ|||||||ᵒ

Excerpts from Nomination Letters for Teacher of the Year

The opportunity to know and work with an extraordinary educator such as Philip Bigler happens rarely in the life of any school, student, teacher, or administrator. When it does, the "heavens ring" and the word spreads instantly through the hallways of the school and neighborhoods of the community. In five short years as a history and government teacher at McLean High School, Phil Bigler's impact on his students and colleagues alike resulted in two Norma Dektor Awards for Most Influential Teacher in 1995 and 1996, selected by the senior students, and two nominations as McLean Teacher of the Year, selected by the faculty...

As soon as Phil arrived at McLean High School teaching the freshman World Civilization course and sponsoring the yearbook staff, I began hearing about how terrific he was. It was not long before students and parents began telling me about how they had become enchanted by history, a subject that had previously held little relevance to them. I began hearing about the trips of the Jefferson Historical Society, a new school club that Mr. Bigler organized to take weekend trips to the many historical sites in this region. Students told me that not only was history now their favorite subject but that they wanted to study it in college. When it was announced that Mr. Bigler would also be teaching Advanced Placement American Government, the guidance office was inundated with requests to be in his sections. In fact, the enrollment of this very difficult and demanding program instantly doubled. Students who were academically capable but had never pushed themselves to work hard were reaching for new challenges thanks to the remarkable abilities of Philip Bigler to make history truly alive.

Philip Bigler's annual presentation on the Kennedy assassination became a legend, with students and teachers from throughout the school asking to see and hear it. I loved dropping in unannounced on his classes to see what interactive historical experience the students were having. I witnessed game show formats with the contestants using an impressive buzzer and light system that Mr. Bigler had designed. The level of excitement among the students to demonstrate mastery of factual information and analytical insights was wonderful. There was never such a thing as a "dry" lecture. Every presentation featured slides, laser discs, video tapes, recordings, and music to fully envelop the students in the environment and context of the historical moment under discussion. Mr. Bigler organized frequent guest speakers. He organized joint projects with his counterpart at Langley High School in which students from each school argued one side of a current case before the U.S. Supreme Court. Each time I heard about or observed him in action, I was in awe of the quality of his teaching, the variety of learning modalities that he incorporated and the incredible preparation that all of this required. For any teacher to reach the high level of accomplishment that Mr. Bigler exhibits daily in his classroom would be a lifetime career goal. To achieve this in tandem with his other professional accomplishments truly defies imagination…

Elizabeth Lodal
Principal, McLean High School

Phil is the kind of teacher we should all aspire to be. He is a powerful, dynamic and charismatic presence in the classroom. His wealth of knowledge, his warmth and caring, and his clear values have earned him the respect of students and colleagues alike. Year after year he is asked by students to speak at National Honor Society functions and graduation ceremonies. In a field where style is often glorified over substance, where sheer numbers seem to prohibit individual attention, and where the margins between right and wrong often become blurred, Phil emerges as a model educator and a truly gifted teacher of history.

As a classroom instructor for nearly two decades, the author of four books, and a former historian for Arlington National Cemetery, Phil knows his subject matter better than any high school teacher I have ever worked with or observed. More importantly, he is able to share this knowledge with his students in a way that helps them not only learn facts and figures but also make important connections between past and present. Ancient history comes alive through the use of simulations, role playing, multimedia lectures and group projects. Students do such things as build models of Greek temples, write issues of *The Roman Times*, put on medieval banquets, and create fact-based videos on the Islamic religion. Our freshmen had fun in Phil's class, but they also worked hard; and the high quality of their products was a tribute to the standards Phil set and his ability to motivate and inspire.

Phil motivates students not only with a profoundly personal engagement of history but also with a strong sense of caring for his students as individuals. In sum, they care deeply about him. When a student's beloved cat was run over by a car, Phil wrote the girl a personal note and insisted that I do the same. His letter was both sincere and sensitive; nothing about it was perfunctory. A gesture such as this might seem insignificant by itself, but the consistency of Phil's caring and the cumulative effect of his compassion cannot be underestimated. Without question, Phil is one of the kindest people I have ever met.

Finally, Phil's clear sense of ethics makes him a compelling figure in the classroom. I found myself mesmerized watching him interact with students on ethical issues. Phil insists that students treat each other and their teachers with respect. He cares that they make good decisions in their lives, and he helps students understand that even such simple actions as being on time to class or taking the trouble to make up a test are measures of one's character and form a foundation for future success.

Phil himself practices what he preaches without the hypocrisy that often plagues modern role models. He is trustworthy, reliable, and honest. He does what he says he will do and does it better than you would ever expect. He is one of the few people I know I can count on when I need help, and his energy for helping seems endless.

Priscilla Boyle
English Teacher and Teaching Partner

With a resume that includes impressive titles, such as the author of four books, a former Arlington Cemetery historian, and a teacher with twenty year's experience, it is easy to see how qualified Mr. Phil Bigler is to receive this year's Agnes Meyer Outstanding Teacher Award. But to judge Mr. Bigler's competency solely on these impressive achievements would be an injustice, because there is a lot more than knowledge to Mr. Bigler in the classroom: imagination, commitment and love.

Simulations, Jeopardy, mock trials, conventions, and elections, projects and field trips. Sound like fun? You bet it is. When I first met Mr. Bigler in the fall of 1991, as I sat in my first high school history class, I looked around at the classroom. As it was then, and continued to be over the next four years, completely decorated in Americana, political memorabilia, campaign signs, and posters, corresponding to the subject matter, it was impossible to remain disinterested. Throughout my high school career, I sat in a total of four of Mr. Bigler's classes: an introductory history class, two yearbook classes, and a government class. During this time, I was a citizen of a Greek polis, filmed *Antigone* and *1001 Arabian Nights*, ate hummus, and was a Roman Jeopardy finalist. Senior year, I tried to balance the budget, represented Missouri (which is the "Show-Me" state, in case you were wondering) in the "1995" GOP convention and endorsed Warren Rudman as the Republican candidate. I also helped run Kennedy's 1960 campaign in a computer simulation, and defended the eighth amendment in front of the "Supreme Court" (Mr. Bigler). By the time I'd graduated I'd been through weekend tours of Colonial Williamsburg and Arlington Cemetery, courtesy of tour-guide Bigler. And since our yearbook camp happened to be in Pennsylvania, we of course went to explore the historic Gettysburg battlefields during our free time. Needless to say, by the time the government AP exam rolled around at the end of senior year, students were extraordinarily well prepared; one student said afterwards, "even though he wasn't there, I could hear Mr. Bigler's voice telling me the answers.

In yearbook, Mr. Bigler challenged us to set high goals for ourselves and our work. Then he equipped us with the means to achieve them. We were all trained to be good writers, photographers, designers, editors, teammates. Under Mr. Bigler's tutelage we were introduced to innovative and up-to-date technology, and quickly became proficient in not only standard word-processing, but specialized design applications.

There was a wall in Mr. Bigler's room dedicated to past students, "the wall of fame," which we were promised a spot on if we behaved and performed well. The criteria were simple: honesty, kindness, respect and hard work, all of the elements of good citizenship and humanity. Act accordingly, and you would succeed both in class and in life. Mr. Bigler always reminded his students that there are two paths in life, the high and the low, and that once you find yourself on the wrong path, it's never easy to get back on the right one. In class, Mr. Bigler eagerly discussed ethical, both historical and contemporary, issues. One former student, now a sophomore at UVA, told me, "I often find myself thinking about a lot of the things Mr. Bigler said back then."

He welcomed students to speak to him when they found themselves in a moral dilemma, or needed help resolving personal problems. Mr. Bigler is special because he allows himself to be more than a teacher and a mentor: he allows himself to be a trusted confident and close friend.

Amanda Neville
Former Student

I first met Mr. Bigler my freshman year at McLean High School. He taught my World Civilizations history class. From the first day that I walked into his class as a freshman, I felt at ease with him. It was easy to see that he was dedicated to teaching because of all the new and inventive ways he came up with to enhance the curriculum. One of my most vivid memories of his class would have to be the simulations he used to help the class better understand the time period we would be studying.

Mr. Bigler's approach to teaching history was very different. He focused on the past cultures and ways of life, not just on dates. Through the simulations, it felt as if we went back in time and actually witnessed what was going on. His class was very "hands on." Mr. Bigler assigned many projects, but every member of the class would have a different twist to it, so that when we presented it we would learn new facts from each other. I looked forward to attending his class every day because he always made it so interesting and his lectures never came straight out of a textbook.

The new approaches to teaching did not stop with my class. Over the four years I watched Mr. Bigler change his lesson plans so that they were more personal to each class. I remember during my junior year, when I walked into his World Civilizations History class, he was having a huge luncheon banquet. I felt that I had traveled back in time because the room was decorated with the students' medieval projects, Madrigal music played in the background. And everyone was laughing. It was time for the students to present their project. There were wandering minstrels, lectures, and entertainment. In just one unforgettable class period, they learned about the culture and history surrounding that period.

Throughout my four years in high school, I also got to know Mr. Bigler on a more personal level. He was the yearbook advisor. At the end of my freshman year as a staff writer, Mr. Bigler asked me if I would like to be a section editor. By my senior year, I was the editor-in-chief of the publication and we worked together closely. Every time there was a deadline, he was with us until the building closed for the night. He worked so hard to upgrade the computers and get new ones so that everything was done on computer. We had an amazing book, thanks to Mr. Bigler. Whenever someone had a problem, Mr. Bigler was always there, whether it had to do with the yearbook, school, or was a personal issue. He was so approachable...

It was an honor for me to have had Mr. Bigler as a teacher and advisor. He is a terrific teacher and friend. There has never been a more dedicated, caring, and trusting person. Everyone he comes in contact with can vouch for that, especially his students. Mr. Bigler was elected by my class to be our Convocation speaker because he truly inspired us. He accepted nothing less than excellence from all of us, and he worked with us every step of the way to achieve that.

Emily Wu
Former Student

Appendix C

Philosophy of Education

An old proverb asserts that "Civilization begins anew with each child." As an educator, I have found this statement to be both a vision of optimism as well as a dire warning. On one hand, our students are the intellectual heirs to Plato, Aristotle, Augustine, and Newton; the inheritors of a rich legacy of human progress traversing three millennia. Conversely, if we fail to successfully teach and educate our young people, we are just one generation removed from barbarism. I have always seen my role as a teacher to facilitate student learning in what will be their life-long quest for knowledge, to help ignite in students the spark of enlightenment, to motivate their interest, and to cultivate their minds.

These are no small goals, especially given the numerous distractions that daily bombard modern teenagers. Indeed, television, our greatest rival for their attentions, seems to proselytize situational ethics, blurring distinctions between right and wrong while even the nightly news has been reduced to little more than tabloid journalism which sensationalizes tragedy and makes the casual viewer immune from the horrors of evil. The public schools are routinely accused of exacerbating this lamentable situation by being "value neutral" in its curricula. However, I have been fortunate to teach in schools in Fairfax County where the reverse is true and where the faculty has a strong commitment to imparting proper values and ethics. These societal norms are not culturally biased but instead convey the basic ways in which human beings interact with one another. Respect, honesty, and responsibility are just a few of the expectations that I have for my students, and as a history and government teacher, I have a unique opportunity to show how ethical values have impacted people over the centuries. There are countless illustrative stories that have powerful lessons which convey meaning to our students' lives—stories of triumph and tragedy, of heroes and villains, of right and wrong. As President Harry Truman once surmised, "The only thing new in life is the history you don't know.

In my classroom, I make extensive use of historical simulations. Students participate in a wide variety of activities in my courses: they become members of a Greek *polis* living in Periclean Athens; they take a caravan to Mecca while learning Islamic history; they debate the issues facing 19th Century women at the Seneca Falls Conference; they wage a fierce computer simulation of the dramatic 1960 presidential campaign; they write detailed letters based upon a historical persona and argue the minute details of Constitutional law in mock trials. These units make the past come alive while empowering students first by making them partially responsible for their own education and secondly, by emphasizing important research, writing, and public speaking skills. The simulations are, in fact, quite rigorous academically and are content-driven. I am a firm believer that a student should and must know something after completing my class and I have found that those among us who constantly lower their teaching standards in an effort at accommodation, in the end only succeed in reinforcing mediocrity.

I also believe that reading should be a major component of all Social Studies courses. It has been accurately observed that books are to the historians what test tubes are to the scientist. Reading remains the primary way we learn and accumulate knowledge and although all of the new computer technology, from CD-ROMs to the Internet, is exciting and has a valid role in the classroom, for a student who cannot read, there will be little benefit from even these high motivational devices. Steve Allen put it succinctly in the preface of his book, *Meeting of Minds*, "For the man who cannot read, Dostoevski and Bacon might as well have lived on another planet, Aristotle and Aquinas might as well have never been born." Over the course of a year, my students are assigned several outside readings to supplement their textbooks. These have included James Michener's *The Source*, John F. Kennedy's *Profiles in Courage*, Michael Shaara's *The Killer Angels*, Christopher Matthews' *Hardball*, and Peggy Noonan's *What I Saw at the Revolution*. Likewise, students are encouraged to read other important works outside of the classroom environment, for both credit and personal enlightenment. I have tried to convince them that there is nobility and dignity in spending a Saturday night at home with a book.

I was once told by my principal that to be a teacher is to be forever an optimist. My educational philosophy is based upon this crucial fact and is grounded in the belief that all students can and should learn. I also have come to believe in an educational system where excellence is expected and quality the norm.

NOTE: Ayn Rand eloquently explained the importance of developing a philosophy in a speech to the West Point Corps of Cadets entitled, "Philosophy: Who Needs It?"

"But the principles you accept (consciously or subconsciously) may clash with or contradict one another; they, too, have to be integrated. What integrates them? Philosophy. A philosophic system is an integrated view of existence. As a human being, you have no choice about the fact that you need a philosophy. Your only choice is whether you define your philosophy by a conscious, rational, disciplined process of thought and scrupulously logical deliberation —or let your subconscious accumulate a junk heap of unwarranted conclusions, false generalizations, undefined contradictions, undigested slogans, unidentified wishes, doubts and fears, thrown together by chance, but integrated by your subconscious into a kind of mongrel philosophy and fused into a single, solid weight: self-doubt, like a ball and chain in the place where your mind's wings should have grown." (March 6, 1974)

Appendix D

Speech to the National Teacher of the Year Selection Panel

March 2, 1998

I t is an honor and a pleasure for me to speak to you today at this special forum to celebrate education, public schools, and teaching. I have been privileged to be part of this wondrous profession for over 20 years and I have come to believe that our public schools are the greatest hope for our nation's posterity and political well-being. Our schools continue to represent the most cherished and precious ideals of American democracy, for we teachers are committed to educating each and every child regardless of income, race, ethnicity, mental or physical impairment, or any other pre-existing condition.

It wasn't always so.

In the late 17th Century, the royal governor of the Virginia colony, William Berkeley, saw public education as a dangerous threat to the established order. He wrote, "I thank God, there are no free schools nor printing [in Virginia], and I hope we shall not have these [for a] hundred years; for learning has brought disobedience, and heresy…into the world, and printing has divulged them, and libels against the best government. God keep us from both."

Fortunately, a century later, wiser minds prevailed. Abigail Adams believed that a general education was vital to both the health and well-being of the nation. "Youth is the best season wherein to acquire knowledge," she wrote, "tis a season when we are freest from care, the mind is then unencumbered and more capable of receiving impressions than in an advanced age—in youth the mind is like a tender twig, which you may bend as you please, but in age like a sturdy oak and hard to move."

In 1786, Thomas Jefferson, the sage of Monticello and arguably the greatest man of this millennium, urged the Virginia state legislature to establish a universal system of free public schools and that these facilities be made available to rich and poor alike. His vision was partially realized with the establishment of the University of Virginia in 1819. Its mission continues to serve as a model for all academic institutions and is a powerful inspiration for educators: "This institution will be based on the illimitable freedom of the human mind," Jefferson wrote. "Here we are not afraid to follow truth wherever it may lead, nor to tolerate any error so long as reason is left free to combat it."

Today, we teachers proudly stand firm as the caretakers of civilization, the last true bastion against the onslaught of barbarism and tyranny. Education remains the greatest gift that any society can bestow upon its people, for knowledge provides judgment in time of crisis; solace in periods of despair; perspective on occasions of joy; and in daily life—contentment. Moreover, no government, no economic condition, no person can ever deprive an educated person of their mind or of what they know.

This universal truth is readily apparent in the life of Admiral James Stockdale. At the age of 37, the United States Navy sent him back to school with virtually no restriction as to a course of study. Stockdale took advantage of this unique opportunity to pursue the humanities and while at Stanford, he confronted an age-old paradox that has confounded mankind since creation—If we inhabit a truly just universe, how is it possible for good people to come to tragic ends? Why do tyrants and dictators thrive and prosper with impunity? How can good and evil exist simultaneously?

Stockdale found many of his answers through his in-depth reading of the first century Stoic philosopher, Epictetus. *The Enchiridion,* or "Manual" provided a pragmatic and remarkably modern guide for living a virtuous life even during times of great adversity. Three years later, on September 9, 1965, Stockdale's A-4 jet fighter was shot down while on a bombing mission over North Vietnam and he was destined to remain a prisoner of war in Hanoi for the next 7 ½ years. Throughout this brutal confinement, Stockdale endured personal humiliation, daily torture, and physical degradation—and he did so alone, forcibly separated from the companionship of his fellow Americans. Despite this incomprehensible ordeal, Stockdale credits his humanities education and his reading of Epictetus for helping him to persevere and to survive.

The truth is that our own education is a continuous process and that we learn the important lessons of life only through hard work and by tackling difficult tasks. No one can accurately predict what the future holds or what lessons taught in school or gleaned from reading a book will ultimately hold relevance.

Several years ago, I was teaching a class in Contemporary Issues. One of our ongoing topics was the issue of terrorism. At the beginning of each class, I would post a computer printout of incidents that had occurred the previous day throughout the world. The sheer number of terrorist attacks was staggering and they seemed to transcend virtually all geographical boundaries and political systems. Finally, we decided to focus on one specific event, the hijacking of TWA Flight 847, in an effort to better understand the motives and goals of such people. The plane was on a routine flight from Athens to Rome when it was seized by two armed men who had somehow eluded airport security and smuggled guns and hand-grenades onto the aircraft. For the next two weeks, the entire world's attention was transfixed as the plane and its captive passengers crisscrossed the Mediterranean. Early on, the hijackers singled out Americans and Jews for particular punishment. While the plane was on the ground at the airport in Beirut, Lebanon, they murdered a young Navy diver, Robert Stethem, and callously threw his body onto the tarmac. He is, incidentally, buried just across the Potomac at Arlington National Cemetery and his grave continues to represent the tragic human toll of terrorism. To this day, it is adorned with fresh flowers placed there by his loving parents who continue to mourn their son's loss. Robert ultimately proved to be the only fatality in this bizarre hijacking. The lives of the other passengers aboard TWA 847 were saved through the heroic efforts of the plane's purser, Uli Derickson. Virtually all of my students were fascinated by her story and many of them took the personal initiative to write to her in Arizona.

A few weeks later, Uli responded with an evocative letter that provided perhaps the most profound lesson of the entire school year. She wrote: "A few years after I came to America I became a flight attendant. How many of your students I wonder have sat in a classroom and said to themselves, 'I can't imagine what good this course is ever going to be for me. How can it possibly help me? What am I doing here?' I am married to a TWA pilot. Two years after we were married, he was sent to Saudi Arabia…and in a flash, I went from being a liberated American woman to being a woman in a Moslem society. After two weeks of this sort of life, I thought to myself, either I am going to go crazy, or I am going to do something productive. So, I went to school and I learned Arabic. Little did I know that ten years later, it would save my life, and possibly the lives of 147 others…It is my belief, that any one of your students in the years to come could just as easily be handed a similar surprise or maybe even a worse one than what was handed to me on June 14, 1985—a surprise incidentally, I would rather not have been given, but we can't always be choosy about what life decides to schedule for us." Indeed.

It is our duty as educators to establish a rigorous core of knowledge for our students in order to prepare them for the exciting challenges of the 21st Century as well as for the uncertainties of life. By the time they graduate from high school, our students should have, at minimum, studied the Declaration of Independence, the Constitution, and the Bill of Rights, along with the other great documents in American history. Moreover, they should have read Homer, Voltaire, Shakespeare, Twain, Douglass, and King, for these and other important literary luminaries represent the cumulative efforts of over 3,000 years of human civilization. It was no mere coincidence that as a boy living on the remote frontier, Abraham Lincoln read Thucydides' *History of the Peloponnesian War*. Later, as president, when he faced a similar dramatic struggle, Lincoln could recall that the great Pericles had once stood before the dead of Athens and there justified his city-state's bloody struggle with Sparta as a holy crusade to preserve Hellenic culture. So, too, in 1863, Lincoln would stand at Gettysburg at the new national cemetery and in 272 carefully crafted words, poetically explain the Union cause and the necessity of continued sacrifice so that "...government of the people, by the people, and for the people shall not perish from the earth." As Harry Truman once so accurately observed, "The only thing new in life is the history that you don't know."

The word "school" is derived from the Greek root meaning "leisure." Some 2,500 years ago, for a brief moment in time, the center of civilization was anchored on the shores of the Aegean. There, a remarkable group of people established a society where learning was seen as a virtue and where knowledge was a daily pursuit. To be a teacher is to be forever an optimist and I believe that our own American golden age is still before us. It will be created and nurtured by a new generation of students dedicated to their own personal enlightenment and to the advancement of mankind.

Thank you.

Appendix E

oʻ|ııııʻ|ıʻo

National Teacher of the Year Rose Garden Ceremony

THE WHITE HOUSE
Office of the Press Secretary
For Immediate Release April 24, 1998

REMARKS BY THE PRESIDENT
IN HONORING THE NATIONAL TEACHER OF THE YEAR
PHILIP BIGLER

The Rose Garden
3:22 P.M. EDT

THE PRESIDENT "…You know, this is the Rose Garden, and from these steps we have, at various times, paid tribute to our bravest soldiers, our pioneering astronauts, our greatest athletes. Americans who, in offering up their personal best made our spirits soar, and sometimes changed the course of history, and in so doing, earned the title of "hero." But nothing could be more fitting than to celebrate the men and women whose great deeds are too often unsung, but who, in offering up their personal best every day, help to create those other heroes. For every soldier, every astronaut, every scientist, every athlete, every artist can thank in no small measure a teacher, or more than one, for what he or she ultimately was able to become.

In that sense, we celebrate heroes here today who build up our children and America's future. We're especially glad to honor this year's National Teacher of the Year, Mr. Philip Bigler, but all the other teachers, too. I'm sure he would be the first to say -- and I'm sure all of you would be the first to say -- that you really stand here in the shoes of tens of thousands of others who every day do their best to lift our children up. Your tools have changed over the years -- textbooks have been updated, slates have given way to computers. But the most important tools -- the heart and soul and compassion -- are still the same. The passion for opening young minds to knowledge; the unshakable faith in the potential and possibility of every child; the commitment every now and then to stay after class to help a struggling student; the vigilance to answer every child's discouraged "I can't" with a determined "Yes, you can."

Our national honoree, Philip Bigler, brings all these gifts to his history classes at, appropriately, Thomas Jefferson High School for Science and Technology in Virginia. For more than 20 years, his students haven't just studied history, they have lived it. He's transformed his classroom into a virtual time machine, challenging students to debating each other as members of rival ancient Greek city states; as lawyers before the Supreme Court; as presidential candidates named Thomas Jefferson and John Adams.

Through these historic simulations, his students have learned lessons about democracy and the meaning of citizenship, lessons that will last a lifetime -- lessons we want every American to know.

We need more teachers like Philip Bigler and all our other honorees in every classroom in America today. For it is they who can make our schools the best in the world. It is they who can guarantee that America will have another American Century in the 21st century…Now, I close with these words, so that we can give our honoree the last word: The great Daniel Webster once said, "If we work upon marble, it will perish. If we work upon brass, time will efface it. If we rear temples, they will crumble into dust. But if we work upon immortal minds, we engrave on those tablets something that will brighten to all eternity."

Thank you, Philip Bigler, for brightening those minds to all eternity. (Applause.)

PHILIP BIGLER: Thank you. Mr. President, Secretary Riley, Senator Robb, Congressman Davis, distinguished guests: Today, we bring you the good news in public education. Teachers representing all the states, the District of Columbia, Guam, Puerto Rico, the Marianas Islands and the Department of Defense are here today. They, in turn, represent the thousands of other dedicated and talented professional educators who at this very moment are working the daily miracles in our nation's classrooms. They are our country's unsung heroes, committed to teaching every child regardless of income, race, ethnicity, mental or physical impairment or any other preexisting condition. We take pride in our vocation and we join in this celebration of teaching professional excellence.

We also honor our students. And, Mr. President, today I'm very honored to have four students from Thomas Jefferson High School for Science and Technology here. I would like to introduce to you, Mr. President, representing Thomas Jefferson, their humanities classes in Fairfax County Public Schools: Sandi Lin -- Sandi, would you please stand. I would also like to introduce to you Leon Scott. Leon, would you wave since you're standing already? Katelyn Shearer, who is standing next to him. And Emily Spengler, who is over here as well. (Applause.)

Mr. President, also here is one of my other former students from McLean High School, Amanda Neville. Amanda, would you please stand? Mandy is a senior now -- (applause) -- at your alma mater, Georgetown University, and she's preparing to go on to graduate school this fall. And I'm very proud of these young people. Thank you for coming.

When I began my teaching career some 23 years ago at Oakton High School, I never dreamed that one day I would be invited to the White House and to be recognized by the President of the United States for my work as a classroom teacher. But my mother and father could, because they, like all parents, wanted the best for their children and they had the highest aspiration for us. The parents and teachers of this nation represent a powerful coalition for quality public schools, and we, working together, can assure educational excellence.

My former principal at McLean High School who is also present today, Elizabeth Lodal -- Elizabeth, please stand -- (applause) -- once imparted these words of wisdom to me. "To be a teacher," she said, "is to be forever an optimist." Each day, we teachers are privileged to glimpse the future, and I believe that our American Golden Age is still before us, and it will be a time when learning is cherished and scholars are revered.

Thank you, Mr. President, for inviting us here today and for all you're doing to support our public schools. Thank you.

Available at: http://archives.clintonpresidentialcenter.org. A DVD of the ceremony is available through CSPAN. See http://www.c-spanvideo.org/.

National Teacher of the Year

Each day, we teachers are privileged to glimpse the future, and I believe that our American Golden Age is still before us, and it will be a time when learning is cherished and scholars are revered.

Philip Bigler

Appendix F

Great Reads for Social Studies Classes

I always send reading lists home to the parents and post this information online. Likewise, I emphasize that a student's book selection must be done with parental involvement and with their permission.

Allen, Frederick Lewis. (2000) *Only Yesterday: An Informal History of the 1920's*. New York: Harper Perennial Modern Classics.

Alvarez, Everett Jr. and Anthony S. Pitch. (1989) *Chained Eagle: The True Heroic Story of Eight-And-One-Half Years as a POW by the First American Shot Down Over North Vietnam*. New York: Donald I. Fine, Inc.

Ambrose, Stephen. (1996) *Undaunted Courage: Meriwether Lewis, Thomas Jefferson, and the Opening of the American West*. New York: Simon & Schuster.

Bennett, William. (2007) *America: The Last Best Hope Volumes I & II*. Nashville: Thomas Nelson Publishers.

Berton, Pierre. (1977) *The Dionne Years: A Thirties Melodrama*. New York: W.W. Norton.

Beschloss, Michael R. (1986) *May-Day: Eisenhower, Khrushchev and the U-2 Affair*. New York: Harper & Row Publishers.

Bigler, Philip. (2009) *Liberty & Learning: The Essential James Madison*. Harrisonburg: The James Madison Center.

Bishop, Jim. (1984) *The Day Kennedy Was Shot: An Hour-by-hour Account of What Really Happened on November 22, 1963*. New York: Greenwich House.

_____. (1984) *The Day Lincoln Was Shot*. New York: Gramercy Press.

Blaine, Gerald w/ Lisa McCubbin. (2010) *The Kennedy Detail: JFK's Secret Service Agents Break Their Silence*. New York: Gallery Books.

Brands, H.W. (2006) *Andrew Jackson: His Life and Times*. New York: Anchor Press.

_____. (2002) *The Reckless Decade: America in the 1890's*. Chicago: University of Chicago Press.

Highly motivational history books encourage students to read. It is important for teachers to provide students with a choice of books for each and every unit.
(www.corbisimages.com)

Browkaw, Tom. (1999) *The Greatest Generation Speaks: Letters and Reflections*. New York: Random House.

Brown, Dee. (2007) *Bury My Heart at Wounded Knee: An Indian History of the American West*. New York: Holt Paperbacks.

Capon, Lester, ed. (1988) *The Adams-Jefferson Letters: The Complete Correspondence between Thomas Jefferson & Abigail Adams & John Adams*. Chapel Hill: University of North Carolina Press.

Caro, Robert. (2012) *The Passage of Power: The Lyndon Johnson Years*. New York: Knopf.

Carroll, Andrew, ed. (1997) *Letters of a Nation*. New York: Kodansha International.

Chang, Iris. (1997) *The Rape of Nanking: The Forgotten Holocaust of World War II.* New York: Basic Books.

Colbert, David, ed. (1997) *Eyewitness to America: 500 Years of America in the Words of Those Who Saw it Happen*. New York: Pantheon Books.

Crawford, Alan Pell. (2009) *Twilight at Monticello: The Final Years of Thomas Jefferson*. New York: Random House Trade Paperbacks.

Davis, Burke. (1982) *The Campaign that Won America: The Story of Yorktown*. New York: Eastern Acorn Press.

_____. (1988) *The Civil War: Strange & Fascinating Facts*. New York: Wings Publishers.

Douglass, Frederick. (2002) *Narrative of the Life of Frederick Douglass: An American Slave, Written by Himself*. New York: Bedford/St. Martin's Press.

DuBois, W.E.B. (2005) *Souls of Black Folks*. New York: Simon & Schuster.

Ellison, Ralph. (1995) *Invisible Man.* New York: Vintage Press.

Faust, Drew Gilpin. (2008) *This Republic of Suffering: Death and the American Civil War.* New York: Alfred Knopf.

Ferling, John. (2005) *Adams vs. Jefferson: The Tumultuous Election of 1800.* New York: Oxford University Press.

Fenn, Elizabeth. (2002) *Pox Americana: The Great Smallpox Epidemic 1775-82.* New York: Hill & Wang.

Frankl, Viktor E. (1992) *Man's Search for Meaning.* Boston: Beacon Press.

Gallagher, Hugh. (1999) *Splendid Deception: The Moving Story of Roosevelt's Massive Disability and the Intense Efforts to Conceal it from the Public.* St. Petersburg: Vandamere Press.

Grant, Ulysses S. (2006) *The Personal Memoirs of U.S. Grant.* New York: Aegypan Press.

Grunwald, Lisa and Stephen J. Adler. (1999) *Letters of the Century: America 1900-1999.* New York: The Dial Press.

Hillenbrand, Laura. (2003) *Seabiscuit: An American Legend.* New York: Ballantine Books.

_____. (2010) *Unbroken: A World War II Story of Survival, Resilience, and Redemption.* New York: Random House.

Horwitz, Tony. (1999) *Confederates in the Attic: Dispatches from the Civil War.* New York: Vintage Press.

_____. (2011) *Midnight Rising: John Brown and the Raid that Sparked the Civil War.* New York: Henry Holt & Company.

_____. (2008) *A Voyage Long and Strange: Rediscovering the New World.* New York: Henry Holt & Company.

Huxley, Aldous. (2006) *Brave New World*. New York: Harper Perennial Modern Classics.

Jakes, John. (2001) *On Secret Service*. New York: Signet.

Jefferson, Thomas. (1984) *Thomas Jefferson: Writings: Autobiography, Notes on the State of Virginia, Public and Private Papers, Addresses, Letters*. New York: Library of America.

Kennedy, Caroline. (2005) *A Patriot's Handbook: Songs, Poems, Stories, and Speeches Celebrating the Land We Love*. New York: Hyperion Publishers.

King, Martin Luther. (1990) *Letter from Birmingham Jail/I Have a Dream Speech*. New York: Perfection Learning.

Koestler, Aruthr. (1984) *Darkness at Noon*. New York: Bantham Books.

Labunski, Richard. (2008) *James Madison and the Struggle for the Bill of Rights*. New York: Oxford University Press.

Larson, Erik. (2004) *The Devil in the White City: Murder, Magic, and Madness at the Fair that Changed America*. New York: Vintage Press.

Lengel, Edward G. (2011) *Inventing George Washington: America's Founder, in Myth and Memory*. New York: HarperCollins Publishers.

Lord, Walter. (2004) *A Night to Remember*. New York: Holt Paperbacks.

Mallon, Thomas. (2012) *Watergate: A Novel*. New York: Pantheon Press.

Manchester, William. (2008) *American Caesar: Douglas MacArthur 1880-1964*. New York: Back Bay Books.

_____. (1996) *The Death of a President*. New York: BBS Publishing.

_____. (1980) *Goodbye Darkness: A Memoir of the Pacific War*. Boston: Little, Brown and Company.

Margolis, Jon. (1999) *The Last Innocent Year: America in 1964*. New York: William Morrow and Company, Inc.

Massie, Robert. (2011) *Catherine the Great: Portrait of a Woman*. New York: Random House.

_____. (2000) *Nicholas and Alexandra*. New York: Ballantine Books.

Matthews, Christopher. (1996) *Kennedy & Nixon: The Rivalry That Shaped Postwar America*. New York: Simon & Schuster.

McGinniss, Joe. (1993) *The Last Brother: The Rise and Fall of Teddy Kennedy*. New York: Simon & Schuster.

McMillan, Sally. (2009) *Seneca Falls and the Origins of the Women's Rights Movement*. New York: Oxford University Press.

McPherson, James M. (2002) *Antietam: The Battle that Changed the Course of the Civil War*. New York: Oxford University Press.

Michener, James. (1984) *The Bridges at Toko-Ri*. New York: Fawcett Publishers.

Millard, Candice. (2011) *Destiny of the Republic: A Tale of Madness, Medicine and Murder of a President*. New York: Doubleday.

_____. (2005) *The River of Doubt: Theodore Roosevelt's Darkest Journey*. New York: Anchor Books.

Miller, F. Thorton. (1991) *The Wolf by the Ears: Thomas Jefferson and Slavery*. Charlottesville: University of Virginia Press.

Minear, Richard H., ed. (1999). *Dr. Seuss Goes to War: The World War II Editorial Cartoons of Theodor Seuss Geisel*. New York: The New Press.

O'Reilly, Bill and Martin Dugard. (2011). *Killing Lincoln: The*

Shocking Assassination that Changed America Forever. New York: Henry Holt and Company.

Orwell, George. (1984) *1984.* New York: Signet Classics.

Paine, Thomas. (2005) *Common Sense and Other Writings.* New York: Barnes and Noble Classics.

Rand, Ayn. (1995) *Anthem.* New York: Plume Books.

Rowe, James. (1971) *Five Years to Freedom: The True Story of a Vietnam POW.* New York: Ballantine Books.

Shaara, M. (1996) *The Killer Angels: The Classic Novel of the Civil War.* New York: Ballantine Books.

Sides, Hampton. (2010) *Hellbound on his Trail: The Stalking of Martin Luther King, Jr. and the International Hunt for his Assassin.* New York: Doubleday Books.

Solzhenitsyn, Aleksandr. (2009) *One Day in the Life of Ivan Denisovich.* New York: NAL Trade.

Stockdale, Jim. (1995) *Thoughts of a Philosophical Fighter Pilot.* Stanford: Hoover Institute.

Swanson, James. (2010) *Bloody Crimes: The Chase for Jefferson Davis and the Death Pageant for Lincoln's Corpse.* New York: William Morrow Press.

_____. (2006) *Manhunt: The 12-Day Chase for Lincoln's Killer.* New York: HarperCollins Publishers.

Tuchman, Barbara and Robert Massie. (2004) *The Guns of August.* Novato: Presidio Press.

Washington, Booker T. (1995) *Up from Slavery.* New York: Mineola Dover Thrift Editions.

Weintraub, Stanley and Rodelle Weintraub. (2000) *Dear Young Friend: The Letters of American Presidents to Children.* Mechanicsburg, PA: Stackpole Press.

Wheelan, Joseph. (2003) *Jefferson's War: America's First War on Terror, 1801-1805*. New York: Carroll & Graf Publishers.

White, Theodore. (1961) *The Making of the President 1960*. New York: Antheneum Publishers.

Wilber, Del Quentin. (2011) *Rawhide Down: The Near Assassination of Ronald Reagan*. New York: Henry Holt and Company.

Wills, Garry. (2006) *Lincoln at Gettysburg: The Words that Remade America*. New York: Simon & Schuster.

Winik, Jay. (2006) *April 1865: The Month that Saved America (PS)*. New York: Harper Perennial.

Wolfe, Tom. (2008) *The Right Stuff*. New York: Picador Press.

Oxford University Press has published 23 titles in its *Pivotal Moments in American History* series. All of these books are written by excellent scholars and are very readable. For more information see: http://www.oup.com/us/catalog/general/series/PivotalMomentsinAmericanHistory/?view=usa

Another outstanding series is the *American Presidents* series published by Times Books. Each volume is written by a renowned historian and is a concise biography of an American president. Available at: http://www.americanpresidentsseries.com/.

Appendix G

Music and Film for Use in Social Studies Classes

Music

Many of these songs are now available as MP3 downloads or are on YouTube.

"Allentown," (2001) *Billy Joel: The Essential Video Collection*, DVD, New York: Columbia Music Video.

"The Ballad of the Green Berets," (2007) *The Ballad of the Green Berets* (Barry Sadler), CD-ROM, BMG Music.

"The Battle of New Orleans," (1987) *Johnny Horton's Greatest Hits*, CD-ROM, New York: Columbia Records.

"Born in the U.S.A.," (1990) Bruce Springsteen. *Born in the U.S.A.* New York: Sony Records

"The Death of Emmett Till," (1972) *Broadside Ballads,* Vol. I (Bob Dylan), CD-ROM, Folkway Records.

"Eve of Destruction," (2009) *The Best of Barry McGuire*, CD-ROM, Santa Monica: Geffen Records.

"If You're Reading This," (2008) *Tim McGraw's Greatest Hits* Vol. 3, CD-ROM, Nashville: Curb Records.

"Goodnight Saigon," (2001) *Billy Joel: The Essential Video Collection*, DVD, New York: Columbia Music Video.

"Leningrad," (1997) *Billy Joel: Greatest Hits Volume III*, DVD, New York: Columbia Music Video.

"Mr. Garfield," (2002) Johnny Cash. MP3 download available on Amazon.com.

"Rasputin," (1992) *Boney M: The Greatest Hits*, CD-ROM, London: BGM Records.

"Rodeo," (2003) *Copland conducts Copland*, CD-ROM, London: London Symphonic Orchestra.

(www.comstock.com)

"Should've Been a Cowboy," (2004) *The Best of Toby Keith*, DVD, Nashville: Mercury Records.

"Sink the Bismarck," (1987) *Johnny Horton's Greatest Hits*, CD-ROM, New York: Columbia Records.

"Symphony #9," (1990) *The New World*, composer Antonin Dvorak, CD-ROM, Chicago: Chicago Symphony Orchestra.

"The War Was in Color," (2006) Carbon Leaf: *Love, Loss, Hope, Repeat*, CD-ROM, New York: Vanguard Records.

"We Didn't Start the Fire," (1997*) Billy Joel: Greatest Hits Volume III*, DVD, New York: Columbia Music Video.

"We Shall Overcome," Mahalia Jackson (2001) *God Bless America*, CD-ROM, New York: Sony Music Corporation

---

*Some of these films are rated "R" and are not appropriate for uncensored use in middle or high school classrooms. There are, however, suitable chapters that can be used effectively but it is important that before using **any** film, a teacher previews the content for appropriateness and acceptability based upon community standards and in compliance with school district regulations. If a subject is controversial, it helps to send a permission slip home to parents along with the option to opt out. You should also check with your school system concerning its policies on showing videos as part of classroom instruction.*

1776, (2002) DVD, directed by Peter Hunt, Columbia Pictures.

4 Little Girls, (1997) DVD, directed by Spike Lee, HBO Home Video.

American Graffiti, (2005) DVD, directed by George Lucas, Universal Pictures.

Apollo XIII, (2008) DVD, directed by Ron Howard, NBC Universal.

Becket, (2008) DVD, directed by Peter Glenville, MPI Media Group.

The Conspirator, (2011) DVD, directed by Robert Redford, Roadside Attractions.

Dances with Wolves, (2011) DVD, directed by Kevin Costner, MGM.

Death of a Salesman, (2003) DVD, directed by Christian Blackwood, Image Entertainment.

Dr. Strangelove or: How I Learned to Stop Worrying and Love the Bomb, (1999) DVD, directed by Stanley Kubrick, Columbia Pictures.

"The Deerslayers," *The Last of the Mohicans*, (1992) DVD, directed by Michael Mann, Twentieth Century Fox.

The Flight (The Taking of Flight 847), (1988) VHS, directed by Paul Wendkos, Lions Gate Studio.

Fort Apache, (2007) DVD, directed by John Ford, RKO Radio Pictures.

Grapes of Wrath, (2004) DVD, directed by John Ford, 20th Century Fox.

Glory, (2000) DVD, directed by Edward Zwick, Columbia TriStar Home Video. (*Although this film is rated "R" for violence and language, it is still the best Civil War film ever made. It may be appropriate to have an opt-out lesson for students along with a signed parental approval form*).

Inherit the Wind, (2001) DVD, directed by Stanley Kramer, United Artists.

"King's Repose," "The French Line," and "For England," *Henry V*, (1989) DVD, directed by Simon Rattle, MGM Pictures.

The Last Days, (1998) DVD, directed by Steven Spielberg, October Films.

Life is Beautiful, (1997) DVD, directed by Roberto Benini, Miramax Films.

The Lion in Winter, (2001) DVD, directed by Anthony Harvey, MGM Pictures.

A Man for All Seasons, (1998) DVD, directed by Fred Zinnemann, Columbia Pictures.

The Making of the President 1960, (1963) directed by Mel Stuart, David L. Wolper Productions. (Available on DVD from http://www.mediaoutlet.com).

"Memorial" and "Omaha Beach," *Saving Private Ryan*, (1999) DVD, directed by Steven Spielberg, Dreamworks Entertainment.

Mississippi Burning, (2001) DVD, directed by Alan Parker, MGM Pictures.

Nicholas and Alexandra, (1999) DVD, directed by Franklin J. Schaffner, Columbia Pictures.

"Oh Boy," *The Buddy Holly Story*, (1999) DVD, directed by Steven Rash, Columbia Pictures.

Patton, (1999) DVD, directed by Franklin Schaffner, 20th Century Fox.

"Prologue and Credits" and "The Day the French Came," *Heaven & Earth*, (2000) DVD, directed by Oliver Stone, Warner Brothers Pictures.

"Prisoner Delivery" and "All Virginia was Here," *Gettysburg*, (1993) DVD, directed by Ronald Maxwell, Turner Pictures.

A Raisin in the Sun, (1991) DVD, directed by Daniel Petrie, Columbia Pictures.

The Right Stuff, (1997) DVD, directed by Philip Kaufman, Warner Home Video.

Soundtrack of a Revolution, (2010), directed by Bill Guttentag, Docurama.

Tora, Tora, Tora, (2006) DVD, directed by Kinji Kurosawa, 20th Century Fox.

Walt Disney on the Front Lines, (2004) DVD, Walt Disney Video distributed by Buena Vista Home Entertainment.

The Wizard of Oz, (2010) DVD, directed by Victor Fleming, Warner Home Video. (*This can be used as part of the study of the Progressive period using the lesson plan devised by Henry Littlefield in the early 1960's*). See: http://www.amphigory.com/oz.htm.

The Wonderful, Horrible Life of Leni Riefenstahl, (2003) DVD, Kino Video.

Two excellent resources on evaluating films for accuracy and for use in history class are:

Carnes, Mark, ed. (1996) *Past Imperfect: History According to the Movies*. New York: Henry Holt and Company.

Wilson, Wendy S. and Gerald H. Herman. (1994) *American History on the Screen: A Teacher's Resource Book on Film and Video*. Portland, Maine: J. Weston Walch.

Lists are continually updated at http://www.appleridgepublishers.com

Appendix H

*Outstanding Software and Digital
Resources for Teachers*

*Whenever you purchase software it is important to ask
the publisher or distributor if there is educational pric-
ing. There are several online stores that sell exclusive-
ly to schools, teachers and students at substantial discounts.*

- **AnimationFactory.com**: This website provides teachers and students with an incredible array of animat-
  ed clip art, video clips, PowerPoint backgrounds, and
  web material. It is a subscription-based service with
  a small annual fee. http://www.animationfactory.com

- **ArcSearch**: This is the proprietary search engine for the
  collections of the National Archives. It allows students to
  research the Archives' online collections and to download
  digital materials which are in the public domain. Virtually all of the resources can be used freely by students in
  presentations, reports, and websites without restriction.
  http://www.archives.gov/research/arc/how-to-search.html

- **The Birthday Chronicle**: Developed by Ken Kirkpatrick software, the Birthday Chronicle allows teachers to print out "This Day in History" sheets for students. It is a great way to acknowledge students on their special day and can likewise serve as a daily history lesson for the class. http://www.kksoft.com

- **Comic Life**: This program has a very easy user interface and allows students to produce their own comic book pages using their own digital photographs. It is a highly motivational program that gives students the opportunity to maximize their creativity while dramatizing and illustrating historical events. http://comiclife.com/

- **DonorsChoose.org**: This website allows teachers to post online projects that require additional sources of funding. Donors are far more likely to contribute to educational projects when they are confident that they know exactly where their money is going and that their funds directly benefit students. Online donations can be made directly using PayPal.

Students at Bethesda-Chevy Chase High School enjoy playing a competitive game of classroom Jeopardy as part of their course content review.
(Philip Bigler)

- **Dover Images**: Dozens of CD-ROMs are available with excellent clip art images and historical photographs. These include *Civil War Illustrations, American Historical Illustrations and Emblems, Vintage New York City Views, Great Photographs from Daguerre to the Great Depression,* and *Famous Americans.* Images are in the public domain and can be used freely on website and in student projects. A detailed printed catalog is available from the publisher. http://www.doverpublications.com

- **EarthStation1.com**: This company provides wonderful history DVD's and CD-ROMs at minimal cost. It is a great resource for audio files, photographs, art work, and public domain films. Students can use these resources for reports and PowerPoint presentations. http://www.earthstation1.com

- **Foundation for a Better Life**: The organization's website provides teachers with outstanding motivational PDF posters that promote positive values for students. Schools can also request a free DVD of the Foundation's public service announcements which can be effectively used with individual classes or school-wide assemblies. Several audio files are also available for download. http://www.values.com

- **Inspiration:** *Inspiration* is a low cost software program that enables students to produce mind maps, graphic charts, and other visual diagrams which can be easily exported into PowerPoint or other presentation formats. The program is highly intuitive and easy to learn. www.inpiration.com

- **Interact:** *Interact* publishes several outstanding historical simulations including "Great American Confrontations," "The Court-Martial of Lt. William Calley," "The Civil War," "Socrates," "The Greeks," and "American Letters." These are teacher-developed activities and are highly motivational. Classroom activities can be easily adapted for

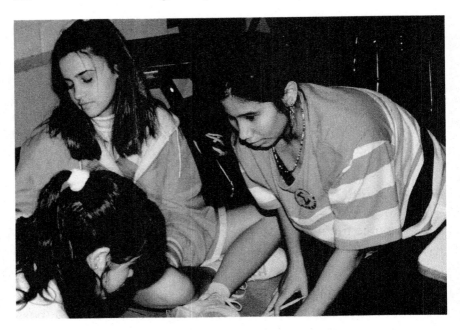

Spartan Thinzar Nyun (right) plans her group's construction of a Greek temple as part of a histrorical simulation in World Civ. Interact *publishes a wide range of highly motivation activities which help get students enthused about history and involved in their own learning.* (Philip Bigler)

students of all abilities and adjusted to accommodate individual class time restrictions. http://www.teachinteract.com

- **Muvee Reveal:** Muvee software allows students to make their own digital film productions quickly and efficiently. Pictures and movie clips can be easily imported into the software which can be produced effortlessly by using Muvee's numerous creative preset templates. One of the most useful templates for history classes is "Turn Back Time" which converts a production into an old black-and-white film complete with scratches. Students can use their own music for their films or use the provided stock audio files. http://www.muvee.com

- **Oyez:** This website is maintained by the Chicago-Kent School of Law and provides online access to current and historical Supreme Court cases. Most landmark cases have audio files of the oral arguments for students to listen to and to use in projects. http://www.oyez.org

- **The Pharaoh's Scribe:** Also by Ken Kirkpatrick, this program allows students to produce a cartouche with their name in Egyptian hieroglyphics. http://www.kksoft.com

- **PowerPak Pro for Powerpoint:** This CD-ROM offers templates for 24 PowerPoint games including Jeopardy, Family Feud, Wheel of Fortune, and the $64,000 Pyramid. The software is easy to use and can be customized to meet your own curricular needs. http://www.ftcpublishing.com

- **Trainers Warehouse**: The Trainers Warehouse offers a wide variety of presentation aids including digital timers, PowerPoint templates, and video warmups. There is also a wide array of clickers and buzzers available which are ideal for classroom use. http://trainerswarehouse.com

- **Voki:** On the Voki websites, students can create their own avatars which can be embedded in websites or used with student projects. Schools can purchase a classroom license for a small fee. This allows the teacher to assign various projects and to assess student work before publishing it to your own proprietary site. http://www.voki.com

- **Walden Fonts**: You can buy CDs of historical fonts including "Minute Man," "Wild West Press," "The Civil War Press," "William Shakespeare," and "Old State House." These typefaces allow students to produce authentic-looking historical documents. Many of the sets include period clip art and historical signatures. http://www.waldenfont.com

- **Wordle**: This site allows students to create graphic renditions of word passages. It is particularly effective using historical speeches or famous quotations. Using PhotoShop or another digital picture editor, it is possible to add background pictures to make stunning posters for the classroom.

A Wordle using Lincoln's Gettysburg Address. Students can produce a wide variety of creative posters using Wordle and a photo editing program. (National Archives/Philip Bigler)

Bibliography

Above and Beyond: A History of the Medal of Honor from the Civil War to Vietnam. (1985) Boston: Boston Publishing Company.

Albom, Mitch. (1997) *Tuesdays with Morrie: An Old Man, a Young Man, and Life's Great Lesson.* New York: Doubleday.

Allen, Steve. (1978) *Meeting of Minds.* Los Angeles: Hubris Press.

Aurelius, Marcus. (2002) *Mediations.* trans. Gregory Hays. Norwalk, CT: Easton Press.

Augustine, Norm. "The Education Our Economy Needs," *Wall Street Journal,* September 21, 2011, p. A17.

Benning, Victoria. "Jefferson High's Bigler Simply Loves Learning," *Washington Post,* January 29, 1998, VA-1.

"Between Me and You: Quotes of the Year," (1995). *Time Annual 1994: The year in Review.* New York: Time, Inc.

Bigler, Philip and Stephanie Bishop, eds. (2007) *Be A Teacher: You Can Make a Difference.* St. Petersburg, Florida: Vandamere Press.

Bigler, Philip and Karen Lockard. (1992) Failing Grades: A Teacher Report Card on Education in America. St. Petersburg, Florida: Vandamere Press.

Bigler, Philip. (2005) *In Honored Glory: Arlington National Cemetery: The Final Post.* St. Petersburg, Florida: Vandamere Press.

_____. (1984) "John Leacock's 'The Fall of British Tyranny' in the Whig Propaganda Offensive: The Personalization of the Revolution." Master's Thesis, The College of William and Mary.

Bolt, Robert. (1962). *A Man for All Seasons*. New York: Vintage Books.

Bolotin, Norman & Christine Laing. (2002) *The World's Columbian Exposition: The Chicago World's Fair of 1893*. Urbana: University of Chicago Press.

Borowitz, Albert. (2005) *Terrorism for Self-Glorification: The Herostratos Syndrome*. Kent, Ohio: Kent State University Press.

Buckley, William F. "Today We are Educated Men," *Townhall*, June 2011.

Carr, Nicholas. (2010) *The Shallows: What the Internet is Doing to Our Brains*. New York: W.W. Norton & Company.

Chaddock, Gail Russell. "America's Top Teacher Gets Teens Out of Their Seats and Into History," *Christian Science Monitor*, May 5, 1998, p. D7.

Chang, Iris. (1997) *The Rape of Nanking: The Forgotten Holocaust of World War II*. New York: Basic Books.

The Congressional Medal of Honor: The Names, The Deads. (1984) Forest Ranch, California: Sharp & Dunnigan Publications.

Conroy, Pat. (2010) *My Reading Life*. New York: Nan A. Talese/Doubleday.

Cullen, Dave. (2009) *Columbine*. New York: Twelve, Hachette Book Group.

Dallin, Alexander. (1985) *Black Box: KAL 007 and the Superpowers*. Berkeley: University of California Press.

Frankl, Viktor E. (2008) *Man's Search for Meaning*. Boston: Beacon Press.

Ginsberg, Benjamin. (2011) *The Fall of the Faculty: The Rise of the All-Administrative University and Why It Matters*. New York: Oxford University Press.

Hendra, Tony. (2004) *Father Joe: The Man Who Saved My Soul*. New York: Random House.

Hill, David. "Mr. Bigler's Big Adventure," *Teacher* magazine. Available at: http://www.edweek.org/tm/articles/1998/09/01/03teach.h10.html

Hirsch, E.D. (2009) *The Making of Americans: Democracy and Our Schools*. New Haven: Yale University Press.

Horwitz, Tony. (2008) *A Voyage Long and Strange: Rediscovering the New World.* New York: Henry Holt and Company.

Robert Hughes. (1997) *American Visions: The Epic History of Art in America.* New York: Alfred A. Knopf.

Jamieson, Edward L., Ed. (1995) *Time Annual 1994: The Year in Review.* New York: Time Inc.

Kanner, Bernice. (2004) *The Super Bowl of Advertising: How the Commercials Won the Game.* Princeton: Bloomberg Press,

Kaple, Deborah, Ed. (2011) *Gulag Boss: A Soviet Memoir.* New York: Oxford University Press.

Knox, Bernard, ed. (1993) *The Norton Book of Classical Literature.* New York: W.W. Norton, pp. 304-305.

Lake, Thomas. "The Way It Should Be," *Sports Illustrated,* June 29, 2009, pp. 56-63.

Littlefield, Henry. "The Wizard of Oz: A Parable on Populism." Available at http://www.amphigory.com/oz.htm.

McCullough, David. (2001) *John Adams.* New York: Simon & Schuster.

Michener, James. (1989). "The Saintly Men of Safed," *The Source.* Norwalk: Easton Press

_____. (1962) "When Does Education Stop." from http://www.asahi-net.or.jp/~xs3d-bull/michener.html.

Minear, Richard H., ed. (1999) *Dr. Seuss Goes to War: The World War II Editorial Cartoons of Theodor Seuss Geisel.* New York: The New Press.

Noonan, Peggy. (1990) *What I Saw at the Revolution: A Political Life in the Reagan Era.* New York: Random House.

Ohio Industrial Commission v. Mutual Film Corporation (236 U.S. 230) from http://supreme.justia.com/us/236/230/.

Pearce, Joseph. (2001) *Solzhenitsyn: A Soul in Exile.* Grand Rapids: Baker Books.

Pietrusza, David. (2008) *1960: LBJ vs. JFK vs. Nixon: The Epic Campaign that Forged Three Presidencies.* New York: Union Square Press.

Plato. (2000) *The Apology.* Translated by Hugh Tredennick and Harold Tarrant. *The Last Days of Socrates.* Norwalk, CT: Easton Press.

Poole, Robert M. (2009) *On Hallowed Ground: The Story of Arlington National Cemetery.* New York: Walker Publishing Company.

Ravitch, Diane. (2010) *The Death and Life of the Great American School System: How Testing and Choice are Undermining Education.* New York: Perseus Books Group.

Rakove, Jack, Ed. (1999) *Madison: Writings.* New York: Library of America.

Rand, Ayn. (1999) *Atlas Shrugged.* New York, Plume Publishing.

Reid, T.R. "The Making of an Empire," *National Geographic*, July, 1997, pp. 12-41.

Roquemore, Joseph. (1999) *History Goes to the Movies: A Viewer's Guide to the Best (And Some of the Worst) Historical Films Ever Made.* New York: Main Street Books.

Scharff, Virginia. (2010) *The Women Jefferson Loved.* New York: HarperCollins Publishers.

Shetterly, Margie. "School Master," *Montpelier*, Summer, 1998, pp. 12-17.

Shenk, David. (1997) *Data Smog.* New York: HarperCollins Publishers.

Aleksandr Solzhenitsyn. (1976) *Warning to the West.* New York: Farrar, Straus and Giroux.

Stockdale, Jim. (1995) *Thoughts of a Philosophical Fighter Pilot.* Stanford, CA.: Hoover Press

Movies, Film and Documentaries

"American Teen: The Movie." Retrieved August 28, 2010, 2010, from http://www.americanteenthemovie.com/.

"Growing Up Online." *Frontline.* PBS Video, from http://www.pbs.org/wgbh/pages/frontline/kidsonline.

"Two Million Minutes." Retrieved August 28, 2010, from http://www.2mminutes.com/.

Acknowledgments

Over the past few years, Lee Congdon and I have regularly gotten together for long and enjoyable lunches at Harrisonburg's own version of "Cheers," the Boston Beanery. These are always welcomed occasions and have become, happily, more frequent since our mutual retirements from our long careers in public education. We often use these sessions to discuss the world's deteriorating political situation and our society's ethical decay. We have both personally witnessed the decline of history education in our schools, where rampant political correctness and dogmatic ideological agendas now pose serious threats to intellectual integrity and freedom of thought. It is our nation's students who are the victims of this education malpractice and now our very civilization is imperiled.

Lee urged me to write a book that would chronicle my career as a high school history teacher. I have resisted doing so because such a reflection is, by its very nature, intensely personal, and I cherish my innate sense of privacy. But as our education system continues to self-destruct, I have finally relented, hoping that an honest and forthright professional autobiography will serve as a testament to the nobility of teaching and will simultaneously honor the many students who have influenced and blessed my life. I am deeply grateful to Lee for his ongoing encouragement in this project. He remains my intellectual mentor and his high standards of scholarship and personal integrity continue to be an inspiration.

Likewise, my wife, Linda, has been a constant source of support throughout the 30 years of our marriage. She has always encouraged my professional endeavors and has had her own remarkable career as a Spanish teacher.

In my retirement, I have been fortunate to be able to continue to teach and to work with many pre-service educators. It is personally gratifying for me to see a new generation of talented, gifted young people who are motivated by a strong sense of ideal-

America's Future--Pre-service teachers from James Madison University: Ellen Vest, Samantha Lippy, Abby Jamison, Instructor Philip Bigler, Meaghan Leon, Hannah Prestiy, and Phoebe Stevens. (Philip Bigler)

ism in their quest to make a difference. In many ways, they remind me of myself during my undergraduate days at Madison College. It is my fondest hope that these new teachers, despite all of the odds and obstacles, will someday be able to restore sanity to our schools by demanding intellectual honesty and by promoting independent thought. They are our nation's hope and our civilization's future.

INDEX

National Teacher of the Year

Philip Bigler

Philip Bigler is available to speak at conferences, back-to-school events, in-service activities, and other educational forums. His presentations are highly motivational and inspring. Copies of *Teaching History in an Uncivilized World* and *Be A Teacher: You Can Make a Difference* are available at a bulk discount to schools, conferences, and educational institutions. For further information or to contact Mr. Bigler, please contact Apple Ridge Publishers at:

info@appleridgepublishers.com

http://www.philipbigler.com